UNEMBEDDED

UNEMB

SCOTT
TAYLOR

EDDED

TWO DECADES OF
MAVERICK WAR REPORTING

Douglas & McIntyre
D&M PUBLISHERS INC.
Vancouver/Toronto/Berkeley

Portions of this book have been published in *Esprit de Corps* magazine
or in the author's previous works published by Esprit de Corps Books. Elements of Chapter 6,
"Crime and Corruption in the Canadian Military," were originally published in
Bernd Horn, ed., *From the Outside Looking In: Media and Defence Analyst Perspectives on Canadian
Military Leadership*, published by Canadian Defence Academy Press in 2005.

Douglas & McIntyre
A division of D&M Publishers Inc.
2323 Quebec Street, Suite 201
Vancouver BC Canada V5T 4S7
www.dmpibooks.com

Library and Archives Canada Cataloguing in Publication
Taylor, Scott, 1960–
Unembedded : two decades of maverick war reporting / Scott Taylor.

Includes index.

ISBN 978-1-55365-292-2

1. Taylor, Scott, 1960–. 2. War correspondents—Canada—Biography.
3. Foreign correspondents—Canada–Biography. I. Title.
PN4913.T39A3 2009   070.4′333092   C2008-906216-7

Editing by John Eerkes-Medrano
Jacket and text design by Naomi MacDougall
Jacket photograph by Katherine Taylor
Photos courtesy of Scott Taylor (unless credited otherwise)
Maps by Eric Leinberger based on original maps by Katherine Taylor

Printed and bound in Canada by Friesens Corporation on acid-free paper that is forest friendly
(100% post-consumer recycled paper) and has been processed chlorine free.

Distributed in the U.S. by Publishers Group West

We gratefully acknowledge the financial support of the Canada Council for the Arts,
the British Columbia Arts Council, the Province of British Columbia through the
Book Publishing Tax Credit, and the Government of Canada through the Book Publishing
Industry Development Program (BPIDP) for our publishing activities.

To all those who have supported
and encouraged me along the way . . .

And to all those naysayers and cynics
who unwittingly served only to strengthen my resolve

"The first casualty when war comes is truth."

U.S. SENATOR HIRAM JOHNSON, 1917

"... it was a case of people adapting their
memories to suit their sufferings."

THUCYDIDES, *History of the Peloponnesian War*

CONTENTS

1

GETTING THE STORY

BECOMES THE STORY

Tell us who you are working for, and
your execution will be quick and painless.
IRAQI INSURGENT

MOSUL, IRAQ, SEPTEMBER 10, 2004, late afternoon—I was awkwardly seated, cross-legged on the floor. Apart from the woven rug upon which I sat, there were no furnishings in the large room. Thick blankets had been hung over the windows, blocking out most of the bright afternoon sunshine. Nevertheless, the room was stifling hot. In the doorway to my left was a lanky young Arab man with a Kalashnikov assault rifle. Across from me, Zeynep Tugrul—my Turkish colleague and fellow captive—was seated on the far edge of the rug. Her hair was covered with a headscarf, and her eyes were fixed on the floor in front of her. Any attempt by us to communicate or even make eye contact only angered our Arab guard.

Behind me, unseen, a third captive was bound hand and foot and stuffed inside a tiny alcove. An Iraqi resident of Mosul, this

1

man had been a driver for UNICEF when the insurgents apprehended him. Like Zeynep and me, he had been accused of spying
for the Americans. I dared not turn around to see him, but I could
hear him praying quietly.

Through the doorway behind the guard, we could also hear
an animated debate underway in Arabic—essentially, a bidding
war between several factions of the Iraqi insurgency to determine which of them would gain possession of the prisoners. The
three of us had originally been captured in the Turkmen enclave
of Tal Afar by a chapter of Ansar al-Sunnah—al Qaeda's branch
in Iraq. A subsequent full-scale American attack against their Tal
Afar stronghold had forced our captors to flee into the open desert and eventually led to us being brought into this empty house
in a middle-class Mosul suburb. Until this point in our captivity
Zeynep had been able to understand our guards' Turkmen dialect, but as the conference concluded, we soon learned that we
were now the property of an Arabic extremist faction known as
the Students of Islam.

Our guard moved aside, and several of his colleagues entered
the room. They immediately moved behind me and began berating the UNICEF driver in Arabic. Wrapping a thick rope around
his neck, they pulled him roughly out of the alcove and towards
the room's only door. Without warning, one of the guards kicked
out viciously at the prone prisoner's struggling body. Not dar-
ing to turn my head, I heard the UNICEF driver let out a muffled
shriek of pain as they dragged him down the hallway.

Our guard was momentarily distracted by the sight of his colleagues hauling away the trussed-up captive, and Zeynep and I
briefly locked eyes. Her expression of hopeless fear mirrored what
I was feeling. Suddenly aware of our exchanged glance, the guard
shouted angrily at Zeynep, and her eyes immediately returned

2

to stare at the rug in front of her. Within minutes, four of the Students returned to our room. Brushing past the guard, they moved directly behind me and forced me into a kneeling position; my hands were tied behind my back, and I was blindfolded with one of their red and white headscarves. Throughout this, they gave me gruff instructions in Arabic. My failure to comprehend resulted in them striking me in the back of the head several times with closed fists.

Only after I was completely trussed up did my interrogator enter the room. I could sense him as he seated himself a few feet in front of me. "We know you are a spy," he said in nearly flawless English. "Tell us who you are working for, and your execution will be quick and painless."

I could sense the other Students close behind me. The sweat from the blindfold was already seeping into my eyes, and fear was welling up in my guts. Throughout the previous three days of captivity I had often been interrogated like this, but the cumulative effect of trying to disprove a negative was taking a toll on my nerves. When first apprehended, I had been confident that the whole thing was simply a misunderstanding. I believed that my Canadian passport and press credentials would prove my identity as a journalist from a country that had remained neutral during the U.S. invasion. I had also possessed a DVD video camera, a 35-mm Minolta, notepads and various other trappings of my trade. All of this, including our identity cards and money, had been taken from us in Tal Afar. When the United States began its attack, an air strike on the insurgent headquarters had left this vital material buried under a pile of smoking rubble. Now that we had been transferred to a new set of captors in a different city, it seemed impossible to prove my identity, let alone disprove the allegation of being a spy.

"Tell me why you came to Iraq," my interrogator continued. I dug deep in my psyche to draw upon my military training. Kneeling as upright as possible—as though standing at attention on a parade square—I delivered my responses in the matter-of-fact, respectful-of-authority tone used when reporting to a superior officer.

"My name is Scott Raymond Taylor. I am a Canadian journalist and I entered Iraq on September 7. The purpose of my visit is to report on the humanitarian crisis created by the U.S. invasion." Only through a conscious effort did I refrain from punctuating this statement with the military's compulsory "Sir!"

"You are lying! You are an American pig!" my interrogator replied. "Why did you visit Tal Afar?"

At this moment, Zeynep—who had remained in the room to witness my questioning—attempted to voice a caution to me. Before she could utter anything more than my name, the Students moved in quickly and, at the instruction of the interrogator, forcibly removed her to the hallway.

During previous questionings the lack of English speakers among the Turkmen insurgents had meant they had relied on Zeynep to translate for them. Unbeknownst to me, Zeynep had deliberately altered many of the answers that I had truthfully given so as not to invoke the anger of our captors. One of these issues was the fact that we had visited Phil Atkinson, a Canadian acquaintance of mine at the U.S. base in Mosul, before heading to Tal Afar. It was Atkinson who had advised us that a major U.S. attack against the Turkmen insurgents was imminent and that we should steer clear of that region until the dust settled. Not wishing to miss out on observing such a major story first-hand, we had ignored his advice and headed straight into the Tal Afar hornet's nest. Zeynep had realized that any disclosure of our

4

visit to the U.S. base and prior knowledge of the American attack would probably convince the Turkmen that we were spies and result in our immediate deaths. She had fabricated an entirely different tale for them, and I had remained blissfully unaware of her subterfuge.

As events unfolded, her abortive interruption served its purpose. When the questioning resumed, my interrogator switched gears and began asking me about my "alleged" journalism credentials. Which agency did I work for? Although it was only one of a number of international outlets that published my syndicated reports, I always emphasized the fact that I worked for Al Jazeera's English-language news agency. Throughout more than an hour of subsequent questioning, every one of my answers, including my Al Jazeera connection, was greeted with "You are a liar!"

Finally, my interrogator interrupted one of my answers: "Enough! We are finished here." I could hear him stand up and move behind me. Instructions were given in Arabic, and my hands were untied. A suddenly friendly voice told me that I could remove my blindfold and asked if I would like any water or tea. I untied the sweat-soaked scarf from my eyes and politely asked for both water and tea. I slowly moved from a kneeling to a sitting position and tried to rub some circulation back into my inflamed knee joints. In short order, a teenage Arab boy entered and placed a small glass cup of tea and a frosty tumbler of water on a carpet in front of me.

A tremendous sense of relief flowed through my body. The interrogator and four Students all smiled at me as they filed out of the room. I drank the water thirstily and was surprised to see that even the guard was going through the door, leaving me alone in the room. As I leaned forward to pick up the hot cup

5

of tea, I noticed a slight movement to my left. The guard was peering from the edge of the door frame with an impish grin on his face. Thinking he was trying to play a mind game on me, I returned to my tea. At that moment they burst into the room.

The lead man wore a balaclava, and the rest had their scarves wrapped around their faces, revealing only their eyes. I saw that they were carrying ropes and sticks, and they came in fast. Instinctively, I rolled to my right side—away from them—and tried to get to my feet. There was nowhere to go, and I was not even upright before the first attacker kicked both my legs from under me. I went down hard, and a knee in the small of my back knocked the wind out of me. One man lashed my hands together behind my back, while another used his headscarf to both blindfold and gag me. Still trying to regain my breath and hyperventilating in fear, I could taste and breathe my attacker's sweat from his scarf. My feet meanwhile had been lashed, about shoulder-width apart, to a wooden pole. I was dragged into the small alcove where the UNICEF driver had previously been kept. Two of the Students heaved up on the pole and pulled my feet above my head.

I knew what was coming next, and the panic threatened to consume me. Although I had been out of uniform for more than twenty years, I willed myself to hold it together for—of all things—the honour of my old regiment. *Don't let those bastards have the satisfaction of breaking a Princess Pat,* I told myself. I mentally vowed not to cry out in pain for at least the first twenty blows.

Biting deep into the gag, I braced myself and began to pray. It didn't take them long to reach a total of twenty blows. As small clubs beat the side of my thighs and whiplike reeds slashed the bottom of my feet, the pain was excruciating. When the twenty-first blow struck, I screamed "Fuck!" into my gag. This response would be repeated with each successive blow until the clubs induced a charley-horse spasm to grip my entire body. At these

6

moments I would scream out "Jesus Christ!" in a single extended exhalation until the pain receded.

After several minutes of this beating, my interrogator returned to resume his questioning. His allegations were the same as before, but now whenever my muffled, gasped replies were greeted with "Liar!" a series of blows would follow until I convulsed.

"You told me you are not a practising Christian, yet you are calling on your saviour for strength," said my interrogator. "That makes you a liar."

On that cue, the batons once again pounded into my already badly bruised thighs. As the spasms wracked my body, my stomach muscles tightened, my back came off the ground and again I bit down on the gag and screamed, "Jesus Christ!"

The line of questions suddenly took a bizarre turn: "Tell us how the locator disks work." I had absolutely no idea what he was talking about, and I replied accordingly. "Liar!" he said. And the blows fell again. After my third denial of this same question, the interrogator became furious. He bent down and punched me viciously in the face. Although he was off balance and struck me at almost the full extension of his reach, my head was on the floor, so my nose absorbed the full blow. I could taste the warm blood pooling in my mouth, and I knew he had broken the cartilage. The punch had also partially knocked aside my blindfold. For the first time I could see my attackers, and the thought of being able to brace for the blows brought a small sense of relief. The sensory deprivation of the blindfold had only served to magnify my fears, as the imagined fear is often more powerful than the reality.

"How do the locator disks work?" Again, I could only reply that I didn't understand the question. This time my interrogator did not immediately utter a response. Instead, he took one of the small batons from his colleague, stepped back a pace, tested the

7

weight of the weapon and suddenly brought the club full force against the side of my left foot. The entire impact struck the edge of my baby toe, disintegrating a section of sock, shattering the bone, removing the toenail and sending a shower of blood onto the shirt of one of the Students holding up the pole. My interrogator's shout of "Liar!" as he struck was immediately echoed by my convulsion and an even more prolonged "Jesus Christ!"

Having vented his fury for the moment, my interrogator calmed down a little. "When they first searched your belongings, the emir himself found a strange metallic disk in your wallet. He took this from you, and it was on his person the following night when the American missile miraculously struck his vehicle and killed him. We believe that you came to Tal Afar to plant that disk prior to the attack, and now I'm asking you to tell me how they work."

My brain was racing now as I realized he was referring to my regimental coin. This memento is issued to every member of the Princess Patricia's Canadian Light Infantry upon graduation from battle school, and I had always kept mine in my wallet as a good-luck charm. In Tal Afar, after I had been strip-searched, the insurgent leader, the emir, had been the one to find the large silver medallion in my coin pouch. I had been asked to explain what it was. Since we were suspected spies, the notion of a journalist carrying a regimental coin would have been difficult to explain. Seizing upon the illiteracy of our captors and their lack of worldliness, a quick-thinking Zeynep had defused the situation before I could reply. In a condescending tone, she had told the emir that it was a token for pay telephones in Turkey. Satisfied with that response, the emir had proudly pocketed my coin.

Before attacking the insurgents in Tal Afar, the U.S. military had maintained a continuous aerial surveillance of the city. As such, the emir's Land Rover would have already been a clearly identified "leadership target." True to the U.S. military's counter-insurgency doctrine, a guided Hellfire missile had been launched from an unmanned Predator drone to eliminate the emir before the main assault commenced. The sophisticated American track-ing and guidance systems had nothing to do with my coin. It would still take a lot of explanation to convince my interroga-tor of that fact and, furthermore, that my regimental memento was the innocuous keepsake of an ex-soldier. "It was a telephone token," I replied. "Liar!" And the blows continued.

At this point in the torture I became detached from the physi-cal pain. It wasn't that my brain didn't still register each and every hit, but I was now convinced that I was about to die. I had already given all the possible answers that I could. There was nothing to confess, and so I believed I was to be beaten to death. I continued to respond to the questions, and my nervous system still reacted with reflexive convulsions to the pain. I began to focus on the pain. I knew that the human body could only absorb so much punishment before the brain shut down into a protec-tive blackness. As such, I found myself willing the next blow to take the pain to the next unbearable level so that I could escape the hell I was enduring. Fear was no longer upon me, because I didn't think I might die; I *knew* I was being killed, and I simply wanted to end the agony as quickly as possible.

My mind was also able to disassociate from the present, and while I would not describe it as an experience of being out of body or of having my life flash before me, I did conjure up images of loved ones in order to make my peace and say my farewells. There were a lot of goodbyes to say—it had been a long trip from a childhood in suburban Canada to a blood-spattered torture chamber in war-torn Iraq.

9

ARTIST INTO COMMANDO

Beer mugs smashed down, heads were split
open, tables were upended and, above the shrieks
and cries, the mess hall resonated to the
chant "San Fernando! San Fernando!"

THE WOEFULLY UNINFORMED COMBATANTS
OF SAN FORTUNATO PLATOON

MY EARLIEST MEMORY IS OF a small hotel in Taxco, Mexico, in 1966. At the time I was just five years old, and my father, Raymond, had been attempting to teach me how to tie my own shoes. When his patience expired, I was informed that the rest of the family—my mother, Mary, and elder sister, Tracey—would be taking a siesta. I was to continue practising tying bows until I got it right, and that had better be before they awoke, "or else." I can't recall what the "or else" entailed, but suffice it to say that the threat left a lasting impression on me. The fact that I had not yet mastered the art of tying my shoes by that age indicates I was no child prodigy. The incident also highlights the fact that I was introduced to travelling off the beaten path at a very early age.

My father was a graphic artist whose employment at a large studio in Toronto put him in the lower-middle-class income bracket.

11

Despite the financial constraints of a modest paycheque and the fact that my parents had two toddlers in tow, international travel was an annual event for the Taylor family. Transatlantic commercial flights were still a novelty then, so to fulfill their penchant for European exploration, my parents packed us onto a Montreal-bound train; there, we boarded a Cunard ocean liner and set sail for England in 1967. For the next eighteen months, my father worked in central London, and Tracey and I attended grade school. We were the only Canadians in an otherwise all-English school, and our accents set us apart as outsiders. Making a presentation about the far-off and exotic land from which I had travelled, I revealed to my classmates that my maternal grandmother, Pauline, was a full-blooded Mohawk Indian. I had always been immensely proud of that fact, and it now paid an unforeseen dividend. In those days, even in England, Hollywood-inspired kids loved to play cowboys and Indians, and now my new-found friends were delighted to be able to play the game with the real McCoy. During the school holidays our family either crossed the English Channel to explore the Continent or made sightseeing trips across the width and breadth of Great Britain.

Although he had been too young to serve in the Second World War—just turning fifteen as the hostilities concluded—my father had nevertheless always had a keen interest in all things military. As a hobbyist he had amassed an enormous (my mother claimed "insane") amount of William Britain's military miniatures. From those legions of thousands of lead soldiers came some of my first toys. In an effort to add some battlefield realism to them, I apparently had a penchant for removing the heads from the figurines. Although this resulted in my possessing entire battalions of headless soldiers, I recall my mother always finding me new, intact units from my father's seemingly limitless collection. Usually this occurred while he was away at work.

When we arrived in London, I was advised by my father that I had reached a new plateau on the climb towards manhood—I was to start purchasing my own lead soldiers. Pulling together my tiny allowance, tooth-fairy money and monetary gifts from relatives, I would eagerly anticipate the monthly trip downtown to Hamleys toy shop. At that time, Hamleys, the largest store of its kind in the world, still sold Britain's miniatures as children's toys.

On one such venture into central London we witnessed the annual ceremony of trooping the colour in honour of the Queen's official birthday. Thousands of British soldiers were on parade that day, resplendent in their scarlet tunics, white belts and bearskin hats. When we returned home to our tiny flat that night, I couldn't wait to go out into our garden to recreate the entire spectacle. Although my fledgling collection consisted of only a handful of intact soldiers, it was augmented by a large contingent of the battered and headless variety. A child's imagination cannot be underestimated, and in my mind the review I assembled rivalled the one that Queen Elizabeth had inspected earlier in the day. From that moment forward, I knew I wanted to be a soldier.

ON RETURNING TO Canada from our England adventure, we moved back into our small three-bedroom Scarborough bungalow. After living in the cramped London flat wherein my sister and I slept in the living room, our Canadian home seemed palatial. At this time my father decided to open his own art studio. The trade-off of gaining his personal freedom by being his own boss in exchange for the loss of a steady income was a perpetual cause for concern and discussion at the dinner table. The fact that my father's studio was in our basement and that my mother did the accounting meant that the business was more or less a family affair. Although my father possessed a tremendous talent as an illustrator, commissioned artwork was not something from which he could generate a solid income. The meat and potatoes of his studio work were the labour-intensive graphics and lay-outs required for assembling mail-order catalogues. To expand his skill set and hone his talents, my father continued to take life drawing courses and sculpture classes and to sketch landscapes whenever we travelled.

Although he was never affiliated with any political organiza-tion, my father was Green in his beliefs and lifestyle long before the Green Party ever existed. We never owned a family car, or a television, for that matter. The calculated savings of not operat-ing an automobile were set aside for the travel fund. The long cold walks to school and the weekly chore of hauling groceries home in a bundle buggy were more than offset by our trips to Europe, North Africa, the Mediterranean and the Caribbean.

Raymond would research our potential destinations with an eye for anything that was not yet a tourist trap. When tourist travel to Fidel Castro's Cuba re-opened in 1972, we were among the first batch of visitors. The U.S.-imposed embargo had resulted in strict rationing and a tremendous shortage of most commodi-ties. For the average Cuban, even toilet seats were hard to come by, and most of the newly opened hotels didn't have any. Predict-ably, the majority of visitors in the Canadian tour group griped and complained about almost everything. At one breakfast sit-ting, a member of our group triumphantly announced, "Hey, I know what's wrong with this butter—it's not salted." It was a minor point, but it was the final straw for Raymond Taylor. He took Tracey and me aside and explained that his disagreement with such complaints related to the use of the word *wrong*— a term that haughtily implied that whatever we Canadians did was "the right way." His lesson was that what made Cuban butter *different* was the absence of salt, and his point that different was not wrong was something I never forgot.

At home the absence of a television was a different matter altogether, as my parents wanted Tracey and me to develop our reading skills rather than waste time in front of what they called "the idiot box." At the time I certainly felt I was missing out on something magical. Schoolyard discussions invariably focused on the previous evening's television programs, which certainly curtailed any active participation on my part. I can recall that in 1969 my friend Bill Newton, at the age of eight, organized a petition to keep *Star Trek* on the air after it had been cancelled in its third season. Bill was a pretty easygoing kid, but this was something he took very seriously. I could only imagine that this *Star Trek* was a program of such incredible quality that it inspired my friend to go door to door, begging neighbours for their signatures. Only in hindsight do I realize that my parents were correct when they told us we weren't really missing anything on television.

To further encourage our reading habits, the Taylors held an annual family contest. The books we read were recorded, by title and page count, on a chart that included weekly and monthly totals. Since the winner was determined by the most pages read by year's end, numerous challenges arose over such things as the percentage of photos and the point size of the text. Throughout this period, my interest remained exclusively military history. Our local suburban branch library had only a limited collection of non-fiction books pertaining to war, and with the pressure of the family reading race I soon exhausted this resource. I had to search further for new titles and, as a result, became a regular subway commuter to visit the downtown central Toronto library.

In addition to ingesting military knowledge, I also had the desire to bring historical battles to two-dimensional visual life. I was lucky to have inherited some of my father's artistic talent, and from a very early age I was encouraged to develop my drawing skills. While some youngsters went off with their fathers on early morning hunting or fishing trips, we would get up early on Saturday mornings, cycle to a scenic location and set up our easels. My father would explain the basics of the composition he had chosen, and we both would begin painting the same scene. The gradual movement of the sun across the morning sky altered our primary light source and meant that the sketches had to be completed quickly. For me, the greasy bacon-and-egg breakfast at a diner that followed these sessions was usually the highlight of the outing. I always felt I was competing with my father, and my art—while good, for a youngster—was certainly never in his league. Compared with my peers, however, I was regarded as a terrific artist, and art was always my strongest subject at public school. When the time came to choose a curriculum for my high school studies, my decision to pursue a career as an illustrator had already been made.

The local collegiate had just introduced a vocational art program that offered a total of four art credits per year, which was essentially half of all my classes. Although I took the mandatory science, math and English courses at the advanced level, this charted path of vocational art precluded the possibility of my applying to university. My heart was set on following in my father's footsteps. Nevertheless, what seemed to be a straight-A student's clear-cut and easily attainable career objective was about to encounter a formidable hurdle—the discovery of booze and the opposite sex.

IN THE VOCATIONAL art program at Wexford Collegiate I had met and become friends with a guy who could best be described as an early bloomer. At fifteen years of age he was already six foot one, was shaving regularly and had a muscular form enhanced by his dedication to bodybuilding. As a pair, we looked like those *Looney Tunes* cartoon dogs—I was Chester, the bouncing terrier puppy, and he was Spike, the bulldog. He was terribly shy and had developed a crush on a girl in the ninth grade. I knew this Katherine Kirkness as she had been a year behind me in public school. We had competed against each other in a public-speaking competition and had shared an advanced English course. The terror I had felt on addressing the school assembly had left my legs shaking, and I had been surprised when she told me how much she "enjoyed" giving speeches. As soon as she arrived at Wexford in September 1976, she launched a campaign to get herself elected to student council. It was during her election speech that my friend Spike first noticed her and developed his consuming crush.

Before the Christmas break, I had convinced him to summon the courage to ask Kathy out. She turned him down flat, and he was devastated. Being a good friend, I offered to intervene and help make his case for him. Not having much experience in talking to girls myself, I waited until New Year's Eve to make the introductory phone call. I had a job working as a dishwasher at a downtown restaurant, and despite the fact that I had just turned sixteen the night before, the older serving staff included me in their celebrations. Fortified with a little liquid courage, I took my supper break at around ten o'clock and headed to the pay phone. Kathy's father was in the midst of a party and seemed surprised that a boy was calling at that hour for his fifteen-year-old daughter. When she came on the phone, I dutifully—and drunkenly—lit into her for not giving Spike a chance. She explained that he was not her type—too big and intimidating. When I asked her what kind of guy she was looking to date, she said someone with a

17

good sense of humour that could make her laugh. I said, "Like me?" and when she replied, "Yes," Spike immediately became my ex-friend.

FROM THAT TIME forward, my high school studies took a back seat to both the emotionally charged development of my relationship with Kathy Kirkness and the lure of teenage drinking parties. By grade thirteen, I was eighteen years old and of legal drinking age. I had a well paid part-time job at a local lumberyard and could therefore afford several large mugs of beer every lunch hour at Frank Vetere's, the licensed pizzeria just a block from the school. On some afternoons, my mates and I returned to class drunk; on other afternoons, we didn't return at all. Even with my partial and often-inebriated attendance, I was able to maintain a respectable average grade of 70 per cent. As I was beyond the government-designated age of majority, teachers concerned with my underachieving were helpless to intervene.

Parents, however, have their own laws. Suffice it to say that their methods persuaded me to rethink my parameters, alter my circle of friends and concentrate on salvaging the possibility of a post-secondary education. I subsequently applied to my father's prestigious alma mater, Ontario College of Art (OCA). This school had a great reputation and enrolled only one in ten applicants. Acceptance was based on a candidate's portfolio and interview results.

Working out of a sense of desperation, I quickly completed a couple of ambitious large-scale murals, along with a series of smaller works, to illustrate my knowledge of the basics such as composition, perspective and design. What had appeared to be really slick, professional-looking artwork in the high school classroom suddenly seemed amateur and childish when I had to display it in front of my art college entrance judges. A couple of anxious weeks later, though, I was as surprised and delighted as my parents were to learn that I had been accepted to OCA. There were a couple of months left in my school year, and I already had enough credits to earn my diploma, so—having achieved my desired goal—I simply stopped going to class. My rationale was that I did not need the aggravation of attending an advanced English course; as a future illustrator I would not have to write anything for the rest of my life.

MY EXPERIENCE AT Ontario College of Art was both challenging and frustrating—and, ultimately, disappointing. Most of the faculty members were male, and since they also constituted the entrance judges, the majority of the students were female. Most of the teachers still practised their trade in the art field and taught college only as a sideline. For some, that hobby seemed to be more about selecting their next wife than about educating a new generation of artists. Some of my instructors were on their third, fourth or, in one case, fifth student turned spouse.

The first year was a foundation course in which everyone was to acquire an education in all art forms before choosing a specific direction—commercial, fine art, sculpture and so on—in their second year. We were all encouraged to express our individuality, and I have to admit that my penchant for researching and illustrating historical military scenes set me apart from many of the students on the experimental fringe who felt that hallucinogenic drugs and nudity were part of the larger art scene.

One of the instructors who had the most influence on me was an illustrator named Huntley Brown. He was an incredibly talented artist and a terribly grumpy curmudgeon. He challenged students, freely used the term *crap* to describe that which warranted it, would not tolerate excuses and, unlike many of his lecherous peers, would not hesitate to reduce a pretty girl to tears

19

with his criticism of her work. His specialty was editorial illustration, bringing the written word to life in a vivid form. What he stressed was making a scene believable, and he believed that in order to achieve this, the illustrator needed to observe and draw people all the time. If a sketchbook wasn't handy or a drawing not practical in a certain circumstance, he wanted his students to study the image so that they could recreate it on paper later. Such mental exercises as simply trying to envision the height of a table relative to that of a chair—in my case, researching the correct weapons and uniforms for a military illustration—led me to constantly consider things from the perspective of "How would I draw this?" That art of visually studying life to make possible subsequent detailed recollection was the most important lesson I learned at OCA.

Within the creative confines of the art college campus there existed a very healthy underground music movement. The new wave era and the punk movement were at their height, and OCA was a breeding ground for new bands. Martha and the Muffins had a top-ten single with "Echo Beach" during their fourth year at the college, and the keyboardist from the Spoons was in my first-year class. I had played the drums for several years before college and felt the urge to join in the punk movement. I met Gordon Wilson, a very talented guitarist who shared my interest in illustrating military subject matter, and the Offenders were born. There was some initial teething trouble as we sorted out the rest of the lineup. In the end, my sister's boyfriend, Rick Winkle (vocals), and his mate, Terry Lipitkis (bass), filled the bill. Somehow we convinced OCA administration to allow us the use of a studio, and we spent the summer of 1980 rehearsing and compiling a song list of twenty tunes. The sound was a danceable punk with a touch of rockabilly, resulting from Wilson's unique guitar style.

20

Playing the Toronto bar scene was a tremendous and often heady experience as we picked up a solid following and began to feature at several major venues. Even though the money we made was increasing, our expenses seemed to grow in proportion, so we all worked additional jobs to support the Offenders. But trying to juggle a full course load at art school, the dream of a rock-and-roll band, a part-time job as a waiter and my relationship with Kathy Kirkness was proving too much to handle. She had followed me from Wexford Collegiate to pursue her own studies at OCA. Combining occasions, on April 9, 1981, I presented her with a birthday gift in the form of a diamond ring, and we were now formally engaged to be married. Although she fully supported the Offenders, she was not as wilfully blind to our commercial potential as I was. The rest of the band wanted to take out a collective loan to pay for a self-produced record. After a long deliberation I realized it was time to move on, and in December 1981 I officially quit the Offenders.

Once again it seemed that my life was on a well-plotted course. Graduation was around the corner. A job awaited me at my father's art studio. My wife-to-be would graduate the following year. We would marry and settle down to a quiet life in the suburbs.

When this scenario fully hit home, I packed a small bag and headed straight to the nearest armed forces recruiting centre.

COMING IMMEDIATELY AFTER my experience at art college and the Toronto music scene, basic recruit training was, not surprisingly, a shock to my system. I had read numerous accounts of boot camp, the most memorable being Leon Uris's book *Battle Cry,* and had watched the Hollywood adaptations ranging from the ridiculous (comedies such as *Stripes*) to the romantic (*An Officer and a*

21

Gentleman) to the brutal (*Full Metal Jacket*). I would soon discover that observing the transformation from civilian to soldier is far easier than actually experiencing it first-hand.

At twenty-two years of age I was older than most of the recruits and was one of the few college graduates. The other members of my platoon were a coast-to-coast sample of Canadians and came from all walks of life. What we had been before joining the Canadian Forces, including our family lineage or social status, meant nothing now. Freshly shorn of our civilian hairstyles and equipped with barrack boxes and kit bags full of our new uniforms, we were all equals in the eyes of the training staff. Individuality was something to be repressed and replaced with a collective oneness. We all had the same haircut, we all wore the same uniform, we drilled until we all could march in synchronized step, our beds were starched to a rock-solid state of precision and we slept anywhere but in the bed. Every item we had access to was either issued by the military or considered an inspected item.

Every morning's inspection by the training staff covered the entire kit list: clothing pressed until you could shave with the creases, footwear polished to a mirror-like standard and all personal hygiene items presented in pristine condition. Items such as toothbrushes and razor blades therefore had to be duplicated—one was for inspection, and one for use. The utensils we actually used had to remain hidden during the inspection in the one container that was designed for personal use—a shoebox. Inside this small cardboard container we also had to edit down all the contents that would give any glimpse of our former selves. Overnight we had to decide what was important enough to remain in the shoebox, and in so doing we recruits unwittingly defined our own personalities. Photos of loved ones were taped to the inside of the lid (often those "loved" ones had been clipped from a *Penthouse* magazine), and every inch of space was carefully packed to maximize usage. If, for instance, a soldier was really into country music, he might squeeze in a Walkman cassette player, a headset, some batteries and two or three tapes. Avid readers could tuck away a couple of dog-eared paperbacks. In retrospect, it was an amazing exercise in deciding what was important to you at that point in your life.

My box included a fair amount of stationery, as I had promised Katherine that I would write to her every single day. She had not been too pleased with my sudden career change and the fact that it would entail us now entering a long-distance relationship. The promise to write to her daily had been made without my really understanding the physical demands of recruit school. The days were filled from dawn to dusk with drills, classroom sessions and physical education. Meals were something to which we were marched in three-rank columns, and then, with instructors bellowing at us to hurry up, we inhaled rather than ate the food. Sleep was almost non-existent, because sleep deprivation was part of the process of mentally breaking down the recruits. Nevertheless, I kept my promise to Katherine. The daily entries of my boot camp experiences predated the modern blogs but essentially served the same purpose. Not only was I compiling a running record of my transition into a soldier, but I was also gaining tremendous practice in written storytelling. Unlike high school English projects that concentrated on analyzing other people's writings, I now had to convert my own adventures into a written form.

Once the first phase of our training was complete, we received our regimental coins and prepared to settle into garrison life in Winnipeg. The platoon with whom I had gone through battle

23

school had become a tightly knit cadre during that seventeen-week process. Initially there had been a lot of violence among the group to establish an internal hierarchy or a pecking order. Fist fights in the barracks were a common way to let off steam and settle scores. The instructing staff officially denounced such violence but unofficially encouraged it. The only thing worse than being bullied was the victim reporting the abuser to the senior non-commissioned officers. This would inevitably result in group punishment for the entire platoon, something like a ten-kilometre run in full kit. The whistle-blower would then be left to face the animosity of everyone in the barracks.

A challenge from the outside was a different story. Shortly after I had arrived at Canadian Forces Base Wainwright, our platoon was only at half strength, and we were awaiting another batch of new recruits before our actual battle school training would begin. Each platoon was named after a regimental battle honour to help us understand our forefathers' legacy. One night we were drinking at the junior ranks' mess when a fellow from Gothic Line platoon deliberately bumped into one of our mates. Never one to shy away from a challenge, Private Rekydal (also known as "The Duck") immediately let fly with his fists. Other members of the Gothic Line jumped into the fray, and the Duck was quickly overwhelmed. From the bottom of the pile he shouted, "San Fernando! San Fernando!" We immediately took up his battle cry, and every one of us leapt to defend the honour of our platoon. Beer mugs smashed down, heads were split open, tables were upended and, above the shrieks and cries, the mess hall resonated to the chant "San Fernando! San Fernando!"

By the time the military police arrived at the scene, most of the Gothic Line boys had fled the field. We were marched back to our barracks under escort, still exhilarated by our victory and still chanting "San Fernando! San Fernando!" Our warrant officer, who had been rousted from his home, was awaiting us at the entrance to our Quonset hut. He lined us up in three ranks and informed us that there would be a forced march the following morning to teach us all a lesson. As an old paratrooper, Warrant Officer Bert Scott had no problem with the fact that we had fought as a unit. He was proud of that. But we needed to learn that our platoon was actually called *San Fortunato*, not San Fernando.

BACK IN TORONTO, Katherine was having difficulty convincing her parents about the merit of the upcoming wedding. In fact, even on the way to the ceremony her father pulled the car over to the side of the road and gave her a last opportunity to back out of the marriage. While her parents had their doubts about me as a suitable groom, they were also concerned about the fact that we were going to move to Germany immediately following the honeymoon. Katherine was about to confront a two-pronged clash of cultures: we were going to have to adapt to living in Europe, and she was going to have a crash-course entrance into the military environment. Shortly after our battalion arrived at the base in Baden-Soellingen, I was sent off on the annual six-week NATO exercise known as Fallex. Most of the nine platoon members were single, and the few wives who were left behind were forced to set up their homes on their own. By the time I returned from Fallex, we already had two cats, Katherine was conversational in German and she knew practically every resident of our village.

Our platoon commander, "Super Dave" Hirter, had good news for me when we returned to the base in Baden. He had been selected to command the Princess Patricia's Canadian Light Infantry (PPCLI) platoon that would be sent on the French commando

25

course that year. Although the forty candidates for the commando course were drawn from all over the battalion, Hirter had secured me a place on the team. We immediately launched into a month-long vigorous preparatory course before heading down the Rhine River to the French *entraînement commando* facility that was situated on the German side, opposite Neuf-Brisach. For the next three weeks French army instructors would put us through a gruelling set of confidence courses to test our fear of heights and close confines, teach us unarmed combat techniques and train us in the art of making improvised explosive devices.

Although we were already fit, disciplined infantry soldiers, the commando course took the personal challenge of soldiering to a whole new level. As the Canadian contingent, we were attached to a French army company and based at the same training compound as units from the United States, Germany and Britain. Naturally enough, Super Dave wanted his platoon to show all these nationalities just how good Canadian soldiers were—even if we killed ourselves in the process.

Balancing out Super Dave was PPCLI Warrant Officer Jim Decoste. Although he was only thirty years old at the time, Decoste had enlisted at the age of seventeen. He already had completed the U.S. Army Ranger course, and the fact that Super Dave respected his experience was probably instrumental in us all surviving our commando training. That is not to say that Decoste wasn't hard core; in fact, he was a strong proponent of the "train hard, fight easy" school of thought. That was best exemplified by his behaviour during the big Escape and Evasion exercise. Halfway through the commando course an entire platoon would be pronounced "captured," and then, under the watchful guard of the French army, the captives would be trucked across the Rhine River into France. The destination was an old castle, where the

26

captured soldiers were beaten and interrogated with frightening realism by Decoste. The objective was for the platoon to pool its wits and wisdom under pressure and to plot an escape. The ultimate goal was to return to our barracks on the German side of the border. All local police forces and military units were notified to apprehend fugitives if they were spotted.

Corporal Kevin Tucker was my partner in the commando course; he had won a gold medal in the 800 metres at the brigade track meet, while I was the reigning champion of the 1,500 and 5,000 metres. Considering that we were the two fastest soldiers in the entire brigade, right off the bat we decided to do what we did best and made a run for safety. Before the trucks even crossed into France, Tucker and I had managed to overpower the French soldier guarding us and leapt out over the tailgate. We were fortunate to be in the rearmost truck in the convoy, and our departure wasn't noticed by those driving the vehicle. While watching the tail lights disappear, Tucker and I saw a third form flip out from under the canvas flap on the French truck and hit the asphalt with a sickening thump. It was another member of our platoon, one who had the unfortunate nickname of "Spaz." We were just about to tell him that our chances of escape would be better if we split up when Spaz revealed that he had a 100-Deutschmark note sewn into a flap in his combat boot. Since the instructors had removed all our wallets and identification when Tucker and I were "captured," Spaz suddenly became a welcome member of the team.

We had to remain on the loose until the exercise ended on the following dawn. Feeling cocky, we "liberated" civilian clothes from a backyard clothesline and "borrowed" three bicycles. We rode to the next village, entered a smoky *gasthaus*, took a table near the rear exit and ordered a meal. We conversed quietly among ourselves, nursing our beers and Spaz's 100 Deutsch-marks, furtively glancing at the door whenever a new patron entered. Close to midnight, we settled our tab, bid *auf wiedersehen* to the barmaid and set off on our bicycles again.

Once back at the commando school we saw that French military police were actively patrolling the gates. Luckily we were able to climb a fence and gain access to the unobserved vehicle compound by using our civilian clothes to negate the barbed wire. Lying in the shadows beneath a truck, we waited for our colleagues to return from their ordeal. When they did finally appear, we three simply emerged from our hiding spot and mingled with the crowd. Most of the others were bleeding and bruised from Decoste's interrogation techniques. I thought to myself, *Thank God I missed out on that.*

In addition to playing the role of interrogator, Warrant Officer Decoste was also one of the few bilingual soldiers in our platoon. As such, he had become the translator for our French army instructors. However, there was very little translating required for the unarmed combat training courses because the combat techniques were graphically demonstrated, using unsuspecting "volunteers" as guinea pigs. Whenever the combat instructor would single out a candidate for a demonstration, a little gulp of fear escaped from the chosen one. We dubbed this French sergeant "Doctor Demento" because in whatever move he was about to show us, his victim was going to get hurt.

In one such case, Corporal Kennington flinched just before Demento's attack and as a result received a kick right in his testicles instead of his inner thigh. At first we didn't realize what had happened, because Kennington didn't utter a sound. He dropped face first, began convulsing and appeared to be biting the grass and chewing the dirt. Medics were called forward. Turning him

28

over onto his back and with his feet apart, they gingerly retracted his testicles from where they had been lodged, up inside his pelvic muscles. Once both testicles were back, dangling where they belonged, Demento told Kennington that there would be a five-minute breather before he would demonstrate the move again. This time Kennington did not flinch.

THE COMMANDO COURSE ended in a suitably dramatic fashion, with all of the bone-weary survivors marching up a winding road to the deserted ruins of an ancient French castle. There, in the grey dawn drizzle, we formed ranks in the overgrown courtyard and received our coveted commando badges from a grizzled French colonel. Bearing a swooping eagle overlaid on a sword and backed with a leather tab, it was a great-looking badge and we could hardly wait to affix it to our dress uniform. Immediately after our return to Baden-Soellingen, Super Dave Hirter put my name forward for the section commander's course. It would have meant a promotion to master corporal and a pay raise, but it would have also entailed another thirteen weeks away from home. I had promised Katherine that I would not re-enlist beyond my basic three-year engagement, and I told Super Dave that it would be better to assign that slot on the section commander's course to a career soldier. I asked instead for the three-week parachute training course that I had always wanted to complete and that I felt I could sell to Katherine. Petulantly, Super Dave told me the jump courses were only for career soldiers.

Instead, I was sent back to Canada to complete the seven-week combat intelligence course, and I was immediately transferred from 9th Platoon to Warrant Officer Decoste's intelligence section in battalion headquarters. There were only six of us in this

29

small section, and we operated in close confines both in the garrison and in the field. In uniform, Decoste was a true military mentor—tough, fit, fair and dedicated to both the profession of arms and the regiment. In our off-duty hours, despite the rank difference, Katherine and I became close friends with Jim and his wife, Janice.

ALTHOUGH I HAD hung up my uniform, Katherine and I were still very much enthralled with living and working in Germany. We both had become fluent in German and had established some strong friendships with our fellow villagers. Once we had entered into their confidence, many of the older Germans were eager to discuss their Second World War experiences. The area where we lived had been "liberated" from the Nazis by Moroccan soldiers in the Free French army, and few of the village's households had not been violated in some manner. Raping and looting had been rampant, and the locals still harboured a resentment for the suffering they had endured. This was an invaluable opportunity for me to get beyond the "drums and bugles" historical accounts that I had studied all my life. Here was the other side of the story—the suffering of the vanquished that is rarely recorded by the victors.

30   Katherine had worked as a figure skating coach at the base since shortly after our arrival. The coaching job involved her working early mornings, late evenings and weekends at the arena to coincide with her students' class times. Her status as a civilian professional meant that upon my release from the military we became members of the officers' mess. This overnight jump from the junior ranks' club to consorting with officers was a quantum leap in status. I took a temporary art position at the Canadian Forces' television station and later became the base's graphic

artist. My position as a civil servant entailed the traditional nine-to-five workday. With our conflicting schedules, both of us had plenty of time to pursue outside freelance art contracts.

In 1987 I was contacted by Bill Fogarty, a Canadian living in Germany who published English-language magazines. He needed an art director, and I leapt at the opportunity. I kept the base job, but in the evenings I laid out his editorial pages and designed his ads. Fogarty was a real character—almost a living caricature. He had been living in Europe for so long that his passport had expired, and with no German work permit, he existed completely outside of any government regulations. He paid cash for his printing contracts, had a small apartment in Luxembourg but lived out of his car or at his advertisers' lodgings on a contra arrangement. His magazines—*Euroski* and *Golf Travel*—were entirely driven by advertiser revenue, and his primary clients were resorts and hotels hoping to attract U.S., Canadian or British service personnel stationed at NATO bases in Germany.

By the time I met Fogarty, his flagship, *Euroski,* had been in publication for nearly a decade. He rarely passed through Baden-Soellingen, so we arranged things so that, whenever possible, I would travel to meet him on the weekends. It was a great gig for both Katherine and me as we were being paid to travel to all of Europe's most luxurious ski destinations and to experience some of the most amazing hotels and restaurants.

Fogarty's love of publishing was limited to the sale of advertising. He wasn't concerned in the least with editorial content—other than to produce a repetitive series of glowing "reviews" for his clientele. Fogarty banked on the fact that most of his advertisers had, at best, English as a second language and thus were unlikely to discover that all of his reviews were almost identical. Fantastic photographs were available to him free of charge from various tourism boards, and it was a simple task for me to compile a slick-looking publication at virtually no cost.

We had earlier convinced Fogarty to switch his printing contract to the local German printer we used near the base. However, one of the main production costs in those days was the laborious process of colour separations. In 1988, Fogarty travelled to Thailand, where he found a colour film studio that could produce his separations at a fraction of the price he was paying. Administration was never a strong suit for Fogarty—he had banker boxes full of random files and a shoebox cluttered with old receipts—and working for him provided a unique set of challenges. He had a ravenous appetite for fine food and an insatiable thirst for alcohol. This, coupled with the sedentary lifestyle associated with living out of his car, had resulted in him sporting a Buddha-like belly and in him aging well beyond his years. Most of the aggravation he suffered resulted from the absence of an organizational system. Jovial when things were going well, Fogarty could fly into a purple-faced rage when he encountered difficulties. He was, however, a shameless maverick, and I learned the basics of the publishing trade from him by closely studying both his merits and his faults.

Eventually Katherine and I tested the waters with a couple of our own projects. We produced an illustrated history magazine for the PPCLI's regimental seventy-fifth anniversary and a full-colour air show program for the base in Baden-Soellingen. The PPCLI project included the commissioning of twenty-five original battle illustrations, which I researched and designed before Katherine rendered the final paintings. The air show program was the first completely entrepreneurial publication that we financed through the sale of advertising to local merchants. Following in Fogarty's footsteps, we more than halved our production costs by flying to Bangkok for our colour separations.

We established our own business arrangement with a Thai company while enjoying the sights and sounds of the Orient. Both of these projects proved to be financially successful and resulted in our amassing a tidy little nest egg. Even after a celebratory safari to Kenya, a trip throughout the Mediterranean and a junket to Norway, we still had ample funds.

Katherine and I were only twenty-seven years old, healthy and fit; we were travelling the globe, conducting business in Europe and Asia, holding down two jobs each, working in our chosen fields, doing creative and challenging projects. And we were financially secure.

We had no way of knowing it then, but things were about to change dramatically.

3

TICKET TO ADVENTURE

It was like the world's greatest superpower
went to war against the Flintstones.

A U.S. SENATOR

AS MUCH AS WE HAD loved our German experience, in the summer of 1988 Katherine and I decided to return to Canada to seek
out new challenges. We had initiated a proposal with the Royal
Canadian Armoured Corps to produce a series of paintings as
well as an illustrated history book for their upcoming fiftieth
anniversary. This was to be a long-term project that would allow
us to continue travelling and publishing internationally. We
hoped to wrap up the contracts and the research in Ottawa in a
couple of months and to be living—and painting—in Paris before
Christmas.

Our flight home from Canadian Forces Base Lahr to Canadian
Forces Base Trenton was the regularly scheduled air force shuttle. At that point, the Canadian Department of National Defence
owned and operated five Boeing 707 passenger planes. These aircraft flew coast-to-coast milk runs across Canada almost daily and
were used to sustain the flow of personnel and families based in

Germany. This was essentially a mini-airline, complete with flight attendants, and I noted that it did not have anything in the way of on-board entertainment—no audio system, no inflight movies and no seatback reading material. Without any distractions at hand, Katherine and I discussed the feasibility of publishing an inflight magazine for the Canadian air force. By the time the 707 touched down on the CFB Trenton runway, we had written out a rough business plan, complete with the title "Esprit de Corps" and a logo design. The concept was to use the uniquely targeted distribution of military passengers to attract advertisers who wished to promote their products to service personnel. As a quarterly magazine, each issue would have a readership of close to 100,000, and by printing *Esprit de Corps* on quality paper we needed to print only 5,000 copies. In our initial proposal, we offered the Department of National Defence full editorial oversight and prepublication approval, and as our title suggested, this inflight magazine would be bilingual. Most importantly, we were going to deliver the magazines to the air force at absolutely no cost. All we asked was that the flight attendants ensured that the copies were placed in the seatbacks—and replaced with new copies when they became tattered. Even this request would only redirect the manpower already required to update the safety pamphlets that the air force was paying to print and place in the seatbacks. We offered to include the safety information, along with flight route maps and squadron histories, in each of our editions. So there would be no cost, no additional labour and a savings on printing safety pamphlets, and every passenger would have an entertaining journal to read while flying. How could Defence say no to that?

It didn't take us long to discover that junior officials in the Canadian military make a career out of saying no. Katherine and I had spent our first two weeks in Ottawa drafting logos and letterhead and researching other military publications to list potential advertisers. We were convinced that this concept could really take off, and we took the train to Trenton to make our sales pitch to a navy lieutenant who had claimed that the decision was his alone to make. We wore our most business-like suits and were eager to impress him with our dedication and professionalism. At the gatehouse, we called him and he advised us not to bother signing in through security; instead, he would meet us at the air terminal cafeteria. Twenty minutes later, dressed in casual work dress, he entered and approached our table, shaking his head: "Not going to happen." He handed back our proposal with the seal still unbroken. Checking his watch, he informed us that he was late for another meeting and left without so much as shaking our hands. On the three-hour train ride back to Ottawa that night, I vowed to Katherine that this magazine was "going to fucking happen." What had earlier been opportunistic enthusiasm for the project had now become a consuming personal quest.

Rather than trying to work my way up from the bottom, I decided to go straight to the top. The very same proposal, marked "Personal and Confidential," was sent to air force commander Lieutenant General Larry Ashley in Winnipeg. A number of phone calls to Ashley's office failed to produce anything more than confirmation from his secretary that my package had been received. A week later, I tried my luck again. This time my heart sank when the secretary informed me that Ashley had indeed looked at my proposal and had returned it to the attention of the same navy lieutenant in Trenton. Hearing my disappointment, the secretary dropped her voice to a whisper and said, "I'm not supposed to tell you this, but the commander has approved your proposal." The exultation over this victory was doubled by the thought of Navy

Lieutenant "Not going to happen" getting the directive from a three-star general to make it happen.

We had convinced the air force to accept a freebie. Now all we had to do was convince national advertisers to commit the money necessary to make this thing take flight.

IF EVER THERE was a fortuitous time to launch a military magazine in Canada, it had to be the winter of 1988–89. The Progressive Conservative government was in power, the Cold War was in full swing and Prime Minister Brian Mulroney was in lockstep with U.S. President Ronald Reagan. The U.S. policy of the day was to increase military spending in conventional weaponry and in the weaponization of space to the point where the Soviet Union would go bankrupt trying to keep pace. As a good ally, Canada had drafted a new Defence White Paper in 1987, which was intended to get us to do our bit to spend the Soviets into oblivion. The author of this ambitious new blueprint for our military was Defence Minister Perrin Beatty. He envisioned a large-scale increase in regular force personnel; the purchase of four hundred new main battle tanks; a revitalized militia equipped with 1,200 northern terrain vehicles; four new fleets of helicopters to replace the existing Sea Kings, Chinooks, Kiowas and Twin Hueys that had reached their expiration dates and the most controversial procurement of all—twelve nuclear-powered submarines. After decades of Canadian soldiers being regarded as the poor cousins in NATO because of their aging equipment, Canada was suddenly about to leap to the front of the pack in one massive orgy of defence spending. International weapons manufacturers descended upon Ottawa like a band of tomcats catching a whiff of a feline in heat.

As a publication, *Esprit de Corps* was an unproven entity, but our intended readership of military passengers was certainly the

group whom these defence contractors wanted to influence. Our
ad rates were also far cheaper than those of any of the existing
trade publications, and these corporations had large budgets
set aside to pursue massive military contracts. With our low
overhead, we didn't need a seat at the table with these major
advertisers; as it turned out, even the table scraps we were given
were enough to make our magazine a reality.

We published *Esprit de Corps*'s first two issues at the same time
to minimize travel expenses. We did the typesetting and layout
at our printer back in Germany, flew the colour separations to
Thailand and then returned to Germany to finalize the printing
as our contract with the air force stipulated delivery of the magazines to the base in Lahr. The original editorial policy was aimed
at providing entertaining features that would have a shelf life
extending beyond the proposed circulation dates. Travel, fashion
and history articles were interspersed with cartoons and cross-
word puzzles. We couldn't afford to hire writers, so Katherine and
I churned out the copy. With our collective background in visual
arts and the fact that we had to pay twenty-five cents a word for
translation, these inflight magazines were big on illustrations
and light on text. And, since we had to obtain Department of
National Defence approval for all editorial content prior to publication, it was pointless to pen any commentary that might be
the least bit controversial.

In its infancy, *Esprit de Corps* was fun, entertaining and not at
all independent. But now that it had become a reality, the magazine was also a ticket to adventure. One that I was quick to cash
in.

IN MARCH 1989, just as the first copies were rolling off the presses,
I received an invitation to join HMCS *Ottawa* for a three-day
cruise off the coast of Halifax. Having read C.S. Forester's entire

39

Horatio Hornblower series before the age of twelve, I had deliberated for a long time at the recruiting centre before choosing the infantry over the navy. My experience aboard the *Ottawa* convinced me that I had made the right decision.

With a length of about 113 metres and a beam of about 13 metres, the frigate HMCS *Ottawa* was one of the smaller ships in the Canadian fleet. However, to my untrained eye and from the perspective of the jetty, she seemed to be a towering battleship. Crossing her deck, I was welcomed aboard by the officer of the watch and ushered below to the tiny cabin that I would share with three lieutenants. A full tour of the ship was followed by a hearty breakfast in the wardroom. Everyone was in good spirits, and in addition to the normal complement of the *Ottawa*'s officers, there were a half-dozen young Sea King helicopter pilots on board. This exercise, called a salty dip, was a standard familiarization cruise to give those newly minted pilots a taste of life at sea. It would also be the first time that they would be required to land their helicopters on a pitching and rolling deck. Needless to say, they all were a little apprehensive.

The lines were cast off, and *Ottawa* paid her respects to the other navy ships moored in their berths as we edged out of Halifax harbour. There was a brisk easterly wind blowing, and beyond the outer limits of McNabs Island we could see whitecaps cresting some rather large waves. I had joined the Sea King pilots on the outside bridge to watch Commander Mike Pulchny, *Ottawa*'s skipper, navigate the frigate out to sea. The lookout, a young Newfoundlander, advised us landlubbers, "It's going to get rough; you'd best get some crackers into ya." One of the pilots thanked him for the suggestion but said that wouldn't be necessary as we'd all just finished a full breakfast of bacon and eggs. "Try not to get that on my boots then," was the Newfoundlander's only answer.

40

Just past the outer harbour the *Ottawa* began to lurch and roll with the waves. I had been told that as long as you can see the horizon line, you can brace for the movement and therefore avoid any motion sickness. This is a lie. Within thirty minutes of the frigate hitting the rough water all of the pilots and I had gone to the guardrails at least once to let loose our innards. Commander Pulchny and the other officers had gone below into the enclosed bridge, and only the Newfoundlander on lookout remained on the upper deck to witness our growing discomfort. This veteran sailor calmly advised the pilots that they would not be flying anything that day as the weather conditions were approaching a "sea state six." We had no idea what that scale entailed, but the very next wave loomed as large as a barn in front of us. "This one's a greener," the sailor said excitedly, and to illustrate his point the old *Ottawa*'s bows bit deeply into the oncoming wave. The entire forecastle was submerged, and the crashing water parted at the base of the forward gun turret. All too slowly the bow re-emerged, appearing to float briefly on thin air before sliding down into the next deep trough. "Greener," said the sailor again, and this time he could have been describing the pallor of the rest of us, who were bent over the starboard rail.

After my third round of vomiting, my stomach was completely empty, yet my body seemed insistent on trying to turn itself inside out via convulsions. Eventually the pilots and I were led, one by one, down into the smoke-filled pilot house, where Pulchny and the duty officer were grinning from ear to ear. The warmer air below decks, combined with cigarette smoke and our inability to see the horizon line, worsened things more than I would have thought possible. Finally, I was lifted into my bunk by a couple of my unimpressed new cabin mates.

It had not been three hours since we had left the jetty, and we were supposed to be at sea for the next three days. What had

41

seemed in principle like a wonderful life experience had in practice become a living nightmare. I drifted off into a fitful sleep.

When I awoke, the ship was dead calm on the water, and the engines had been shut down. I climbed out of my bunk and was delighted to discover that my nausea had abated. Seeking out the wardroom, I learned that HMCS *Ottawa* had returned to the safe confines of Bedford Basin in Halifax harbour to wait out the storm. The "good news," they told me, was that the following morning we would try again. The winds were expected to drop off, and the waves would diminish to what they called after-swells. I was informed that these swells were often far more sickening than the whitecaps we had previously experienced. Thankfully, this forecast proved incorrect, and although I was queasy and anxious, I was at least able to function for the remainder of the voyage. In fact, I managed to get a lift a few times in the Sea Kings as they practised their deck landings both day and night. Pitted against the backdrop of an otherwise empty expanse of the Atlantic Ocean, *Ottawa* suddenly appeared very minuscule. I could not help but marvel at the steady nerves that the pilots required to bring their Sea King down onto the moving and rolling helipad.

During this initial outing I was also impressed with the camaraderie among the ship's company. At this stage, combat ships still had male-only crews, which allowed for an off-duty atmosphere that was lewd and crude, to put it mildly. Although it presented an entirely different set of challenges from my experience in the combat arms, the navy environment—aside from the motion of the ship—was something I enjoyed.

WITH *ESPRIT DE CORPS* still very much in its infancy, Katherine and I continued to develop other publishing projects. We subcontracted our colour separation service to other printing

42

companies, coordinated book printing in Singapore and Hong Kong, and produced a number of air show programs and aviation books in Canada. Through our work with the organizers of the Ottawa air show, we had a solid contact with the Canadian Warplane Heritage Museum in Hamilton, Ontario.

The museum had contracted us to produce a glossy guidebook for visitors to purchase at its gift shop. Housed in old wooden air force hangars that dated back to the Second World War, the museum was a piece of living history. Its collection of aircraft was unique in that they were all still maintained in airworthy condition. The museum had a Hawker Hurricane fighter, a Grumman Avenger torpedo bomber and a whole assortment of transport and training aircraft—all of Second World War vintage. The pride and joy of the Canadian Warplane Heritage Museum was one of the last two Avro Lancaster heavy bombers still flying in the world.

To catalogue the entire collection, photographer Mark Lamontagne—a close friend from our stint together in the PPCLI intelligence section—and I were allowed into the hangars after hours. We spent a couple of nights locked in with the airplanes, lighting them, photographing them, exploring them and clambering all over them.

We had arranged for Lamontagne to fly aboard a Beechcraft Expeditor on the third day to conduct an air-to-air photo shoot of the Hurricane and the Lancaster. It was November 12, the day after Remembrance Day, and the museum was putting the Lancaster aloft as part of a special celebration. It had named its "Lanc" after Andrew Mynarski, a wartime aircrewman who had won a Victoria Cross. After his plane was hit by anti-aircraft fire, Mynarski had refused to abandon the tail gunner, Pat Brophy, who was alive but trapped in his turret. Despite the flames, Mynarski tried in vain to free Brophy. As a final gesture, Mynarski saluted his doomed friend and jumped from the stricken plane with a burning parachute. Mynarski died from his severe burns after landing, but by a sheer miracle tail gunner Brophy survived the impact to tell the tale of selfless heroism. For the celebration, museum staff had located three of Mynarski's former crewmembers from that fateful flight—and they were to fly aboard a Lancaster for the first time in forty-five years.

Lamontagne had to be at the airfield by six o'clock for a predawn briefing. When we arrived, there were already about two dozen people gathered around the snack bar. The mechanics and aircrew were all dedicated volunteers who spent hours of hard work conducting tedious maintenance and ground training. Although this was not a public air show, it was still a rare moment for them to bring history to life. The three Mynarski crew veterans had brought their wives along to witness the moment. They were all in their mid-sixties and seemed a little overwhelmed by it all; the last time they had been in a Lancaster it was shot down in flames and their friends had died around them.

Lamontagne boarded the twin-engine Beechcraft Expeditor, and it taxied out toward the runway. After mechanics removed the chocks in front of the Hawker Hurricane, it followed the Expeditor. The last of the veterans was being helped up into the belly hatch of the Lancaster when one of the museum staff walked towards me from the tarmac. "We have one more spot on the Lanc," he said. "Do you want to go up?"

I couldn't believe my luck and immediately raced towards the big bomber.

For the takeoff, I wedged myself into the mid-upper gun turret, from where I could still watch the activity in the cockpit. The din of the four Merlin engines was deafening as the Lancaster gained momentum. The skies were overcast, but there was a pink sliver of light along the horizon of Lake Ontario. We climbed to three thousand feet, and suddenly the Hawker Hurricane came up alongside us to take up station on our starboard quarter. The Beechcraft soon completed the formation, and we flew low over the farmland of southern Ontario. Once airborne, the Mynarski vets underwent a transformation that, had I not witnessed it, I would have found difficult to believe. They were no longer slow-moving senior citizens; they were once again the cocksure teenagers they had been in the Second World War. One of them motioned for me to get out of my turret so that he could take my place. He immediately unlocked the turret ring and traversed the twin .50-calibre machine guns to target the nearby Hurricane. He was clearly having fun. By now we were out over Lake Ontario, and the pilot gestured for me to go down into the bomb aimer's forward cupola. Located in the chin of the aircraft, the bombardier's position jutted well out on its own. Lying prone on a narrow support beam, I had literally nothing below me but a clear glass bubble. It was nerve-wracking enough just to watch the waves roar past below me; I could only imagine how vulnerable a wartime bomb aimer would have felt, watching hostile tracer fire arc towards him.

45

Back on the ground, I was still exhilarated by the experience. It was not yet eight o'clock, but my adrenalin was pumping. Lamontagne was equally excited as the pink and purple sky had made for a fantastic backdrop for the photo shoot. As I looked around the tarmac, I noticed the Mynarski veterans had again become old men. Their youthful spirit had remained inside the airplane, and I only wished that we could have recorded those glorious moments for their wives to see. Instead, the three vets were hustled off to their cars as their mates complained about how cold it had been, waiting for them to land.

ALTHOUGH *ESPRIT DE CORPS* was not a news magazine at this stage, we couldn't help but note that history was in the making throughout the winter of 1989. In October, the Berlin Wall had crumbled and the Soviet Union was beginning to dissolve. Katherine had travelled to West Germany with the Defence department to cover Canadian troops participating in NATO's Fallex training exercise, and she produced an illustrated story that included several references to the Iron Curtain dividing Germany. Before we could get it to press, this feature had been overtaken by world events. In addition, the sudden unexpected thaw of the Cold War had an impact on the defence industry that constituted *Esprit de Corps*'s advertisers. Anxious to cash in on the so-called peace dividend and to slash the ballooning government deficit, the Mulroney government had begun cancelling a number of large defence procurements contracts. The nuclear submarine purchase was nixed, and the main battle tank replacement was shelved shortly thereafter.

For the average Canadian soldier, the day-to-day routine remained unchanged. Jim Decoste had left the 2nd Battalion in Germany to take the officer training course. After being commissioned from the ranks and becoming a captain, he was posted to the 1st Battalion in Calgary. He contacted me and invited *Esprit de Corps* to accompany his unit when it deployed to northern Norway in February. For years Canada had been part of NATO's Allied Command Europe Mobile Force, which was essentially a fire brigade intended to be rapidly deployed to block a Soviet invasion of Norway. The initial quick-reaction force comprised 850 soldiers of PPCLI's first battalion, augmented with artillery, engineers and a helicopter detachment. Equipment such as armoured vehicles and over-snow vehicles remained permanently stationed near the NATO airbase at Bardufoss, Norway. The exercise was really a massive air transport operation that would bring in approximately five thousand troops from the United Kingdom, Germany, Italy, United States and even Luxembourg to augment the local Norwegian defence force. The plan was for a photographer and me to catch one of the first air force flights into Bardufoss, spend a couple of days recording the military buildup at the frozen top of the world and then catch the last Boeing 707 as it headed back to Canada.

Nothing ever goes according to plan on a large-scale operation, and this exercise was no exception. Weather and mechanical problems delayed flights out of Greenland, and the main Canadian contingent arrived ahead of the advance party. Their field kitchens stranded in Canada, the soldiers were on hard rations. Despite the confusion and lack of amenities, my photographer, Rick Raddell, and I were generously hosted by the troops. We were escorted by a pair of public affairs officers, whom the soldiers invariably distrusted. Once out of our handlers' sight, the soldiers offered thick coffee heavily laced with their private rum stash. It tasted horrible, but it did mitigate the −40°C temperature.

As events unfolded, Captain Decoste was on the last flight from Canada. He was the commander of the advance party that had become stranded in Greenland, and he had been frantically attempting to restore order to the burgeoning chaos. Rick Raddell and I had only a brief opportunity to speak with him at the Bardufoss airfield before we boarded the otherwise empty Boeing 707 for our trip home. Decoste was worried that his invitation for us to report on the Norway deployment would backfire because everything had deteriorated into a fiasco. He didn't need to fret as Raddell's photographs were fantastic and my short article focused on the Canadian soldiers' ability to overcome unexpected hardships. *Esprit de Corps's* internal audience would be able to read between the lines, but to a casual observer it was still a positive piece.

As more service members became familiar with the new inflight magazine, we began running a series of ads entitled "Do you want a promotion?" Any unit, ship or squadron could write and invite us to visit them in action, and we would publicize the experience in a subsequent issue. One challenge from the air cadets—to come gliding with their young pilots—resulted in both photographer Mark Lamontagne and I losing our lunches prior to landing.

In August 1990, Rick Raddell and I flew out to Victoria to accept another seagoing adventure at the request of the Edmonton naval reserve unit HMCS *Nonsuch.* Meanwhile, Saddam Hussein was invading Kuwait and the entire world was mobilizing in support of President George Bush Sr.'s Operation Desert Shield. A Canadian flotilla was to set sail from Halifax to enforce the embargo imposed on Iraq. Closer to home, armed Mohawk activists had established barricades at Oka and Akwesasne; when a Quebec police officer was killed, the Canadian army deployed an entire brigade in response. The national media were packed with news stories of the Canadian military gearing up for combat operations at home and abroad, and *Esprit de Corps* was heading to the west coast to cover some "weekend warriors" on a training exercise.

After Raddell and I managed to find our ship at the Canadian Forces Base Esquimalt dockyard, we were somewhat dismayed. "Are you sure they want me to photograph this old relic?" Raddell asked. Our new home was HMCS *Porte Dauphine,* a short, squat, unarmed vessel known as a Gate-class utility ship. Sailing in formation with her sister ship, HMCS *Porte Quebec,* for the

48

next several days it was the site of basic seamanship training along the scenic British Columbia coast. The old Gate vessels could manage only a snail's pace of about eight knots, and without any weaponry aboard these ships it seemed as though the most frequently taught naval practice was that of scrubbing and cleaning the decks.

To add excitement to the exercise and keep the lookouts alert, the first mate, Tim Khaner, occasionally heaved a floatable dummy into the sea. The man-overboard drill was repeated several times each day. At night the two ships would drop anchor and tie up alongside one another so that both crews could hop the rail and socialize with their counterparts. The naval reserve had mixed-gender crews and didn't even attempt to restrict the sailors to a two-beer limit. In fact, the junior ranks' mess sold cases of beer at duty-free prices—about twenty-five cents a can. Needless to say, it was a glum-looking lot of red-eyed sailors scrubbing the deck when we resumed the patrol the following morning.

By lunchtime on the third day of our cruise, boredom had reached its peak for Raddell and me. When I saw the first mate remove the floatable dummy from the locker, I volunteered to add some realism to the next man-overboard drill. Most of the sailors were down below, eating lunch, and it was decided that if I were to jump, I should maximize the surprise by leaping from the flying bridge on the upper deck. Putting on a life preserver and climbing onto the rail, I suddenly had my doubts. The drop was about twenty-five feet, and even at eight knots the water now seemed to be going by at a fair clip. Just before I made my jump, the first mate advised me to leap as far as possible so as not to be sucked into the propeller. I had not even thought of that possibility, but once that seed of fear had been planted, it grew rapidly. I leapt out so far from that rail that I dislocated my shoulder before

49

I hit the water. As I plunged below the surface, all I could hear was the *whumm, whumm, whumm* of the propeller slicing through the water. My left arm had popped back into the socket, but it was all but useless. I frog-kicked as hard as I could away from the ship as I began to surface. When I did pop up above the waves, I was well away from *Porte Dauphine*—so far, in fact, that the lookout didn't see me. Finally, after repeated requests from the first mate ("Are you sure no one is overboard?"), my yellow pants and orange life jacket were spotted.

The alarm bell sounded, and two lifesavers were tossed towards me. *Porte Dauphine* had stopped both her engines, but momentum continued to take the ship well away from me. I knew it would be several minutes before they had lowered the Zodiac and sent the rescue divers out to retrieve me. I swam clumsily to gather up the lifesavers. At this point, I suddenly began wondering about what was below me in the ocean's murky depths. This was the Pacific Ocean, which meant that somewhere down there were sharks and killer whales. What had seemed like a funny stunt was now suddenly a lot less humorous. At first I thought that if I just remained motionless, I would be undetected by any large underwater predator. I had watched all of the *Jaws* movies, and the absence of any dorsal fins in the vicinity only convinced me that this meant they were directly below me. Feeling vulnerable while hanging from my lifejacket, I carefully pulled myself up onto the two lifesavers so that no part of my body was in the water.

The minutes seemed to drag into hours until the Zodiac finally came roaring around the stern of the now-motionless and far-off *Porte Dauphine*. "You've gotta be crazy, sir," said one of my rescuers. "Do you have any idea what's swimming around out here?" I could only mutter something about whatever it was, it couldn't possibly be as frightening as what I had been imagining.

50

Once I was back aboard, the first mate mistook my shivering for a touch of hypothermia. The tumbler of Pusser's Rum he prescribed worked just as well to calm my shattered nerves.

BACK IN OTTAWA, things were changing at such a rapid pace that *Esprit de Corps* had no choice but to expand drastically or cease publication. The air force had decided to convert its Boeing 707 fleet into air-to-air refuellers, the bases in Germany were to be downsized drastically as a result of the collapse of the Soviet Union and, as of April 1991, Canadian Forces personnel would be transported aboard flights chartered by Air Canada. Without any distribution, our little inflight magazine appeared to be heading for extinction, just as nationwide interest in our military was peaking as a result of the steady buildup in the Persian Gulf. After several days of deliberating, Katherine and I decided to go for broke and convert *Esprit de Corps* into a newsstand monthly.

The new format would be news and history, and to make it commercially viable we would publish in English only. As we would be attempting to grow a subscription base and newsstand sales from scratch, it was imperative to retain the seatback distribution aboard the Air Canada military charters. With two years' worth of sample magazines and several letters of glowing praise from senior officials, it wasn't difficult to get the Air Canada representative to agree. The airline had just won this lucrative contract from the Department of National Defence and was anxious to please its clients.

In order to sell the volume of ads required to print the magazine on a monthly basis—not to mention the Herculean task of filling the projected eighty-four-page format with editorial—Katherine and I had to begin hiring staff. We had rented a renovated Victorian-era house in downtown Ottawa, and keeping one

51

bedroom as our private domain, we converted the rest into office space. James Scott had applied for the job as an advertising sales representative, but his real passion was in military history and writing. While he remained responsible for some major advertising accounts, within a few weeks he had become the editor emeritus of the new magazine. In those early days, every member of the growing team had to be a jack of all trades, and Jim Scott as editor was no exception. For example, when one photo shoot for a luggage advertiser required a male model, Jim was required to squeeze into a Second World War sailor suit that was far too small for him. Humility was a job requirement.

We were still publishing the last of the inflight magazines at this stage and selling and designing the new-look monthly. Given the change in lead times, our production cycle was going to have to change as well. We would have to print the magazines in Canada, but the colour separations would still be done in Thailand. It was also at this point that computer graphics were beginning to eclipse the old technology of laborious cut-and-paste artboards. The new technology was outside our experience, so we needed to contract additional artists. The sudden ballooning of personnel and overhead also pushed my limited bookkeeping skills beyond the brink. Until now I had dutifully logged all the payables and receivables in a single notebook, but calculating things like employee source deductions and balance sheets required an office manager. Originally acquired in a temp-agency swap for a failed candidate, Julie Simoneau was hired as an entry-level receptionist. Like Jim Scott, Simoneau rose to the occasion to fill the administrative void. Before long we had eight employees working full time out of our crowded office.

To finance the expansion, we had incorporated the business and sold a handful of shares to family and friends. The business plan seemed solid enough, and our relationship with the senior brass at the Department of National Defence remained positive. In December 1990, I had been invited to join a team of historians sponsored by the Department to visit Canadian troops in the Persian Gulf. When I received the invitation, I was in Germany, finalizing the printing of the last inflight magazine. Since I would be required to fly out immediately upon my return to Canada, official authorization was sent to the base at Baden-Soellingen to issue me with the six required vaccinations. All service personnel had been immunized before deploying overseas, receiving one needle a week over the course of six weeks as part of their gradual workups. When I showed up at the base hospital in Baden, the nurse read the message from National Defence Headquarters with visible concern. "I'm not sure it's advisable to give you all six at once," she said. "I'll need you to sign a personal liability waiver."

At this late stage there was no other option to obtain the required inoculations—and I was not going to be left out of the Persian Gulf trip on a technicality. I signed the waiver and took three needles in each arm. The nurse advised me to go straight back to my apartment and avoid consuming alcohol. I interpreted this to mean that I should get to bed at a decent hour after a couple of pints with my friends.

The next morning I awoke feeling as though I had been on the losing end of a kick fight with Chuck Norris. My shoulders ached so much that I could not lift my arms, my head was reeling and I had a raging fever. I crashed around in the small apartment, knocking over a coffee table and vomited in the garbage can before attempting to climb the staircase. I had trouble convincing my printer, Peter Naber, who lived upstairs and provided a flat for me, that this was more than just a hangover, but then he insisted on taking me to the local hospital. That wasn't an option

53

at this point, because I had to get to Frankfurt airport to catch my flight home. Any delay, and I would miss out on the Persian Gulf junket. Against his better judgement, and more than a little pissed off about the condition of the apartment, Naber helped to dress me, pack my bags and put me aboard a Frankfurt-bound train. Sick or not, I was going to war.

A half-dozen of us designated historians had been selected to make this trip, and our chaperon was Major Dennis Tabbernor. A serving infantry officer, Tabbernor had jumped at the chance to get into the Gulf War theatre, even if only to act as a tour guide. We flew to London's Heathrow airport and caught a Gulf Air flight to our first port of call, Bahrain. It was here that Canada had established a joint headquarters to oversee the operational command and control of both our naval flotilla and the fighter squadron based in Qatar. Commodore Ken Summers had set up his Bahrain command post in a luxurious five-star hotel. Seeing the remains of several lobsters on the room service tray outside the door as we were ushered in to interview Summers, I noted that this wasn't exactly how I had envisioned life on the front line. Tabbernor had already been warned that Summers wanted nothing to do with our delegation. The commodore had advised Ottawa against sending us, and since they had ignored his advice, he determined to make sure our trip was a waste of time.

Our planned visit to the three navy ships patrolling the Persian Gulf was cancelled, and although we would be allowed to proceed via commercial aircraft to Qatar, Summers advised us not to expect much in the way of access to the air force personnel. As we sat there scribbling down Summers's curt dismissal, the portly little commodore folded his arms dramatically behind his head and leaned back in his chair. The back of the chair suddenly gave way, and Summers clutched wildly at the desk to keep from falling to the floor. It was like a scene right out of a Mel Brooks movie, as we historians attempted not to notice the commodore's antics.

Without an official itinerary we sought out the local bars for inspiration. Bahrain was one of the few Gulf States where the sale of alcohol was legal, and it was therefore something of a playground for oil-rich Arabs. At more than US$7 for a beer, drinking was indeed a rich man's pursuit in Bahrain. Nevertheless, the clubs were packed with coalition forces personnel. This was a major naval base for the United States, and many of the allied countries had also established headquarters here. Most of the actual combat forces were massed along the Saudi Arabia–Iraq border and awaited the expiration of President George Bush Sr.'s ultimatum for Saddam Hussein to withdraw from Kuwait. War fever was at full pitch, and the international media were hyping the coming conflict as "the mother of all battles." Iraq's battle-tested army, the fourth-largest in the world, was about to take on the mightiest alliance assembled since the Second World War. The only women in the nightclubs were the Eastern European singers who constituted the entertainment. In between sets, British soldiers in uniform would belt out old classics like "It's a Long Way to Tipperary" and ribald rugby songs. It seemed a rather festive atmosphere for a world poised on the brink of war.

Qatar was a different experience for us, as the strict no-alcohol enforcement all but curtailed any nocturnal activities. Our little delegation was housed in a five-star hotel, but contrary to Commodore Summers's prophecy, the air force squadron was quite receptive to our visit. We toured both Canada Dry One and Canada Dry Two, the Canadian camps established to support the activities of the Desert Cats CF-18 fighter squadron. We spent a couple of days interviewing and photographing the activities of

55

the ground crew and pilots. It was a major U.S. airfield, and the Canadians were just one small group of the large allied air force. Huge transports were landing continually to stockpile a massive amount of ordnance, and fighter jets were constantly roaring off to mount patrols and reconnaissance over occupied Kuwait.

Just past midnight on January 17, 1991, Bush's deadline expired, and within minutes the first wave of the coalition's attack aircraft were pounding Baghdad. Major Tabbernor rousted his collection of historians out of bed and advised us to be packed and ready to depart from Qatar in fifteen minutes. The war had started, and we were catching the first Hercules transport plane back home.

I WAS CHEESED off at having to leave the Persian Gulf just as the hostilities were erupting, but there was plenty of work to consume my energies back in Ottawa. One of the special projects involving *Esprit de Corps* was the production of a series of pin-up posters for the troops. A local modelling agency found a number of volunteers to strip down into bikinis to raise our troops' morale. A local photographer volunteered his own time, and a whole bunch of military props were donated to the cause by the National Arts Centre. Major Tabbernor's wife even got in on the act when we discovered that she had a side business custom-designing bathing suits. We produced a total of six posters—one for each of the ships HMCS *Terra Nova, Athabaskan* and *Protecteur,* one for the Desert Cats squadron and one each for the Royal 22nd Regiment security force and the administration troops.

In advance of our upcoming magazine launch, *Esprit de Corps* had taken out a promotional booth at an Ottawa trade show, and a couple of the models were on hand to promote their posters. One television crew took an interest in our project to boost morale for our troops in the Gulf and eagerly began filming.

Katherine was coming home from Singapore at the time, but my mother-in-law happened to catch the story, which aired that night on the six o'clock news. She didn't catch all the details of the newscast; all she saw was me on the television with a bevy of girls in bikinis. The next call was from Katherine at an airport, asking me why her mother was so upset.

Another project that stemmed from my visit to Qatar was a book about our fighter squadron's experience in its first combat role since the Korean War. I had met Captain Dave Deere at the mess hall in Canada Dry Two, and he told me that he was keeping a written and photographic record of events with the idea of producing a magazine-format souvenir booklet. I told him that the public interest in the war would probably make such a book a commercial success provided it could be produced quickly enough to cash in on the yellow ribbon mania back in Canada. We made a gentleman's agreement to co-publish the unit's history as soon as Deere returned to Canada.

As events unfolded, that return home came quicker than any analyst had predicted. After thirty days of air bombardment, U.S. commander General "Stormin' Norman" Schwarzkopf launched the allied ground offensive on February 24. The dazed, demoralized and dishevelled Iraqi army did not live up to its hype; it simply collapsed after only a token gesture of defiance. Deere's Desert Cats had been assigned to fly defensive combat air patrols out over the Persian Gulf, but once the Iraqis were put to rout, all the allied pilots wanted to be in on the kill. The Canadians were no exception. Our pilots managed to borrow bombs from the U.S. Air Force in order to contribute to the slaughter taking place on the "Highway of Death" just outside Kuwait City.

When the ceasefire was signed, headlines around the world proclaimed the simple word *Victory,* and the stage was set for jubilant homecoming ceremonies. We calculated that we could produce both the book *Desert Cats* and our inaugural monthly edition in time for a May 1 launch date. Eric Tate had come on board at *Esprit de Corps* in February as an advertising salesman, but his personal forte was organizing large events. He had convinced a number of senior politicians and generals to attend our launch as honoured guests, and this in turn guaranteed a media presence along with a wide range of corporate sponsors. A winery donated several cases of its product, the Novotel hotel in Ottawa arranged a contra deal to provide the food and the ballroom and a custom products company produced a wide selection of luggage and merchandise emblazoned with the *Esprit de Corps* logo. To further nail our feet to the floor in advance of the launch, we had notified the local CTV outlet of our intentions. It decided that the Gulf War angle warranted a full segment on one of its locally produced shows, *Regional Contact.* Once that episode had aired, there was no going back.

Production of both our premiere issue and Dave Deere's book, *Desert Cats,* came right down to the wire. In fact, the owner of the printing company personally drove to the hotel the first copies to come off his binding machines. The reception room was already full of dignitaries and media, and the arrival of our magazines and books was a welcome relief. "Just don't let them open the copies of *Desert Cats* while they're at the podium," said the printer. "The glue's not dry yet, and the books will fall apart."

As publisher, it was my job to welcome everyone to the launch, and then I would turn the floor over to Jim Scott. As editor, he was now also to be our company spokesman. I delegated this role to him because I suffered from crippling stage fright. To get through my few lines of welcoming remarks, I had my speech printed in twenty-point, double-spaced type. I rehearsed it repeatedly and made notes in the margin such as "Pause here for laughter."

As it turned out, there was no pausing whatsoever while I kept my eyes transfixed to my script. With my knees shaking, my rapid-fire delivery was given in one long monosyllabic mumble. I had already stepped away from the podium before people realized that my short speech was over. In the media coverage we received on the news that night, not one clip of my speech was used—the entire thing had been unintelligible.

In all other respects the launch was a classy affair and was well attended by politicians and generals. To assist us in distributing our products, a number of elegantly dressed fashion models acted as hostesses. Their task was to circulate through the crowd and hand out the publications after Jim Scott had officially launched them. A female reporter from the *Ottawa Citizen* asked one of the hostesses, "Who are all these pretty girls?" Needless to say, we were shocked the following morning to see the front-page headline "Pin-up Girls Push War Book." A couple of the models had indeed appeared in the pin-up posters, but the only person aware of this was the reporter herself. It was one hell of an introduction to learning how media stories can be spun. Luckily for us, a large number of high-profile attendees took exception to the *Citizen* article, and the following day a full page of angry letters to the editor was published under the headline "Book Launch Coverage Blows Up Storm of Protest." In getting a second round of media coverage, this time positive, we learned that controversy is not necessarily a bad thing—especially when you don't have an advertising budget.

BEFORE THE DUST from our launch had settled, I was on my way back to the Persian Gulf. This time I was on my own. As I was already circumnavigating the globe to bring the colour separations for the next issue to Bangkok, I simply juggled my flight path to include a stopover in Bahrain. The headquarters staff of Commodore Ken Summers had long gone, and the Canadian flotilla had already returned to Halifax harbour. However, when the coalition forces had been massing in Bahrain prior to the hostilities, real estate had been at a premium. With virtually no negotiating room, the Canadian contingent had entered into a ten-year lease of two modern apartment buildings that were to serve as temporary barracks. The war, of course, did not last ten months, let alone ten years, but the Bahraini landlord would not let the Canadian government out of its contract. When everyone else had headed home, one solitary petty officer was left behind as caretaker of the rental properties. Dressed in local robes complete with an Arabic headscarf, this naval finance clerk met my flight. He was friendly and hospitable, but I felt that his prolonged solitude in this forgotten posting was not a healthy situation.

There were no other media outlets interested in covering the Gulf War aftermath, so Commander Richard Melnick had obligingly sent one of HMCS *Huron*'s two Sea King helicopters to pick me up at the Bahrain airport and fly me out to the destroyer. The *Huron* had arrived in the Persian Gulf just as the hostilities concluded. As the fanfare of war reports had morphed into yellow ribbon homecoming ceremonies, the *Huron* had inherited the unheralded task of maintaining the naval embargo of Iraq. In a subsequent article I compared the crew of the *Huron* to a Zamboni driver clearing up the ice after a hockey game as the players and fans headed to the exit. On the ninety-minute flight out over the Persian Gulf, the magnitude of the war's impact on the environment was readily apparent. The horizon to the north of Bahrain was shrouded in a thick pall of smoke and smog. Three months after the retreating Iraqi army had sabotaged the Kuwaiti oil fields, the fires still burned fiercely, and air pollution blanketed the entire region. Similarly, oil-pumping facilities at Kuwait's ports had been destroyed, and millions of barrels of crude oil still coated vast surface areas of the Persian Gulf as far south as Bahrain. Thankfully, the seas remained relatively calm during my three-day voyage aboard the *Huron*, and my seasickness remained under control.

WHEN I RETURNED to Ottawa, events were unfolding that were destined to propel *Esprit de Corps* into a truly independent publication. The Progressive Conservative government had just appointed Marcel Masse as the new defence minister. Since he had a reputation as a flamboyant and arrogant Quebec separatist, I penned an editorial proclaiming his appointment to be a "slap in the face" for our military as they returned from hostilities in the Persian Gulf. Days later, the vice-chief of defence, Vice-Admiral Chuck Thomas, submitted his letter of resignation to the chief of defence staff, John de Chastelain, in protest. In it, he stated that the Canadian Forces were not properly prepared for the future. Fearing that Thomas would leak his comments to the media, de Chastelain and Deputy Minister Bob Fowler took the wind out of the vice-chief's sails by making his resignation public. In the official media release that accompanied Thomas's letter of complaint was a covering letter from de Chastelain, pointing out that Thomas's gesture of self-sacrifice was undermined by the fact he was just six months away from retirement. Unable to refute Thomas's allegations of mismanagement, de Chastelain chose instead to attack his motives. What could have been a major media issue was examined and dismissed by the press corps as trivial bickering between two generals. However, at *Esprit de Corps* we recognized the import of Thomas's

61

resignation, and Jim Scott interviewed him about his concerns for the long-term future of the Canadian forces.

Both the Marcel Masse editorial and the Thomas interview appeared in our second monthly issue, and the Defence department was quick to react. Two days after that magazine hit the newsstands, we received a fax from Air Canada advising us, "Due to concerns over editorial content, the Department of National Defence has ordered Air Canada to cease distribution of *Esprit de Corps* aboard military charter flights." At this point we only had about seven hundred subscribers, and although we were distributing thirty thousand copies nationwide on newsstands, we had no idea of actual sales. Without the inflight passenger distribution *Esprit de Corps* would have no verifiable readership.

After meeting with our entire staff, we concluded that we had no alternative but to fight this decision. Although the Defence department's letter to Air Canada only referred to editorial content, our sources inside the military had told us that the decision had come down from Marcel Masse's office. Until this point, we had never really extended ourselves to the mainstream media, but now that our very survival was at stake we had nothing to lose.

Jim Scott drafted a press release accusing the Department of National Defence of censorship. We photocopied the Air Canada fax, packed our briefcases with copies of the banned magazine and set off for the National Press Building. We had no idea what we were doing, so we simply went door to door asking to speak to reporters. Since the story involved Marcel Masse and the documentation clearly supported our version of events, a lot of media outlets ran items about the military suppressing freedom of speech. After the initial wave of press coverage, the Defence department was furious at the embarrassment we had caused them, Air Canada wanted no part of the dispute and we were still off the charter flights. It was time for us to do some serious poker playing.

At that time, the magazine *Canadian Defence Quarterly* enjoyed a cozy relationship with the Department of National Defence (DND). Although the quarterly was ostensibly independent, all of its editorial content was provided by senior officers in the military, and the entire press run was purchased from Baxter Publications and circulated as an official periodical throughout the Canadian Forces. With no editorial cost and no distribution expenses, Baxter simply sold exorbitantly priced advertisements to the defence industry, which was eager to reach *Canadian Defence Quarterly*'s "official" readership. To keep the senior officials happy with this arrangement, Baxter appointed top generals to the magazine's editorial review board and then hosted them at annual "seminars" in the Caribbean and Las Vegas. We had learned of these under-the-table junkets through the satirical magazine *Frank*. Included on the *Canadian Defence Quarterly*'s board, and a participant in some of Baxter's freebie excursions, was none other than Chief of Defence Staff John de Chastelain.

I called up Deputy Chief of Defence Staff Lieutenant General David Huddleston, whose office had been responsible for my trip to the Persian Gulf, and told him that we wanted our magazines back on the flights. He had been something of a champion for our publication in the past, but this time Huddleston said he was sorry but his hands were tied. I explained that I did not want to threaten DND, but unless our distribution was reinstated within the next forty-eight hours, our claim of censorship was going to change to conflict of interest. At five o'clock that Thursday afternoon, we would issue a press release detailing how de Chastelain was on Baxter's *Canadian Defence Quarterly* masthead, had received

63

personal benefits as a result and then had issued an order that would effectively kill the competition—*Esprit de Corps*. Huddleston warned me that these were serious allegations. I assured him that I had solid proof, otherwise I would not have taken things to this level. I stressed the fact that our only desire was to get back on the planes, not to embarrass DND any further in this matter.

It was an anxious two days for us because there was no further word from or communication with DND. We had just threatened to disgrace the chief of the defence staff, knowing that to do so would finish the dream of *Esprit de Corps*. Not only would our circulation be terminated, but defence advertisers would also distance themselves from us under such circumstances. It would be a noble Samson-like gesture of collapsing the temple on ourselves in order to kill a few Philistines. Since the alternative was to simply cease publishing without a whimper, we really had no choice.

At 4:45 PM—fifteen minutes before the ultimatum was to expire—on Thursday the phone rang. Huddleston began unconvincingly by saying that his phone call was in no way prompted by my threat. His call also confirmed a complete reversal on the part of the military. He said that if we would promise not to go public with DND's reversal on this, he would issue a letter to Air Canada telling them to resume stocking the seatbacks with the current issue. The details were confirmed in a meeting the following day. A brigadier-general from the public affairs branch and a colonel with the judge advocate general met Jim Scott and me at the Elephant and Castle pub in downtown Ottawa. A handshake sealed the deal, and by four o'clock we were back on the charter flights.

WHEN I HAD last stayed at the apartment complex in Bahrain, I had encountered a couple of Canadian combat engineers who were also using the facility as a temporary residence. They were part of 1st Combat Engineer Regiment, which had been deployed into Kuwait as part of the United Nations' operation to assist in the post-war reconstruction. There had been absolutely no media coverage of these soldiers, who had dubbed themselves "The Lost Boys." Immediately following our censorship skirmish with DND, I flew back through Bahrain and caught a connecting flight into Kuwait. It had been a full three months since the ceasefire had been signed, but most Kuwaiti residents had yet to return home.

Kuwait City was full of coalition forces, UN troops, international oil workers and Palestinian labourers. Most of the damage evident on the streets was the result of vandalism by withdrawing Iraqi soldiers. During the war's month-long aerial bombardment, U.S. and allied planes had pounded Baghdad and other cities in Iraq, but they had not targeted the Iraqi army positions inside the occupied Kuwaiti capital. Iraqi troops had vented their animosity towards the United States by destroying symbols of western culture such as Kentucky Fried Chicken and McDonald's outlets; they had also set fire to the International Hotel. Although they probably had intended to destroy the building, they had started the fire on the seventh floor and only managed to burn out the top three storeys. This was one of the few western-standard hotels that had now reopened for business, so I was lucky to get a room on the sixth floor. The smoke damage was considerable, and looters had kicked the door off its hinges, but for US$50 a night it was a place to call home.

I spent the next week travelling around the war-ravaged countryside with the Lost Boys. A large number of the oil fires were still burning, and the skies were often jet black even at midday. Maverick oil-field firefighting veteran Paul "Red" Adair was frequently seen in the lobby of the International Hotel, conducting business with various Kuwaiti sheiks and businessmen. Adair's teams were bolting the fires and capping the wells, but their task was being made more difficult by competing freelancers. As oil-

65

field owners were paying a set fee for each well that was capped, opportunists were rushing about containing the easy fires. If the Iraqis had blown a well above ground, the fires burned relatively cleanly and therefore were less difficult to extinguish. When saboteurs dug down and ignited subsurface explosions, dirty fires resulted, with out-of-control geysers of flames billowing black smoke. The capping of clean fires only increased the underground pressure of the shared oil and gas deposits, therefore increasing the size of the dirty fires.

Inside the city, the large-scale presence of U.S. military police and international troops belied the widespread lawlessness that existed among the residents. Most Kuwaiti citizens had fled when the Iraqis had invaded, but the largely Palestinian labour force had remained behind. There was not a lot of love between the workers and their employers, and in the post-war vacuum the Palestinians had collected vast stores of abandoned Iraqi weaponry. Arms bazaars flourished throughout the city. A brand-new Kalashnikov assault rifle with one hundred rounds of ammunition could be picked up for about US$10—the same price as a roast chicken dinner from a roadside vendor.

About three hundred of the Lost Boys were deployed into Kuwait, and they were responsible for clearing safe routes through the desert and building accommodations for UN observers. In this immediate post-war chaos, the United States had close to 500,000 soldiers deployed in the region, with several armoured divisions still well inside the Iraqi border. The UN was to monitor the withdrawal of the coalition forces and re-establish the pre-war boundary.

Just to clear routes in order to set up the observation posts, the Canadian sappers had their work cut out for them. It was estimated that approximately 20 per cent of all the ordnance dropped by the allied air force had failed to explode. Furthermore,

66

the Iraqis had sown massive minefields throughout Kuwait, and in their desperate retreat, artillery shells and munitions had been randomly discarded. Just outside Kuwait City there were still more than four thousand destroyed vehicles scattered along one stretch of Highway 80, the "Highway of Death". Most, but not all, of the Iraqi bodies had been cleared and buried by this point, but Egyptian soldiers were still combing the wreckage to locate additional human remains.

American and allied troops treated the site as if it were a tourist trap, spray-painting graffiti on the wrecks and posing atop shattered tanks, as though they were conquering heroes. No one thought to warn any of these soldiers that a new type of munition had been used in the aerial bombing. Essentially the by-product of nuclear waste, depleted uranium has a density greater than that of tungsten, and scientists had also discovered that depleted-uranium warheads ignited upon impact. Used against armoured targets, such rounds were designed to punch right through conventional hardened steel and then incinerate the crew with a red-hot blast of particles. No one thought to calculate the long-term health effects that the resultant radioactive aerosol might have on the humans exposed to it. That would come later.

Out in the desert, away from the carnage on the main highway, the true scope of the allies' one-sided victory over the Iraqis became even more apparent. With not so much as a single tree to provide cover or camouflage, the Iraqi soldiers had prepared defensive positions by bulldozing sand to create berms. Tanks and armoured vehicles had been dug into these primitive protective positions, but from the air such trenches would have appeared like giant bull's eyes. Anywhere the Iraqis had been entrenched, the berms were cratered from 500-lb. bombs, the hulks of their armoured vehicles blackened and the ground strewn with tiny parachutes from cluster bombs. During the retreat, individual tanks and armoured personnel carriers caught in the open had also been destroyed.

The allies suffered fewer than three hundred fatalities in the course of the war—including accidental deaths and a 30 per cent rate of friendly-fire casualties. Even a conservative estimate, however, would put the Iraqi death toll at well above 200,000. It had not been a battle; it had been the mother of all slaughters. As one U.S. senator summed up the one-sided carnage, "It was like the world's greatest superpower went to war against the Flintstones."

The majority of my studies during my combat intelligence training had been on the identification and recognition of Soviet-built tanks and weapons. The overwhelming majority of the vehicles littering the Kuwaiti desert were the older-model T-54 and T-55 tanks, the numbers indicating the years they were built. These thirty-five-year-old armoured vehicles were the outdated, obsolete equipment that Saddam Hussein had issued to his conscripted militia forces. The Iraqi president's elite Republican Guard—and their more modern T-72 tanks—had all withdrawn to the north before the U.S. attack. These loyal Iraqi troops were now heavily engaged in suppressing internal anti-Saddam revolts. The Kurds had risen in the northern provinces, while in the south the Shiite majority had attacked the retreating remnants of Saddam's army as it fled from Kuwait. Despite all the pre-war U.S. demonization of Saddam as a tyrant and a despot, the massive buildup of American forces—including warplanes—made no attempt to support these Iraqi uprisings. In fact, the U.S. commanders went out of their way to allow the Republican Guard to rearm and regroup.

The Lost Boys routinely patrolled the border area and had located one site that housed an abandoned Iraqi missile battery, including seventeen sophisticated Chinese-built Silkworm anti-ship guided missiles. It was not the job of the Lost Boys, as part of the UN observation team, to secure such weaponry; they simply were to report any findings to the local U.S. commander. One day, the Canadian sappers saw tracks in the sand heading back across the Iraq border and noticed that two of the Silkworms were miss-ing. This in turn was reported to the American colonel, and still no effort was made to secure the remainder. By the end of the week, all seventeen Silkworm missiles had crossed the border, and the Canadians realized that the game being played was not exactly as it seemed.

Within a few months Saddam's battered forces were able to reassert full control over all of southern Iraq, including the vital oil fields around Basra. In the north, his Republican Guard had pushed the Kurdish *peshmerga* back from the outskirts of Bagh-dad to their strongholds in the three northernmost provinces. Iraqi helicopter gunships had blasted the retreating Kurdish reb-els while U.S. fighter jets flew idly above them.

After recapturing the oil-rich Turkmen enclave of Kirkuk, Saddam signed a ceasefire agreement with the Kurds. The two primary Kurdish warlords, Massoud Barzani and Jalal Talabani, retained autonomous control over their territory, while Saddam regained control over all of Iraq's oil production.

As these events unfolded inside Iraq, the Lost Boys were ply-ing their trade in the sun-scorched heat of the Kuwaiti desert with very little support from National Defence Headquarters in Ottawa. No provision had been made to equip the engineers with air conditioning units, and as a result fatigue was becoming a major factor because there was no respite from the heat. Sergeant Dave McCracken called me aside during my visit and explained that officially he was not complaining about the conditions; how-ever, he had made a deal to purchase local air conditioners and to acquire a quantity of lighter-weight desert uniforms directly from one of the departing allied units. Up until this point, the old Canadian combat uniforms, which were designed to provide some protection from biological and chemical weapons, had been a serious cause for complaint among the Lost Boys. The material did not breathe, so it only exacerbated the effects of the heat. The British had a surplus of lighter cotton uniforms, and an enterprising quartermaster had brokered a deal with McCracken to exchange them for some booze. However, a bureaucrat in Ottawa determined that there was no budget to buy the air conditioners and that the acquisition of the cooler British uniforms would have to be processed through all the proper channels. Delivery of new clothing from the United Kingdom would not arrive before the Lost Boys returned to Canada.

Upon my own return to Ottawa, I wrote a straight news story about the combat engineers in Kuwait and a scathing editorial outlining the lack of material support they were receiving. Once again, Jim Scott and I headed down to the National Press Building, and this time we were out to assist the front-line troops. Tim Naumetz, a reporter with Sun Media newspapers, quickly took up the cause, and his story of the Lost Boys—accompanied by my photographs of the engineers in action—ran as a major feature across the entire chain.

Canadians were still very much in the yellow-ribbon, support-the-troops euphoria of the Gulf War victory celebrations. For them to learn that our soldiers were suffering needlessly in the desert struck a nerve. A Defence department unaccustomed to such a critical public glare quickly moved to set things straight. I received a letter of thanks from Dave McCracken shortly thereafter, explaining that within days of the Sun Media article the Lost Boys had both their air conditioners and new British uniforms. *Esprit de Corps* had established itself as a medium that could air issues on behalf of a rank and file that was officially unable to do so.

4

BAPTISM OF FIRE

When my unit takes casualties, it is very
emotional because we are all from the same
village. You know their families.
LIEUTENANT GORAN KARLOVIC, CROATIAN ARMY

IN THE FALL OF 1991, the eyes of the world were on southern
Europe as the violent dissolution of Yugoslavia entered its first
stages. Despite strong U.S. diplomatic pressure on the country's
six republics to remain united under a single federal government,
Croatia and Slovenia had declared independence from Yugoslavia in June 1991. U.S. Ambassador Warren Zimmermann had
encouraged the Belgrade federal government to denounce the
secessions and to mount a military demonstration in response.
Columns of tanks were sent into Croatia and Slovenia equipped
with only Yugoslav People's Army (JNA) blank training ammunition. Tipped off to the ruse, Slovenian and Croatian nationalists
quickly overwhelmed the ominous-looking but otherwise harmless mechanized vehicles. A recently reunified Germany flexed its
new-found diplomatic muscles by defying the United States and
officially recognizing the two republics as independent states. A

couple of limited air strikes by the Yugoslav air force had been the extent of hostilities in Slovenia, but in Croatia things were more complicated.

Inside the administrative boundary of the Yugoslav republic of Croatia lived three major pockets of ethnic Serbs, who had thrived in these villages for hundreds of years since the Turks had forced them out of Kosovo. The Austro-Hungarian Empire had encouraged their relocation because the Serbs would provide a buffer zone with the Ottoman Turks. During the Second World War, when Croatia had been allied to Nazi Germany, residents of Serbian enclaves such as Krajina had been brutally persecuted by the right-wing Croatian Ustashi militias. In the wake of the 1991 Croatian declaration of independence from Yugoslavia, Krajina Serbs had proclaimed their own desire to separate from Croatia. This polarization of nationalist sentiments, fuelled by still-vivid memories of Second World War atrocities against each other, sparked a bloody civil war within Croatia. All Yugoslav males had undergone national service, and weapons were in plentiful supply. Serbs living in the predominantly Croatian areas were expelled, detained or worse. Similarly, Croats living in the Serb pockets were eliminated, and the phrase *ethnic cleansing* emerged to describe the violence and widespread expulsions.

72   By March 1992, the UN had managed to broker a temporary ceasefire in Croatia. Canada had nearly a full brigade stationed in Germany because they were still in the process of shipping their equipment home. When the UN call for peacekeepers went out, the Canadian government jumped at the opportunity. The decision to send a twelve-hundred-man battle group into Croatia arrived just in time for the troops involved. Many of the vehicles had already been loaded aboard trains that were headed for the dockyards in Hamburg when the word came down to reroute

them to Zagreb. I was busy making my own plans to get to the Croatian capital.

ALTHOUGH THE FLEDGLING states of Croatia and Slovenia had been officially recognized by Canada, they had yet to establish any embassies or consulates in Ottawa. Obtaining a visa before my trip proved to be impossible, and travel arrangements were also a little problematic. There were no flights into Croatia; the best I could manage was a Canadian Airlines flight into Milan, Italy. From there I hoped to take a train to the border city of Trieste and then either hire a driver or take a bus to Zagreb. According to news reports, the borders were still closed to casual travellers, and there was no possibility of international rail travel. As fate would have it, when I was changing trains in Venice to catch the Trieste shuttle, I noticed one of the gates showing a 2100 departure time for a train to Udine, Ljubljana and Zagreb. I couldn't believe my luck, but a conductor confirmed that "*si, si,*" this was to be the first train from Italy into Slovenia and Croatia.

There were only two passenger cars, of the older-model second-class variety, with six passenger compartments. There was a score of Italians on board from Venice, but all of them detrained at Udine. Strolling the corridor, I realized there were only two other travellers still on the train: an Australian navy sailor and a fifteen-year-old Slovenian boy. We remained in our private compartments as we reached the Italian border checkpoint.

Police and customs agents casually inspected my passport and briefly looked through my suitcase before moving down the railway car to deal with the other two passengers. Looking out of the window, I saw two other Italian police officers escorting a young Asian woman in handcuffs onto the train. I could hear them talking to her as they placed her in the compartment adjacent to mine.

73

The Italian police then left her on her own and took the handcuffs with them. It was puzzling, but I assumed that she had been denied entrance to Italy and was being sent back to Slovenia.

The train picked up speed, and the Italian border post was soon out of sight. Night had fallen, and it was completely dark outside. After only a few kilometres, the train slowed down to navigate a long curve in the tracks. As the train braked to a halt, I was greeted with a scene straight out of a James Bond movie. Lining the railway platform were about two dozen Slovenian paramilitary border guards wearing leather coats and forage caps and armed with Kalashnikovs. A half-dozen of them had German shepherd guard dogs, and from the station house bright spotlights glared directly into our train.

Of the six guards who entered from my end of the railway car, the first three dealt with the Asian woman while the others crowded into my compartment. After demanding my passport, the leader of the group looked through the well-stamped pages. "Visa? Visa?" he asked in English. I stammered an explanation about there not being an embassy in Ottawa, and seeing his confused look, I repeated my reasoning in German.

Not understanding a word of what I had said, he ordered me off the train. His two companions were already rummaging through my suitcase, and the smell of alcohol coming from the trio was overpowering. Figuring I should keep my luggage with me if I was turned back, I hesitated and gestured at the two guards going through my belongings. The leader took my reluctance to follow his order as a defiant gesture. He aimed his Kalashnikov at me and repeated the demand. I left the train and headed towards the main door of the station house. The searchlights were blinding, but I saw that other Slovenian soldiers with dogs were moving along the tracks and using their flashlights to

74

search underneath the railway cars. I had almost reached the station house door when a shout from behind caused me to hesitate. The next sound was the distinct action of a Kalashnikov being cocked. I put up my hands and turned around. The guard leader used his loaded weapon to direct my attention farther down the platform. There the Australian sailor and the Slovenian boy stood in front of a ticket kiosk surrounded by guards. Someone had taped up a handwritten sign that read "Vize." I obligingly moved to join them.

The Aussie and I whispered introductions, and he asked me what the hell was happening. He had been on a six-month sailing cruise, was unaware of any war in the Balkans and had simply been planning to tour Greece. The price of his entry visa into Slovenia turned out to coincide with all the cash he had in his wallet—about US$220. I had no cash on me, and there was no way these paramilitary types were set up to take Visa or traveller's cheques. One of them spoke some German, and I explained that I was a journalist. This seemed to strike the right note with the commander as he had them bring me a glass of brandy. Through the interpreter he made some statements about the glorious war of independence that the Slovenians had just won. A signal from the conductor cut the conversation short. I was given my entry visa for free and rushed back aboard the train.

My gear was in a shambles, but it seemed as though the guards had found nothing worth taking. I had started to repack the suitcase when both the Aussie and the Slovenian teenager asked if they could join me in my compartment. At least a half-dozen Slovenian paramilitaries were travelling on the train, and they were drinking heavily. We considered it best to stick together for our mutual safety. It didn't take long for our fears to prove well founded.

75

Shortly after the train had got underway, the entire group of paramilitaries came noisily down the corridor. They moved past our door, and the first of them entered the Asian woman's compartment. She screamed and tried to fight off the first one, but after that, she just made pleading, whimpering sounds as they took turns raping her. The Aussie and I discussed pulling the emergency brake handle to stop the train—but what then? These assaulters were also the local authority, they were armed and drunk and we were in the middle of nowhere.

Those paramilitaries in the corridor not involved in the ongoing rape passed around a bottle of brandy and yelled drunken encouragement to their mates. At one point a hatless guard, his leather coat unbuttoned, threw open our door and shouted something unintelligible. "He wants cigarettes," said the boy. The Aussie sailor reluctantly extended a half-empty package of Marlboros, and the drunken rapist took them all. The corridor was soon filled with smoke; the whimpering continued.

When the train slowed to enter the rail yard in Ljubljana nearly two hours later, the guards began pulling themselves together. The brandy bottle was heaved out of the window, uniforms were straightened and Kalashnikovs were slung over shoulders. The guards left the train but remained standing in a group on the platform. When the Slovenian boy climbed down the stairs with his luggage, one of the guards cuffed him on the back of the head and hissed a warning at him—presumably telling him to say nothing of what had transpired.

Only once our train had started to lurch forward out of Ljubljana station did the group of rapists begin to leave the platform. The Aussie and I took turns visiting the bathroom at the end of the car in order to check on the Asian woman. She had turned off the lights in her compartment and drawn the curtains. Neither of us was brave enough to knock on the door.

When we finally arrived at the nearly deserted train station in Zagreb, it was about two in the morning. There were no money-exchange shops open, the Aussie and I had no cash between us, and we had no idea where we were going to stay. Nevertheless, we approached the Asian woman, who had emerged from the railway car and now stood alone on the platform. After what she had endured, we tried to appear as unthreatening as possible and tried to communicate our offer to assist her in any way we could. She had regained her composure, and although she probably could not understand a word we said, her dismissive wave was easily understood. She turned and walked slowly, painfully, out into the deserted streets of Zagreb. The overwhelming sense of impotence and injustice I felt at that moment has not diminished with the passage of time.

I SPENT A COUPLE of days getting my bearings in the Croatian capital. A small UN office had opened, but the staff were not willing or able to assist a foreign journalist, and the Croatian army had only a small press centre. Sandbags had been piled in front of many of the main government buildings, and the red-and-white checkered flag of Croatia was everywhere. Other than a few hastily erected protective measures and displays of nationalistic pride, there was little evidence of this country being locked in a civil war. A helpful Croatian journalist at the army press centre explained that the front lines were located about seventy kilometres southeast of Zagreb, around the town of Daruvar. He provided me with the phone number of a colleague and the name of a friend who was serving in 52nd Independent Battalion in that sector.

The Aussie had found a bus that would get him closer to Greece, albeit via Hungary, Romania and Bulgaria. I bid him farewell at the bus depot and boarded my own coach destined for

77

Daruvar. The seventy-kilometre yardstick turned out to be as the crow flies, because the milk-run shuttle I was on took more than three hours to reach our destination.

Most of the passengers had gotten off the bus before we reached Daruvar. As we approached the town, we saw that the outlying buildings had all been either burned or damaged by gunfire. On the mostly deserted main street all the shop windows had been blown out, and broken glass and bricks littered the sidewalks. The other arrivals quickly took their belongings and disappeared into the empty side streets. At one end of the central square was a small café. Lounging around the outside table was a full platoon of heavily armed Croatian soldiers. I approached this group, and their conversation soon ceased as the soldiers suspiciously eyed the stranger in their midst.

I asked if anyone spoke English. They all shook their heads in the negative. *"Deutsch?"* I queried. Again they all shook their heads. I fumbled through my notes to find the name I had been given. "Goran Karlovic?" This drew an immediate response from a young officer at the far side of the café: "Who wants to know?" I explained who I was and how I had gotten his name, and asked where I could find accommodations. Satisfied with my information, Lieutenant Karlovic told me his men were heading to the front that evening—which explained why they were drinking so heavily—and that a hotel was open on the outskirts of Daruvar. He asked if I were interested in touring the front lines. When I readily agreed, he advised me that a driver would pick me up from my hotel the following morning.

The Hotel Therma turned out to have been a pre-war spa resort that had reopened in order to house the incoming United Nations representatives. It was clean and spartan, typical of communist-era Yugoslavia, and at DM 30 (C$20) a night it was within my tight budget. I noticed that the grounds of the hotel had been

78

heavily shelled and had some massive craters that could only have been made by five-hundred-pound bombs dropped from aircraft. After checking in and dropping off my bag, I retraced my steps to the café.

When I arrived, I found that Karlovic's platoon had left and only four civilians remained. I ordered a *pivo* (beer) and sat at the table next to them. Enjoying my drink, I was busy writing down my initial impressions of entering this devastated war zone. The locals, however, thought I was taking notes of their conversation. As they started questioning me about my identity, the only thing I could think of was to show them my passport and shrug my shoulders. Discovering that I was a Canadian journalist, two of them revealed that they spoke good German, and the group asked me to pull up a seat and join them.

Like most victims of war, they were anxious to tell their story. All four were ethnic Serbs, and three of them were married to Croatian women. All of them had been born and raised in Daruvar. The youngest was thirty-six; the oldest, sixty-two. Until the beginning of the civil war, they had worked as factory labourers at a local munitions plant.

Ironically, when the UN had imposed a wholesale arms embargo on the entire former Yugoslavia, most outsiders hadn't realized that this country was third after the United States and the Soviet Union in arms exports during the Cold War. After Croatia declared its independence, the mixed-ethnic town of Daruvar found itself on the dividing line between Serbian and Croatian nationalist factions. When Croatian paramilitaries seized the munitions factory, Serbs working there had been detained for several months. After a lengthy negotiation to arrange a prisoner swap, the Serbs were taken to the bridge that marked the front line between the warring parties.

"'Go home,' they told us," explained Mirko, the elder Serb. "So

79

we turned around and came home to Daruvar. They thought we would walk to Serbia—but we've never even been to Serbia. This is our home."

The local Croatian militias tolerated the Serbs' presence in the town, but they had lost their jobs. In true fatalistic Serbian style, this did not stop them from sitting in a café and drinking all day. In fact, they insisted on buying one more round apiece—obliging me to do the same.

Dusk was falling as we finished the sixth quart bottle of beer, and it was time to start heading back to the hotel. From far off, a low whistling sound was heard, and the café owner suddenly dimmed the light. About two hundred metres down the street a building erupted into a ball of flames. A fraction of a second later we heard the explosion and then felt the concussion shock wave. The Serbs grabbed their coats and bolted for the door. *"Bombardovanje!"* they shouted.

I heard more whistles and noticed that the café owner had left by the back door. The second and third blasts were almost simultaneous and hit just one hundred metres away. I realized that the artillery barrage was coming straight for my location, and attempted to bolt for the door. I hit the frame with my shoulder and reeled outside. It wasn't the concussion that had rocked me—I was staggering drunk. The horizon line seemed to lurch as I staggered up the street and into an alley, willing the adrenalin to clear my head.

The blast from the next shells threw me to the ground. I was in the middle of an artillery bombardment and was frightened enough to recognize the danger but too inebriated to think of a sensible plan of escape. The Serbian barrage was creeping through Daruvar on a path parallel to the main street. I simply lay curled up in the fetal position in a rubble-filled alleyway. The

80

shock waves had forced the air from my lungs; I could feel the searing heat and sense the shrapnel cutting the air above me, but I could not hear the explosions. I had been temporarily deafened by the blast.

When the bombardment had moved well beyond my position, I could still see the flashes but could not hear them. I put my hands to my ears. They were bleeding. I was drunk, deaf and in the middle of a war, but I was alive. In the pitch blackness I somehow made my way slowly back to the hotel.

I was awoken by the telephone ringing and the front desk clerk advising me that my driver was waiting. My head was pounding, and my ears were still ringing. I could not understand how I had become so drunk on just six quarts of beer. My Croatian army driver, who spoke excellent English, explained that this was a common mistake made by newcomers to the Balkans. The local *pivo* had a 13 per cent alcohol content. In other words, I had consumed the equivalent of six quarts of wine—not beer. As for the bleeding from my ears, he explained that plenty of his comrades of the 52nd Independent Battalion had suffered the same fate from the previous evening's bombardment.

As we arrived at the battalion's front-line trenches, Lieutenant Karlovic was at the command bunker to greet me. He confirmed his driver's estimate that at least fifty heavy artillery shells and twenty rockets had hit the Croatian lines during the night. They had sustained no casualties, but many of the buildings in the vicinity had been hit.

At the age of twenty-three, Karlovic was the acting battalion commander that day. He took me on a tour of his unit lines. He had just completed his national service when the war broke out and had been "elected" to a command position. It was easy to understand why the other Croatians had chosen him as their

81

leader—he was tall, fit, good-looking and charismatic. They were a youthful group, with many sporting long hair and headbands and with knives strapped to their belts in Rambo-like fashion. They absolutely detested the Serbs, whom they claimed were *Chetniks*—the term used during both world wars to describe those loyal to the monarchy.

After a short patrol along the cratered ridge that marked the forward edge of the Croatian position, Karlovic brought me into his bunker. It was here that he lost me. He proudly boasted that his unit was a collection of patriots who had thrown off the repressive yoke of a Serbian-dominated federal Yugoslavia. Karlovic claimed that in order to achieve this remarkable feat, his comrades had been forced to capture weapons from the Yugoslav army. He pointed at his well-armed troops and said, "As you can see, we have been very successful."

What I actually saw were his lies. None of the weapons fielded by the 52nd Independent Battalion had been captured from the Serbs. Everything they possessed—from light machine guns to mortars to rocket launchers to Kalashnikovs—had been manufactured in East Germany. In my lessons at the Canadian Forces intelligence school, identifying the distinctive German production models had been relatively easy because East Germany was the only Warsaw Pact nation to make extensive use of hard plastic in the magazine and stocks. The Yugoslavs produced their own family of Kalashnikov weaponry at the Zastava plant near Belgrade, but they used the more conventional stamped metal parts. Germany (now unified) had not just recognized an independent Croatia on a diplomatic level, but it had also violated the UN-imposed arms embargo by fully equipping the new Croatian forces.

As for discussing the challenges of command at such a young age, a visibly exhausted Karlovic was a little more honest with me. "When my unit takes casualties, it is very emotional because we are all from the same village. You know their families," he said. On December 22, 1991, the 52nd Independent Battalion had been involved in a bloody ambush with Serb forces that left seven Croatian soldiers dead and thirty-six wounded. "That was just three days before Christmas, and it was my job to bring the bodies home for burial," said Karlovic. "That was very difficult."

The fluid movement of troops and widespread ethnic cleansing had settled into a routine stalemate, with both sides well entrenched above the now vacant city of Pakrac. "Just look at this mess," he said, sweeping his assault rifle in a wide arc that encompassed the shattered cityscape. "This is worse than Beirut, and it only took three months to destroy it."

It was only about ten o'clock and the sun in the eastern sky was trying to burn a hole through the morning's cloud cover. "Shit," he said. "They've started early today."

Karlovic pointed to a spot on the far ridge from which rose several puffs of white smoke. We heard the crack of the heavy machine-gun bullets as they cut through the air over our heads and slammed into the concrete walls of the 52nd Battalion's headquarters bunker. To demonstrate his courage to his troops, Karlovic walked slowly back up the exposed slope. I had no choice but to follow him.

By the time we had reached the relative safety of the bunker, the 52nd Battalion was responding to the Serbian machine guns with a 20-mm automatic cannon mounted on a flatbed truck. Other weapons from both sides soon joined the firefight, and Karlovic called for the driver. It was time for me to be on my way.

BACK AT THE Hotel Therma I encountered a number of Canadian officers in the lobby. They were the advance guard of the

83

Canadian contingent being deployed as part of the UN peace-keeping force. I joined Lieutenant Colonel Michel Gauthier of 4th Combat Engineer Regiment for dinner, and he briefed me on what was transpiring. Their armoured vehicles' arrival the previous evening had sparked the Serbian artillery barrage that had nearly killed me.

Apparently, someone had forgotten to advise the Yugoslav army of the UN deployment, and the sound of advancing armour had been mistaken for a major Croatian offensive prior to the ceasefire. As the Serbian shells ranged in on the Canadian position, the soldiers of the 3rd Battalion, Royal Canadian Regiment, had been forced to "crash harbour," which involved everyone rushing into the vehicles, getting the hatches down and scattering in all directions as fast as possible. Several Canadians had received shrapnel wounds, a number of supply vehicles had been damaged and it was believed that two Croatian civilians had been killed.

At this moment there were only about three hundred Canadian soldiers in Croatia, many of them being Gauthier's engineers, who were preparing the way for the nine hundred troops to come. There was a lot of work to be done cleaning away unexploded ordnance and mines and building temporary shelters to house the Canadian peacekeepers. However, before the Croatian ceasefire line could be fully manned by UN observers, all eyes were already looking south to the developing crisis in Bosnia.

At the conclusion of dinner that night, a young armoured-corps captain had been keen to hear my description of the Croatian 52nd Battalion's positions. He offered to take me across the demarcation line so that I could meet the Serbian military. There was a UN convoy scheduled to make the crossing the following morning, and I eagerly accepted the invitation.

We set out after breakfast with a dozen UN observers packed aboard two minivans. Blue United Nations flags flew from the radio antennae, and someone had used white medical tape to fashion crude UN lettering on the hoods and side doors. I was sure that the rental company in Zagreb would be less than impressed when they returned the vehicles. There was no escort for us, and none of the observers were armed.

When we arrived at the Croatian front line, we were halted by heavily armed soldiers about two kilometres from the trenches. We moved forward as a group, observing a large number of knocked-out tanks and badly damaged houses. The village had been the scene of some very heavy fighting in recent days. A young Croatian captain approached and told us there would be some delay before we crossed because another delegation was on its way from Zagreb.

As it turned out, the second group was the personal staff of Indian General Satish Nambiar, the commander of the United Nations Protection Force (UNPROFOR). Word had broken that morning that peaceful negotiations in the Bosnian capital, Sarajevo, had collapsed, and Serbian forces had begun shelling the city. Nambiar's entourage was headed south to see what the UN could do to ward off another all-out civil war. The Croatians had assembled a small guard of honour to salute the UN general when he arrived at the crossing point. Unlike the majority of Croatian troops, this little parade had mostly matching uniforms, boots and headgear. It was obvious that Nambiar was anxious to get back on the road, but he was obligated to inspect the assembled Croatian guard of honour.

As he made his cursory stroll through the ranks, his group mingled with our UN observers and shared their thoughts on what was transpiring. One British major was practically inconsolable over the fact that the Sarajevo Holiday Inn, which had been the headquarters of the delegation of the Bosnian Serbs, was reportedly under fire. "All my luggage is still in my room," he said. "What do you think will happen to it? Who will compensate me for my stuff?" When I realized that he expected an answer from me, I mumbled something reassuringly unintelligible. I could not believe that such a self-involved idiot was worried about a suitcase full of clothes when it seemed that an entire nation was descending into hell.

Another member of Nambiar's staff was the UNPROFOR deputy commander, a Canadian brigadier by the name of Lewis MacKenzie. I had only just been introduced to him and shaken his hand when Nambiar concluded his inspection and the Croatian captain shouted for us to get moving. A huge white flag was handed to one of the Jordanian observers, who led the way towards the Serbian lines. A similar white flag had been run up a pole in the Croatian village, and around the corner of the road ahead, the Serbs had hoisted their own white panel just above the tree line. It was a well-coordinated exercise to give everyone ample time to prepare for our passage. The twenty of us moved across the one hundred metres of no man's land. Glancing back, I could see that the Croatians had gone on full alert and removed the canvas covers from the barrels of their heavy weapons and manned their trenches. Around the blind corner, the Serbian position suddenly came into view. A 105-mm howitzer had been dug into a sandbagged bunker, and its muzzle was aimed directly down the roadway. It was a fearsome sight, and the demolished houses directly in the howitzer's line of fire indicated that the Serbs had used this weapon a lot in the recent battle. However, such use also indicated that these troops had no sense of how to employ artillery properly. This type of a weapon system should have been located five to ten kilometres behind the front lines,

86

and its plunging arc of fire directed by a forward observer. To place the gunners at such risk and to fire the gun on a flat trajectory over open sights indicated to me that these were novice soldiers in possession of lethal hardware.

I was also stunned to see just how youthful the JNA troops were. The majority were still conscripts—perhaps eighteen or nineteen years old—who had been serving their compulsory service to Yugoslavia when the war erupted. One of them, however, a hardened non-commissioned officer, spotted me immediately. Everyone else in our group was in a uniform, whereas I was wearing a leather jacket and carrying a camera bag. As the JNA sergeant pushed through the UN officers to question my identity, everyone moved aside and looked at me with a "How did you get here?" look on their faces. Nambiar, MacKenzie and their group got into the vehicles that were waiting for them on this side of the line and roared off. My Canadian armoured-corps host had tried to argue my case through a translator, but to no avail. "This chap is set on shooting you," he said, jerking a thumb at the Serbian sergeant. "He says he can tell you are a Croat, no matter what your passport says."

Eventually a compromise was reached whereby I would not be granted access to the Serbian side, but I would be allowed to return on my own to the Croatian position. Feeling his job was done, my host rushed off to join the other UN observers, who were already loaded aboard the two remaining minivans. "We'll be back through here at six o'clock," he shouted. "Wait with our vehicle on the Croat side, and we'll get you back to the hotel in time for supper."

With these final instructions he jumped into the rearmost van, and the UN observers were soon roaring out of sight. The Serbian sergeant gestured at me to be on my way. I noticed that behind him his young soldiers were busy hauling down the white

87

truce flag. As I turned to start walking back, I saw the Croatian white flag disappear as well. Adjusting my camera bag securely across my back, hands held well above my head, I walked slowly down the centre of the road—praying none of the Croatians would overreact.

As I reached the dogleg curve in the road, a Croatian soldier shouted a challenge, and I stopped in my tracks. Behind me, still visible, the Serbian sergeant shouted as well, waving his arm to indicate that I should keep walking. I was identifying myself as best as possible by yelling "Canada" and "journalist," but each time I attempted to approach, the Croatian ordered me to halt. Finally the Croatian captain was summoned, and he remembered seeing me with the UN observers. "Are you trying to get yourself killed?" he asked when I entered the trench. "You look just like a Serb, dressed like that!"

I spent the next eight hours in that battered village, taking photographs of Croatian tanks and exploring the deserted streets. I was startled at one point by an old man who came into an alley to empty the contents of a chamber pot into the gutter. Once we had gotten past our mutual shock, he invited me into his farmhouse. Like the rest of the houses in the village, this building had suffered considerable damage. He spoke German, explaining that he had learned the language while serving in an SS unit during the Second World War. He was wearing a filthy camouflage uniform, and his breath reeked of cheap brandy. Pouring two generous glasses of his homemade *slivovitz*, he asked me to follow him upstairs. In one of the bedrooms he had piled sandbags and removed the windowpanes to construct a sniper post. He had a pair of Zeiss binoculars and a bolt-action Mauser rifle that he said he had kept hidden since the Second World War.

Given that he was seventy-eight years old, I asked him if he was still a soldier. Making a derisive gesture towards the main

Croatian position, he said that they prohibited him from officially serving. They did, however, allow him to guard this flank of the village, and he said he was eager to kill some *Chetniks*. His arc of fire was off to the west, overlooking an empty field in the opposite direction of the Serbian front line. I realized that the Croatian soldiers had simply allowed this old man to harmlessly drink himself to death while fighting the last war.

I finished my brandy, pointed to the far edge of the field and said, "*Chetniks!*" He grabbed the binoculars and scoured the horizon. "Where? Where?" he asked frantically. "They're behind that bush, about four hundred metres out," I replied. It was a cheap trick, but I knew it would keep him occupied until either the sun set or he passed out.

As promised, the UN observer team did return to collect me at around six o'clock, and we were back at the Hotel Therma in time for the evening meal. My limited funds were running low, so the following morning I caught the bus back to Zagreb. From there I was able to get a ticket on a train bound for Munich. It was an incredibly roundabout route to Milan to catch my return flight, but it meant I would not have to travel back through Slovenia.

THROUGHOUT THE SUMMER of 1992, the Canadian media focused primarily on the events in wartorn Bosnia. As the senior UN commander located in the besieged capital of Sarajevo, Brigadier Lewis MacKenzie became a household name. With Canadian troops serving at the airport, international media could still venture in and out of the city. Reports on the violence were a standard feature of the nightly news.

There is no question that the situation leading up to the civil war in Bosnia was complicated in the extreme. This was the flashpoint that had ignited the First World War, and it was an explosive tinderbox in the Second World War. Bosnia is also where former empires and three distinct religions came together—Serbian Orthodox Christians, Croatian Catholics and Bosnian Muslims. All these people essentially derived from the same bloodlines, but those now practising the Muslim faith had converted from the Orthodox religion during the five hundred years of Ottoman Turk occupation. The Turks had not forced Serbs to convert to Islam, but they had charged a surtax to anyone remaining Orthodox. Over time, most of the Muslims became the primary residents of the urban centres, while the Serbs and Croatians lived predominantly in rural areas. When they were annexed and incorporated into the Austro-Hungarian Hapsburg Empire, the majority of Croatians converted to Catholicism.

Czarist Russia had always pledged to support the Serbs, whom it regarded as little cousins. With the Bosnian factions used as proxies to wage war on behalf of major imperial powers, the boundaries of Bosnia ebbed and flowed with each world war. When Nazi Germany occupied Yugoslavia in 1941, it toppled the Serbian monarchy and created an independent Croatia that included the territory of modern Bosnia. Croatia became an ally of Hitler's Third Reich, and a Bosnian Muslim ss division was created to combat the predominantly Serbian partisans during the war.

With Russian Red Army forces being the first of the allies to reach the Balkans, the Communist Yugoslav forces were able to secure and control the entire country in the post-war era. The iron-fisted rule of Josip Broz Tito kept the lid on the simmering, but never extinguished, ethnic hatred. During the Cold War, Tito kept his country out of the Soviet Union's Warsaw Pact, and as a result, this neutral communist nation was able to play both the East and the West to establish a vibrant economy. However, following Tito's death in 1980 and a change in policy for the Soviet Union in 1989, those pivotal forces disappeared. Faced with a plunging economy, old hatreds resurfaced. The three nationalist camps in Bosnia were spurred on by the declarations of independence of both Slovenia and Croatia. However, the resultant civil war in Croatia heightened the international community's fears of what would happen should Bosnia decide to withdraw from Yugoslavia as well.

In February 1992, Lord Carrington and Portuguese ambassador José Cutileiro proposed an ethnic power-sharing plan for Bosnia-Herzegovina. Bosnian Serb leader Radovan Karadzic, Croatian leader Mate Boban and Bosnian Muslim leader Alija Izetbegovic all initially accepted the Carrington-Cutileiro peace plan.

It appeared as though war had been prevented; then the United States decided to get involved. Feeling it had been undermined by the Germans in the creation of Slovenia and Croatia, the U.S. State Department wasn't going to miss the boat on Bosnia. The U.S. ambassador to Yugoslavia, Warren Zimmermann, flew from Belgrade to Sarajevo to meet with Izetbegovic. Zimmermann convinced the Muslim leader that the United States would support his administration if it declared unilateral independence from Yugoslavia. Given this support from the Americans, Izetbegovic rescinded his approval of the peace plan and proclaimed the Republic of Bosnia an independent state.

The predictable violence began almost immediately. As the three major ethnic factions polarized or were cleansed into distinct districts, the maps reflected that the Serbs controlled nearly two thirds of the countryside. Western journalists flying into Sarajevo rarely crossed the front lines, so the image they took away was that of a Muslim population besieged by Serbian forces. Most American and many Canadian outlets referred to the Bosnian Serbs simply as Serbs, the implication being that the latter were invading Bosnia. Complex circumstances were dumbed down to a good-guy-versus-bad-guy equation. The Serbs lost the race to win public opinion, assisted in part by some slick U.S.

91

public relations firms who had no qualms about rewriting history. Words like *Serbian juggernaut* were used to describe Bosnian Serb troops, and editorial cartoons depicted the Serbs as Nazis.

Brigadier MacKenzie had tried to provide some balance to the media reporting by repeatedly stating that all sides in this brutal war had blood on their hands. Such comments were not appreciated by the government of Izetbegovic, and the Bosnian Muslims began a smear campaign against the Canadian general that included issuing an arrest warrant for MacKenzie. The charges included the rape and murder of Muslim women who had subsequently disappeared. The allegations were absurd, and when two Bosnian Muslims brought copies of the arrest warrant to the *Esprit de Corps* office in Ottawa, I ordered them off the premises. Such tactics were indicative of the extent of the fabrications that emanated from the Balkan civil wars, which were being waged as much through the media as they were through actual combat.

We had received occasional correspondence from MacKenzie while he was in Sarajevo and had interviewed him for the magazine after the Bosnians successfully managed to have him replaced as UN commander. While we knew that the mainstream media were covering the Bosnian conflict poorly and with little real context, at least they were still covering it. However, the ongoing saga in Croatia was being almost completely ignored, and I decided to head back there in November 1992.

IT WAS MUCH easier getting into Croatia this time. With the Croatian embassy up and running in Ottawa, I was able to obtain a visa before I travelled. Lufthansa was flying regularly scheduled flights into Zagreb, and the United Nations had a full press centre in operation.

When I went to register with the UN, I noticed that right in front of the headquarters Croatian civilians had set up a wall lined with candles. Each brick had a name and date painted on it, and a small group of weeping women were lighting candles. The Croatian translator at the UN press office explained that this wall symbolized the Serb-perpetrated genocide of Croatians during the war. Each brick was said to represent a victim of Serbian ethnic cleansing. Located right outside the press accreditation centre, this sight of crying women and candles became one of the most photographed scenes of the war. It was a brilliant public relations ploy.

Once again I took the bus south to Daruvar, but on this trip stayed with PPCLI's third battalion (3 PPCLI) in its forward positions. The United Nations was now fully deployed into the demilitarized zone between the Serbs and the Croatians. In fact, most of the Canadian platoon's housing had been established in the bombed-out ruins of the city of Pakrac. No civilians had returned to the area, but under the terms of the ceasefire, both warring factions could deploy policemen into their respective zone of control to prevent any possible looting. However, the police were simply the same heavily armed paramilitary types who had been waging the war; the only difference was that now they had been issued with badges. Exchanges of heavy gunfire were a routine occurrence that made a mockery of the term *ceasefire,* and the Canadian peacekeepers were right in the middle of things. Whenever possible, 3 PPCLI launched raids to seize heavy weaponry from the so-called police strongpoints, but this attempt to enforce the UN mandate of demilitarizing the buffer zone only drew the ire of both factions.

I was assigned to Charlie Company because it was experiencing most of the retaliatory attacks. One of the first patrols I set out on was a security detail assigned to protect a pair of Hungarian forensic pathologists. Working for the UN, these doctors were examining corpses for the purpose of identifying and recording

93

war crimes. What Canadian soldiers had originally thought to be a vandalized graveyard turned out to be a mass-murder burial ground. Sometime during the previous winter, Croatian extremists had butchered an indeterminate number of Serbian civilians and dumped their bodies into mausoleums. The high-water table of the region had partially flooded the tombs, and as a result, the untreated bodies had rotted. In some places, hair and flesh remained on the skeletons; in others, the bones were washed white. The stench was overpowering, and I was in awe of the Hungarian doctors who stood in the filthy muck of the mausoleums. They wore hip waders and rubber gloves and used a fine net to search for human remains. When a severed skull came up in the net, the forensic specialist lifted it in his hand, and the last chunk of flesh and scalp slid off the bone to plop into the water-filled grave.

The soldiers of 3 PPCLI would listen intently as the Hungarian called out details to his colleague: "Victim was female, aged between 40 and 50 years. Cause of death was a blunt instrument to the head." To illustrate his conclusion, he put his finger through a hole in the top of the skull. Curiosity got the better of one soldier, who asked, "What do you think would cause a hole like that?" Without hesitation the doctor replied, "Judging by the shards of bone fragments, probably a screwdriver. And from the force of the blow, it was probably driven in with a hammer."

Immediately after giving this gruesome assessment, the Hungarian pulled himself out of the tomb, stripped off his ooze-soaked rubber gloves and started rummaging through his knapsack. He pulled out a thick ham sandwich on a bun, seated himself just metres from the stack of rotting remains and began enjoying his lunch.

While most of the Canadian soldiers had long since lost their appetites, an armoured personnel carrier commanded by

94

Captain Dan Blanc arrived to begin shuttling soldiers back to the company mess hall. Most soldiers passed on the invitation to get a hot lunch, but I decided to go along with Blanc. He was a young, cherubic-faced reservist, and he was keen to see some action. He wouldn't have to wait for long.

After our midday meal we remounted into Blanc's carrier and were joined by a French-Canadian logistics officer. Normally assigned to rear-echelon duties inside the camp, he had expressed an interest in patrolling the deserted ruins. On our way back to the graveyard, Blanc spotted a Canadian combat engineer team at the end of a deserted side street. Instructing the driver to stop in the middle of the intersection, Blanc removed his headset and shouted back to us, "We'll just be a minute. I'm going to see what those guys are up to."

Blanc jumped down from the carrier, ran about ten steps forward and stumbled. There was an instant flash followed by an ear-splitting explosion that rocked the armoured personnel carrier. Blanc remained crouched over in the roadway, frozen in position, trying to figure out if he was still alive. Miraculously, the booby-trapped grenade had been planted to catch the combat engineers on their way out of the side road. A concrete wall had absorbed the shrapnel that would have turned Blanc into hamburger.

Standing in the cargo hatch of the vehicle, I witnessed the whole thing and felt the heat of the blast. Thinking quickly, I snatched my camera and snapped a couple of shots of Blanc still huddled over, the puff of smoke drifting over his head. As he slowly began to stand upright, the combat engineers, who were some two hundred metres down the laneway, began hollering at us. Following their frantic pointing, we saw a Serbian militiaman bolt from the house where the blast had erupted to take refuge in some nearby underbrush. The .50-calibre machine gun in our

95

vehicle was at the half-load, but there was no way for me or any-one else to get into the commander's hatch to cock the weapon and get off a shot before he disappeared. A somewhat dazed Blanc returned to our vehicle, slightly deafened but otherwise okay.

In the meantime, the engineers had mounted up in their two carriers and were rumbling back down towards the main street. The crew commanders trained their .50-calibre machine guns on the Serbian-held ridgeline above Pakrac. Once all three vehicles were together in the intersection, a quick conference took place between Blanc and Master Corporal John Devison, the engineer detachment commander. The two of them decided that discretion would outweigh valour that day, so we beat a hasty retreat. The French-Canadian officer, who had not exited the vehicle, vowed to not leave the safe confines of the main camp again.

There was no question that the Canadian engineers had been the intended target of this attack. They were the only people to have travelled down that deserted spur, and the Serbian soldier had snuck in behind them after they had deployed. Blanc's unexpected arrival from the opposite direction and his decision to advance on foot had foiled the trap. A follow-up investigation found that the grenade had been planted in a second-storey window to do the most damage to personnel standing in the hatches of the armoured personnel carrier. Ironically, Devison's detachment had been searching the yards and wood-line for another mass grave believed to contain additional Serbian victims of Croatian extremists.

The day after our close call was November 11, 1992, and the soldiers of 3 PPCLI conducted a Remembrance Day parade. On the rain-soaked grounds of Camp Pollum, the Canadian headquarters, a bugler played the last post and soldiers reflected on the fate of Sergeant Mike Ralph, who had been killed that August by a land mine. Many felt that the combat engineer had been deliberately murdered.

At that time, Ralph was the first and only peacekeeper to have been killed in Yugoslavia, and a large marble marker had been erected with his name on it at Camp Pollum. Unit wreaths were placed at the base of this marker, and nobody missed noticing that Ralph's name appeared at the top of a large, conspicuously blank space. With a morbid sense of practicality, whoever had commissioned the marker was preparing to add a lot of names to it.

INTO AFRICA,

AND BALKAN ENCOUNTERS

Have you heard the news? We lost
one of our regiment today in Croatia
COLONEL HERB PITTS

BY THE TIME I HEADED back to Ottawa, the crisis in the Balkans was worsening, but as a domestic news item it was already losing the public's interest. There was another UN mission underway at the time that had completely disappeared from view, and that involved the deployment of a peacekeeping force into the Western Sahara in September 1991.

When the mission was first announced, there was plenty of fanfare. Commanded by Canadian Brigadier General Armand Roy, the peacekeeping force was to be composed of seven thousand international troops, including the Canadian Airborne Regiment. *Esprit de Corps* had done a number of articles on the Western Sahara conflict and had even featured a cover photograph of an Airborne Regiment soldier packing his kit bags. From that point on, the whole operation had simply fizzled out

99

of sight. The Airborne never did deploy, and Brigadier Roy's UN command never totalled more than several hundred observers and support staff. Canada was one of thirty-six countries contributing to this UN operation dubbed MINURSO, and the total number of soldiers if deployed was just thirty-two. In keeping with our magazine's Canadian military mandate, I decided to visit this forgotten mission in early 1993.

Just getting there proved to be problematic. Located south of Morocco, the Western Sahara coast lies due east of the Canary Islands. However, as the name suggests, this former Spanish colony, once known as Spanish Sahara, is indeed the westernmost stretch of the Sahara Desert. Populated by nomadic Sahrawi, the only major urban centre was the landlocked capital of Laayoune. Since Spain had withdrawn from the region in 1975, Morocco had laid claim to the territory as a protectorate. As such, the Polisario guerrillas that had fought the Spanish for independence had continued to resist the Moroccans.

After seventeen years of spirited but ultimately futile resistance, the remaining eight thousand guerrillas had been pushed into remote desert camps by nearly 120,000 Moroccan troops. To keep the Polisario raiders at bay, Morocco had constructed a three-metre-high continuous sand berm that stretched more than two thousand kilometres, from Algeria to Mauritania. Manned by well-armed Moroccan infantry and armour and patrolled by fighter aircraft, the berm had effectively contained the Polisario militarily since its completion in 1988. In June 1990, the Polisario leadership had come to an agreement with Morocco to allow a referendum on the future status of this nation. It was this vote that the UN troops were to oversee in 1991. However, when it became apparent that Morocco was bussing in 200,000 returned refugees to add their votes to an estimated Sahrawi population of 75,000, the whole charade was put on hold.

Moroccan authorities were concerned when I applied for a transit visa and cited my destination as the Western Sahara. The only flights into Laayoune were the UN shuttles from Agadir, Morocco, and once I was co-located with Canadian military personnel I would be outside of Moroccan control. I had been able to book an Air France flight out of Charles de Gaulle airport, which would stop in Casablanca before terminating at the beach resort of Agadir.

I had been in contact with the Canadians in Laayoune, and they had booked me on the UN C-130 Hercules that made a regularly scheduled stop at Agadir on Fridays and Sundays. Essentially, it was a rest-and-recreation run to allow UN staff a weekend getaway. I flew overnight from Toronto to Paris, and the Casablanca-Agadir flight departed mid-morning. I expected to have a comfortable six-hour stopover in Agadir to locate the UN ground staff and ensure that all the arrangements had been made.

This timetable went out of the window the minute the Air France Airbus touched down in Casablanca. Immediately after landing, our plane stopped in the middle of the runway rather than taxiing onto one of the aprons. My fellow passengers were all holiday seekers who at first were amused at the sight of a Moroccan emergency vehicle racing along the runway beside us. People were laughing and photographing the overcrowded truck and its frantically waving occupants.

Then we smelled the smoke. Our plane was on fire. Panic broke out immediately among the passengers. People undid their seat belts and began scrambling to secure their possessions in the overhead bins. One idiot in the aisle across from me struggled to get his life preserver on over his head. Children screamed, others prayed, and above all the other noise the cabin crew could be heard shouting at everyone to sit down and remain calm. Over the intercom the flight deck officer yelled the same message: the

101

fire was out, it was only the landing gear, all was okay and stop panicking. Calm was finally restored, and we exited the plane via mobile staircases. For those passengers whose destination was Casablanca, the drama was over. The Agadir-bound passengers, including me, were now stranded with an unserviceable aircraft.

In the immediate aftermath no one knew what the solution would be, so we were herded into the transit lounge. Although a light lunch was soon provided for us, tempers began to flare among the French tourists. One particularly strident individual had made himself the official spokesperson of the group and, fortified with duty-free liquor, he accosted a beleaguered Air France official. I do not pretend to understand a lot of French, but the most-used word in that exchange was a forceful *"Maintenant!"* The drunk wanted an answer right away, and when he grabbed the Air France representative by the shirt front and struck him across the face, I moved in at once to break things up. I'm sure my shouts in English only served to startle both of them, but the Air France fellow thanked me profusely.

When a plan was finally announced, it meant that I would miss my UN connecting flight. It was going to take twelve hours to bring another plane from Paris; in the meantime, Air France would lay on tour buses and a supper downtown.

102   A Moroccan customs official then checked the passports and concluded that fifteen Korean labourers and I were not to leave the transit area. Since the Koreans only had work permits for Agadir, and my transit visa identified me as a journalist, we were considered "undesirables." An armed guard locked the sixteen of us in a luggage cage. I had resigned myself to this fate, when the Air France official spotted me and began berating the customs officer on my behalf. A face-saving compromise was agreed to, whereby the airline official signed for me and my passport

remained at the airport. In the hours we had spent in the Casablanca transit lounge, the Muzak piped into the room had been an instrumental version of the Hollywood classic song "As Time Goes By." It would end and then begin again—the same song, over and over. This musical theme continued aboard the bus, and when we entered the lobby of the Casablanca Holiday Inn, "As Time Goes By" was emanating from a player piano. I began to wonder if the locals knew any other tune.

By the time that Air France's replacement Airbus got us into Agadir, it was about two o'clock on Saturday morning. The airport was almost completely shut down, and the unexpected late arrival of our flight meant that there were few taxis on hand. I searched in vain for any sign of a UN registration desk, and the local officials had no idea about any flight to Laayoune. They also advised me that I could not remain on the airport premises because they were to be locked up for the rest of the night. I successfully managed to convince three French women to share the last taxi with me. I had no hotel reservations, so I thought the best plan of action would be to go to their resort and see if I could get a room. Unfortunately for me, the sleepy-eyed desk clerk confirmed that the neon No Vacancy sign out front was not lying. The French women unloaded their luggage, and the Moroccan driver approached me with a reassuring smile: "Hotel Sheraton, monsieur?" I figured that the Sheraton would be a stretch for my limited travel budget, but I was exhausted after nearly thirty-six hours of travel.

The beach hotels in Agadir line a long, sandy bay, and the Sheraton was the tallest on the skyline. The driver turned through a gate in a walled garden and drove along a large circular driveway that led to the main entrance. I got out, paid him and climbed the stairs. As the taxi drove away, I noticed a chain

103

across the front doors of the hotel. I rattled the doors, and a startled security guard sat up from one of the sofas in the lobby. I realized then that the whole hotel seemed unusually dark, even for this time of night. Looking agitated, the guard approached the doors and pointed at a large sign posted in one of the windows: Closed Due to Renovations. The guard made the universal hand sign of circling a finger beside his head to indicate that he believed I was crazy and headed back into the gloom of the darkened lobby. Picking up my bags, I glanced down the driveway and suddenly realized that my taxi driver had made no mistake in bringing me to this location. There were now four or five other taxis parked at the end of the long driveway. The drivers had formed their vehicles in a line so as to block the roadway. I figured from the flash of a switchblade that they were not interested in offering me a ride.

At the side of the hotel was a staircase and a pathway that led down to the beach. Not liking my odds of talking my way past the cabbies, I ducked down the darkened pathway. Their excited shouts, followed by the starting of a car engine, removed all doubt as to what these Moroccans wanted from me. On one side of the stairs was a tiered garden; on the other was the concrete wall of the hotel. It was a fairly steep decline that stretched about forty metres before opening onto the wide beach. I was already running, but I knew that I could not outdistance my pursuers for long. The weight of my bags added to my exhaustion, and I had no idea where I was going. I heaved both my briefcase and my bag into the pitch-black shrubbery and dove in after them. Branches cut my face as I turned back to face the pathway. I heard the taxi screech to a halt and the sound of four car doors slamming.

I picked up some dirt—I hoped it was dirt—smeared it over my face and groped around for something to use as a weapon. My would-be assailants had rushed past my hiding place with their flashlights probing ahead of them. When they got to the beach, they evidently saw no tracks on the sand and shouted a caution to the one Moroccan who had remained above my position at the car. I could see them begin their search at the base of the pathway, shining their flashlights into the shrubs as they pulled the branches back. The tiered garden went back about six metres, and I noticed that the cabbies were only going in about half that distance. I started to inch backwards, but I was sure they would hear any slight movements. In fact, I was afraid that they could hear my heart pounding, because I could certainly hear it pulsing in my own ears. When they were directly opposite me, I narrowed my eyes as much as possible without completely closing them. I knew that I risked detection of the light reflected from my eyes, but even more I feared not being able to see my attackers.

I managed to find only one rock, the size of a golf ball, and I knew that this would not exactly even the odds against four cabbies carrying switchblades and flashlights. All of a sudden, I was staring directly into the glare. It remained fixed on my face, and I was sure I had been spotted. So sure, in fact, that I was about to resort to my final plan, which was to scream and run like hell. When the light passed, it took me a second to realize that I was still unobserved. But I could taste bile in my throat.

After the cabbies had reached the entranceway without finding any sign of me, they held a long, whispered discussion. The car doors slammed again, and I heard the cab slowly making its way down the gravel driveway. I figured it was a trap and that at least one of them was waiting above to see if this noisy departure would lure me out of my hiding place. I wasn't falling for this ruse. I adjusted my limbs into a more comfortable position and settled in to outwait them.

My fatigue overcame my adrenalin rush, and the sun was well above the horizon when I awoke. I remembered my circumstance and searched for signs of the cabbies. The driveway now contained some panel vans and construction workers, so I decided that I could safely collect my bags. This took a bit of searching as I had really heaved them to the back of the garden. I stumbled down to the beach and walked across the sand to the next hotel. A worker who was setting up the chaises longues and umbrellas looked at me with shock and disgust. This look was repeated by the clerks when I entered the impressive lobby and approached the front desk.

Only when I caught a glimpse of myself in a mirror did I understand how my mud- and blood-stained appearance would give residents of a beach hotel cause for concern. After a quick wash-up in the public restroom, I explained my predicament to the hotel manager. He said he could certainly rent me a room but neither he nor his staff knew of any UN office in Agadir. Another guest was in the process of turning in her room key when she overheard the discussion. "Are you the Canadian journalist?" she asked. "We expected you at the airport last night."

By sheer luck I had turned up at the exact moment to find the very person I needed to locate. After spending the next day and a half relaxing on the beach, I was on my way to Western Sahara.

MY ARRIVAL IN Laayoune was far less dramatic than my escapades in Agadir. The capital of Western Sahara is a small city surrounded by a sea of sand. The heat was immediately oppressive, with daytime temperatures sometimes hitting as high as 60°C. While some temporary portable barracks had been set up at the airport, the majority of the UN personnel were housed at two Club Méditerranée hotels. The UN had reserved a block of rooms that was billed directly to New York as a standing contract.

On my first morning in Laayoune I rose at dawn and set off on a ten-kilometre run to get my bearings and explore the city. As I left the hotel, I noticed a Moroccan soldier casually leaning against the wall and smoking a cigarette. I waved my hand, mumbled "Good morning" and set off on my run. Although I had hoped to beat the worst of the daytime heat, it was already about 35°c when I finished my jog at around seven o'clock. The soldier was not at the entrance when I returned to the hotel. I showered, put on my freshest shirt, enjoyed a hearty breakfast and was setting out on foot for the UN headquarters when the guard reappeared. He was staggering down the street, soaked in sweat, his chest heaving, and he was glaring at me with a mixture of anger and relief. It was then apparent to me that he had been ordered by his commanders to tail me and not to let me out of his sight. He had dutifully attempted to obey but had never expected to run ten kilometres in combat boots. The next morning I noticed a bicycle leaning against the wall beside him when I set out on my morning workout.

By now Canadian General Armand Roy had been replaced, and Belgian Brigadier General André Van Baelen was the MINURSO force commander. Since I was the only foreign correspondent in Western Sahara at the time, it was not difficult to arrange an interview with him. Asked about the United Nations' operation and success to date, Van Baelen was very pragmatic in his response: "Militarily, our role is to observe the ceasefire here, and since there's not been a shot fired in the past eighteen months, I would say we've been successful."

The Canadians were amused to hear the brigadier's assessment. Most of the MINURSO members felt their role was redundant. "The Moroccan military clearly holds the upper hand, and the Moroccan government has made it clear that they will manipulate any referendum," explained Major Tracey, a Canadian observer. "The Polisario no longer have the strength to capture or hold ground. They have lost."

Over the next few days this situation became readily apparent when I saw the massive lots that the Moroccan government had developed to house the voters who would be temporarily repatriated in the event of an independence referendum. Stretching over acres of flat ground, areas had been marked out for caravans; street lights had been erected, and at regular intervals there were primitive concrete toilet facilities. The only things missing were the 200,000 pre-registered expatriates that the Moroccans would bus in for the occasion.

As for the military situation, I was able to catch a flight aboard a UN resupply helicopter out of Samara that was flying north to the Algerian airbase in Tindouf. We had driven to Samara on the only major highway in the region and passed a long-since disabled and disused conveyer belt; it stretched for many kilometres from the now-defunct phosphate mine that had once provided Western Sahara's only major export.

During my overnight stay in Samara, my two Canadian UN observer hosts explained that this tiny village, built around an oasis, was a camel trading and brothel town. Intrigued at what a mid-Saharan red-light district in a predominantly Muslim country would entail, we travelled to that section of the town in the early evening. Our arrival coincided with that of several truckloads of young Moroccan conscripts. Stationed for twelve months out on the fortified sand berm, they were visiting Samara on their mid-tour break for rest and recreation.

In the district there were about a dozen concrete stalls, each covered with a filthy curtain. The Moroccans were lined up about seven deep in front of each stall. The Sahrawi prostitutes were draped in flowing robes, and only their eyes were visible. They sat cross-legged, with their eyes cast downward, while a pimp negotiated a fee from the next soldier in line. When the curtain was drawn back, the prostitute would simply lie back on a mat. The stalls were obviously not that deep, as both the prostitute's and the client's feet remained visible while the business was conducted—usually in short order. There was no wash facility in evidence, and certainly no ablutions were undertaken between customers.

Somewhere nearby was an open-air toilet, so the whole area stank of feces and body odour. I asked my host if anyone had compiled statistics on the suicide rate of Moroccan soldiers. "They keep that pretty quiet, but I'll wager that more are killed by their own hand than the Polisario ever manage to shoot," he said.

The hot chopper flight to Tindouf—covering almost two thousand kilometres directly over Morocco's fortified berm clearly illustrated what little chance the remaining guerrillas had. Given Morocco's complete air superiority and array of heavy weapons, any attempt to break through the formidable berm defences would be suicidal. All the Sahrawi resistance could do was struggle to simply survive in the desert wasteland.

After seventy-two hours of travel, ration pack meals and overnights at forward outposts, it was a tremendous relief to get back to the Laayoune Club Med. I retrieved my key and headed to my room. The door was ajar, and as I entered I noticed that all of my belongings had been searched. The contents were strewn around the room. I thought I had been robbed, but as I turned the corner I startled a smartly dressed Moroccan captain who was sitting on the bed, thumbing through my notebook. Incredulous, I asked him, "What the fuck are you doing in here?" After recovering from his momentary shock, he merely stared at me with dismissive defiance.

"Did you make this mess?" I asked, pointing to my clothes all over the floor. In response, he crumpled up a wrapper and placed it in the wastebasket. He had just eaten all of the Air France chocolate bars I had been hoarding since my flight.

"You ate my candy!" I foolishly exclaimed. He remained silent, casually replaced his forage cap, adjusted it in the mirror, then gingerly stepped over my scattered gear and walked out the door. Without looking back, he held up his hand as a gesture of farewell and disappeared down the hallway.

It had been a rare glimpse into an exotic corner of the world, but I was not regretting the fact that I was heading home the next day.

KEEPING NEGATIVE STORIES out of the limelight is something that every military tries to control, and the Canadian Forces— albeit committed to defending democratic values and freedom of speech—are no exception.

In the spring of 1993, the Department of National Defence was being micro-managed by a powerful bureaucrat who exercised his excessive influence from behind the scenes, fronted by an admiral just promoted into a post he little understood and by a defence minister who was running for the Progressive Conservative party leadership and a chance to become prime minister. With Deputy Minister Bob Fowler calling the shots, Admiral John Anderson out of his depth and Minister Kim Campbell grasping for the golden ring, the stage was set for the Canadian military to enter a perfect storm of relentless media coverage.

Since December 1992, the Canadian Airborne Regiment had been deployed to assist in the U.S.-led coalition to stabilize Somalia, but in early March 1993 a couple of nasty incidents occurred. On the night of March 4, a Canadian patrol shot two Somali looters, wounding one and killing the other, near the Canadian camp in Belet Uen. This sounded like pretty routine stuff in a country rife with lawlessness and armed bandits. Minimal official mention was made of the event, and the media paid it little attention. Inside Defence Headquarters, however, alarm bells were starting to sound. There were rumours that a hole had been cut in the perimeter fence, that food had been placed just inside as a lure and that the two Somalis were unarmed. Furthermore, the Canadian doctor who examined the corpse claimed that the victim had been executed. The leader of the patrol, Captain Michel Rainville, was also well known inside the army as a loose cannon. He had been disciplined before leaving Canada for three separate incidents involving his own soldiers, including one case of sexual assault and torture and another of choking a private into unconsciousness. It was decided to divert any possible media interest in the incident by describing the two Somali victims as saboteurs. Contingent commander Colonel Serge Labbé claimed that detailed maps and weapons were found on the intruders after they were shot. It was a novel twist, but it was also a complete fabrication.

The next incident occurred less than two weeks later. On the evening of March 16, Canadian soldiers captured another Somali looter, sixteen-year-old Shidane Arone. There had been a tremendous increase in the looting problem, and the battle group commander had just changed the policy towards thieves. The Canadian officers told their men to rough up the prisoners a little as a future deterrent, rather than simply turning them over to the local police. In handing over young Arone, Sergeant Mark Boland told his section, "Do what you like to him—just don't kill him."

Unfortunately for all involved, after brutally torturing the Somali teen for several hours, Master Corporal Clayton Matchee

111

finally disobeyed his orders and killed the prisoner. The troops on the ground—despite many of them being inebriated in an advance celebration of the PPCLI's Regimental Day—understood the enormity of what Matchee had done. Messages were passed from the forward base in Belet Uen to Colonel Labbé's headquarters in Mogadishu. Within hours, Labbé had sent a Significant Incident Report to Ottawa, detailing a suspicious death of a Somali local in custody. Labbé advised his superiors that statements and photographs would be forwarded as soon as possible.

But then nothing happened in Belet Uen. Soldiers expected to be questioned by military police, but none showed up. Instead, evidence such as the rope and batons used to torture Arone were quietly collected and disposed of. The doctor at the base, Captain Neil Gibson, drafted a statement that he had only located "two small bruises" on the battered and bloody corpse he had examined. No photographs had yet been sent to Ottawa, and Gibson's falsified medical report seemed to indicate that Arone had simply expired.

The whole incident would have quietly disappeared at this point if it had not been for the troubled conscience of Trooper Kyle Brown. Brown had been with Matchee during the first shift and had helped tie up the prisoner. At Matchee's urging, he had punched Arone a couple of times and then he'd brought out his camera to take some trophy photographs. One of the images showed a badly beaten Arone with Matchee pointing a pistol at his head, and another showed Matchee choking him with a baton. Brown notified Sergeant Boland of this evidence, and after a lengthy conference, the senior non-commissioned officers of 2nd Commando confronted company commander Major Anthony Seward and accused him of a cover-up. With no alternative but to come clean, Master Corporal Matchee was put into custody on the afternoon of March 19.

112

Ottawa was informed of the thwarted cover-up, and police investigators were to be quietly sent from Canada to Belet Uen. However, before detective Warrant Officer Paul Dowd could even book an airline ticket, U.S. special forces personnel were discovered in Matchee's detention cell at the Belet Uen base. They claimed they had seen Matchee hanging from a bootlace, and they were trying to revive the paratrooper. No one could explain why Matchee's two Canadian guards had not seen him first, but the American soldiers' intervention proved timely. Canadian doctor Major Barry Armstrong rushed to Matchee's aid, and although Matchee suffered serious brain damage, he survived.

Pembroke Observer reporter Jim Day, who was travelling with the Airborne Regiment at the time, had seen the commotion at the cell and watched them take Matchee away on a stretcher. The suicide attempt was not linked to Arone's death at this time for the simple reason that no public disclosure had been made of the Somali's murder. Not until April 1, when Day returned home to Canada, did people begin to tie loose ends together. Then the full magnitude of the top-level cover-up became apparent.

On March 30, Paul Dowd, who was now plying his trade in Belet Uen, received a message and wrote in his log book: "Heat coming from somewhere, Matchee's name known in Canada, pressure to prosecute quickly." At the time, Dowd had been in negotiations to have Arone's body exhumed so that another forensic specialist could conduct a full autopsy. However, as soon as the shit hit the fan in Ottawa, the collection of such key evidence was put on hold. Within days, Trooper Kyle Brown was arrested and charged with torture and manslaughter.

The big issue in Ottawa was not so much the horrific crime committed by our soldiers but the attempted cover-up that had ensued. Defence Minister Kim Campbell's name had been checked in the initial Significant Incident Reports, so the first conclusion

113

was that she had tried to squash the scandal in order to improve her chance to become party leader. The fingers of blame were pointing in all directions when Major Barry Armstrong's wife, Jennifer, went to the media with a letter from her husband. After his examination of the corpse from the March 4 shooting, Armstrong had firmly believed that the victim had been killed in cold blood. He had sent memos up the chain of command and had even personally advised Admiral John Anderson when he visited the base in Belet Uen. When it became apparent that no one was going to act on the matter, Armstrong added this cover-up to the already gathering storm clouds.

In a desperate act of self-preservation, the Canadian military began sacrificing the Airborne Regiment. Intense media scrutiny had uncovered the fact that several paratroopers had known affiliations with white supremacist organizations in Canada. The brass threw this allegation into the mix and declared a full internal board of inquiry into not just the incidents in East Africa but also the command and control of the entire Airborne Regiment. While this board, headed by Brigadier General Tom de Faye, was meant to put the issue to rest permanently, all it managed to accomplish in the end was to buy the senior brass a little breathing room. Every new allegation or development that arose over the next few months could be deflected with the press line that it was the subject of an ongoing board of inquiry. It was also an effective gag order, as soldiers with evidence would be required to present their information to the Defence inquiry, and going straight to the media would result in the maximum punishment under the terms of the National Defence Act.

At this stage of things, *Esprit de Corps* was still pretty much on the sidelines of the Somalia story. I had penned some editorials reminding people that paratroopers were "pit bulls, not poodles," and challenged the directive that had ordered our soldiers to abuse prisoners. Other than that, the mainstream media were already indicating that they had no intention of letting this story drop, and we did not need to prod it along.

WHAT THE BURGEONING Somalia scandal did accomplish was to drive an already media-wary Department of National Defence into a full state of paranoid information lockdown. This policy was to hit fully home in September 1993. My wife, Katherine, had been commissioned by PPCLI's second battalion (2 PPCLI) to produce a full set of illustrations to commemorate the battalion's deployment to Croatia. She had originally been expected to visit the unit in the Pakrac region, which was known in UN circles as Sector West. However, just before she left Ottawa, 2 PPCLI was sent down into Sector South to reinforce a French battalion.

Things had been heating up in recent weeks with a re-equipped Croatian army starting to flex its muscles against the ethnic Serbian enclave known as the Krajina. Approximately 250,000 Serbs were living in this dirt-poor southernmost corner within the administrative boundary of Croatia. As with the Serbs in Sector West, they had resided in the Krajina for hundreds of years. When Croatia proclaimed its independence from Yugoslavia, the people of the Krajina declared their own state—complete with their own worthless currency and rag-tag army.

During Katherine's visit, my old friend Captain Jim Decoste hosted her. Despite the chaos of the unit moving into a new area of operations and heightening tensions, Katherine was given plenty of access to take photographs. She didn't just snap the standard patrol and checkpoint pictures of peacekeeping; she also had the troops re-enact some of their recent combat experiences. Since their arrival in Sector South, 2 PPCLI had already had several sharp engagements with both local factions.

On the night of September 9, Katherine could see flashes of

light on the horizon and hear a distant rumbling. Decoste came into the mess hall and advised her that she was to be choppered out as soon as possible. "Big thunderstorm coming," he warned. Within hours, she was en route by UN Sea King helicopter to the airport in Zagreb.

The thunderstorm she had witnessed was in fact the start of a massive Croatian bombardment that rolled through a valley known as the Medak Pocket. In the wake of that artillery barrage, Croatian special forces under the command of an Albanian Kosovar named Agim Ceku quickly rolled through the weakly defended Serbian front lines. Canadian soldiers had been caught in the bombardment and several had been wounded. Remaining at their observation posts, the troops of 2 PPCLI provided a first-hand account of the ebb and flow of the battle. The initial gaggle of wounded Serbian soldiers and fleeing civilians along the main road in Medak had been replaced by determined reinforcements pushing forward into the pocket. Buses, tanks and even armoured trains were rushing into the region from all over the Krajina. For the next seventy-two hours the Serbs and Croatians fought a pitched battle. The Serbian counterattack had successfully halted the Croatian offensive, but General Ceku's troops remained in possession of four Serbian villages. After a series of protracted negotiations, the United Nations convinced the Croatians to withdraw back to the pre–September 9 boundaries. To oversee the withdrawal, 2 PPCLI and the French battalion were to move quickly forward to ensure a UN presence in the buffer zone.

On September 15, two hours past the agreed H-hour for the Croatian withdrawal to begin, 2 PPCLI soldiers began moving forward. Both foot and vehicle patrols were immediately engaged by the Croatians, who seemed determined to violate the agreement.

116

Under heavy machine-gun fire and rocket attack, Lieutenant Colonel Jim Calvin ordered 2 PPCLI to start firing back. This resulted in the biggest battle in which Canadian soldiers had been engaged since the Korean War. An estimated thirty-five Croatians were killed or wounded over the next thirty-six hours, and the Canadians suffered four wounded.

The local Croatian commander finally agreed to withdraw peacefully the following morning. That night, the Canadian soldiers stood and watched as the drunken Croatians went on a final orgy of raping, killing and burning everything that remained in the Serbian villages. When daylight came and 2 PPCLI finally began rolling forward again, the Croatians remained defiantly in place. Land mines had been placed across the road, and anti-tank cannons were aimed menacingly at the lead Canadian armoured personnel carriers.

Aware of what these Croatian criminals had done the night before, the 2 PPCLI troops aimed their .50-calibre machine guns right back at them. It was a Mexican standoff that threatened to erupt into a bloodbath at any point. At that crucial moment, Lieutenant Colonel Calvin played the one trump card he had left to avoid a slaughter. About twenty members of the international press corps—mostly Serbian stringers for news agencies—had tagged along with the Canadians, all of them anxious to enter the smouldering Medak Pocket. Calvin called these journalists forward and conducted his own press conference. Behind him as a dramatic backdrop were the burning ruins of the village of Citlik and the heavily armed Croatian forces. Calvin knew that the Croatians were very aware of the importance of maintaining international support. As the cameras rolled, raising his voice so that the Croatians could hear his comments, Calvin accused them of war crimes.

117

A Croatian officer quickly ordered the removal of the land mines and the barricades and told the journalists he was prepared to refute Calvin's allegations. As the camera crews rushed to scrum the officers, 2 PPCLI took advantage of the momentary confusion and began moving forward. The hasty advance allowed them to secure more than enough evidence to prove Calvin's claims of war crimes. Some of the charred bodies had been burned alive and were still too hot to place into body bags. Every living thing within four villages had been exterminated, and many of the dead animals had been dumped into the water wells to prevent future use of the wells. It was for this operation that Agim Ceku earned the nickname "Commander Scorched Earth" and a promotion from the Croatian high command.

Photographing the remains of the civilians whom they had failed to protect and collecting forensic evidence to support criminal charges, Lieutenant Colonel Calvin vowed to his troops that the perpetrators would be brought to justice. It was a bold statement, one that would prove difficult to enforce given that the entire incident had remained completely out of the Canadian news media. The briefest of news clips from Calvin's impromptu press conference aired on CNN, but no context was included about the extent of the combat, casualties and carnage. Kim Campbell, now the Progressive Conservative party leader, was locked in the middle of an election battle with Liberal leader Jean Chrétien. The only military stories getting any airtime were the lingering allegations of the Somalia cover-up and Chrétien's promise to cancel the controversial $5 billion EH-101 helicopter program.

Even with my close connections to my old battalion and with Katherine being there at the onset of hostilities, *Esprit de Corps* was as much in the dark about the Medak Pocket battle as were the rest of the media. I met Katherine in Toronto upon her return to Canada because she was to present some of her initial sketches to the regimental colonel in chief, whom we had arranged to see. I called Colonel Herb Pitts from our hotel room on the evening of September 18. He asked, "Have you heard the news? We lost one of our regiment today in Croatia."

Of course, I hadn't heard anything as it had not yet been announced to the media.

"Captain Jim Decoste is dead."

I know Colonel Pitts kept talking, but from that point on I did not hear him. My friend and long-time mentor was dead.

Included in her collection of Croatia photographs, Katherine had a whole series of shots depicting Decoste camping it up on a Jeep. They were goofy shots of him pretending to be a fashion model or pin-up girl. We stared at these in disbelief and sickening shock. I called his widow, Jan, in Winnipeg to express my condolences and realized that her composure was rooted in the belief that this wasn't really happening.

With her permission, I notified the Toronto media—the Department of National Defence still had not done so—and provided them with one of Katherine's photographs. Decoste's Iltis vehicle had collided head-on with a Serbian army truck. The driver of the Canadian vehicle, Corporal Stacey Bouke, was badly injured along with the other occupant, Lieutenant Rick Turner. This had happened at the very end of the Medak operation. Despite the extenuating operational circumstances, it was seemingly just an unfortunate traffic accident.

I flew out to the funeral in Winnipeg. Although the 2nd Battalion was still deployed in Croatia, Decoste's passing had brought out the rest of the regiment from all across the country. I had promised myself—for the sake of my mentor—that I would not cry in public, but this promise only lasted until his golden retriever strutted down the church aisle following his master's casket.

At the alcohol-fuelled wake later that evening, most of Decoste's lifetime comrades-in-arms expressed the sentiment that this career soldier would have preferred to die in battle rather than a traffic mishap. Only years later, when the covered-up details of the Medak battle were finally made public, did we realize that Decoste did indeed see the combat for which he had spent his life training.

ON OCTOBER 27, 1993, I boarded a 747 in Bangkok en route to Kai Tak International Airport in Hong Kong. Thanks to our magazine's deal with Canadian Airlines, I was seated in business class, but packed in the "cattle class" seats of the jumbo jet were about 110 Canadian peacekeepers, fresh from their tour of duty in Cambodia. These troops were the last rotation of 92nd Transport Company and among the last UN troops to leave the transit camps in Phnom Penh. Over the previous eighteen months I had visited the Canadian contingent in Cambodia six times. This was the largest UN mission to date—involving more than twenty thousand international peacekeepers—and it had been successfully concluded.

120

The federal election was underway in Canada, and with the difference in time zones and to the international date line, the election polls had closed back home. Shortly after the plane reached cruising altitude, the pilot came on the intercom and announced the just-confirmed results of the federal election. Jean Chrétien and his Liberals had won a stunning majority, the Bloc Québécois were to form Her Majesty's Loyal Opposition and the Reform party had gained a respectable presence in the House of Commons with fifty-two elected members. The Canadian peacekeepers' response to this news was almost unanimous. Both Chrétien as the prime minister and the Bloc as the official opposition drew incredulous laughter, but a loud cheer rang out when they heard the results for the Reform party. After a pause, the pilot said, "The Progressive Conservatives won just two seats, and Kim Campbell was defeated in her own riding." The whole plane cheered wildly. Two troopers with the Lord Strathcona's Horse Regiment opened up their duty-free bottles of rum, and the troops began to celebrate the demise of the Tories.

Somewhat naively, the rank and file (like many in the media and the Canadian public) blamed Kim Campbell and her staff for the cover-up of Somalia. As well, most of these young soldiers had joined the Canadian Forces during the Mulroney era, so they naturally saw the recent budget cuts and project cancellations as evidence of the government's neglect of its armed forces. Only the most senior non-commissioned and commissioned officers recalled the emasculating effects of Pierre Trudeau's anti-military policies on their once-proud institution.

It did not take Prime Minister Chrétien long to make his mark on the Canadian military. Just weeks after his election, he gleefully made good on the Liberals' promise to cancel the purchase of the EH-101 helicopters. The Conservatives had already signed the contract for this $5.2 billion project, and as a result, taxpayers ended up paying more than $500 million in cancellation costs—and the air force continued to fly aging Sea King helicopters into the foreseeable future.

However, Canada's participation in the EH-101 helicopter project was more involved than a simple client-supplier relationship within the aviation industry. As this was an entirely new generation of maritime helicopter, Canada had been a co-developer on the project with the United Kingdom and Italy. Canada's withdrawal from the project meant that our partner countries would now have to shoulder an additional one third of the research and development costs, and without the Canadian fleet purchase the unit price became astronomical. Needless to say, this severely strained relations with our allies, and Chrétien was soon threatening to take things further.

Even with the change in government, the Somalia scandal had not disappeared from the media spotlight, and the Defence department was still in a state of paranoid non-disclosure on all operational issues. In addition, in December 1993, U.S. media outlets reported that an incident had occurred in Bosnia involving a number of Canadian peacekeepers. It had happened at a vital bridge crossing just north of Sarajevo over a river that marked the boundary between Bosnian Serb and Muslim positions. The UN patrolled the two-hundred-metre span of bridge that had the Serbs at the south end and a Muslim detachment at the north. A Muslim sniper had shot a Serb soldier as he crossed the road, fatally wounding him. The Canadian soldiers had immediately taken cover in their bunker, and for the next ten minutes they made no attempt to risk sniper fire to retrieve the dying Serb. A Serbian detachment that included the incensed brother of the deceased came to secure the body and this patrol. Irate at the UN's failure to protect or provide assistance, the Serbs disarmed the Canadians at gunpoint and conducted a mock execution that included the firing of Kalashnikovs directly over the heads of the bound and terrified Canadians.

News of this incident immediately passed to Ottawa, where the brass at National Defence Headquarters decided it was best kept quiet. The story broke in the United States when the UN authorities in New York confirmed it. When the Canadian media got wind of the severity of the circumstances, newly appointed Defence Minister David Collenette made matters worse. Instead of simply admitting that he had been kept out of the loop or demanding an explanation from his generals, Collenette dutifully read his prepared press lines. There was no cover-up in this instance, he said; it was just that such incidents were considered routine in the former Yugoslavia, and therefore no one thought it necessary to issue a press release.

Canadians were outraged at the prospect of our troops— friendly, aid-distributing peacekeepers—being roughed up by thugs in the Balkans. The media attention sparked an anonymous source to make some equally shocking revelations about our troops being involved in combat in Croatia. This veiled reference to the Medak Pocket—along with stories of Canadian snipers and commandos conducting covert ("black") operations in Sarajevo—sent the Chrétien government into full damage control. Another wide-sweeping internal inquiry was initiated regarding the Balkans mission—complete with the same level of enforced non-disclosure as the ongoing probe into the Canadian Airborne Regiment in Somalia.

Yet another lid was firmly placed on yet another boiling pot. Heading off on his first overseas venture as prime minister, Chrétien further played to the Canadian public's sentiments by declaring that he was prepared to withdraw the two peacekeeping contingents in the former Yugoslavia. Unless other countries stepped up and took some additional risks to ensure the safety of our troops and the success of the UN mission, Chrétien would bring our soldiers home. It was brave talk for a man who was about to learn how little clout Canada carried on the world stage. Chrétien's first stop was London, England, where he met with Prime Minister John Major at 10 Downing Street.

The smiling, confident politician who entered that meeting was far from bombastic when he contritely left several hours later. Not only would our troops remain in Yugoslavia, but a member of the Privy Council called the office of *Esprit de Corps* to say, "Canada just bought four British submarines as part of the EH-101 cancellation." Our informant said that the British had just mothballed their new fleet of Upholder class diesel-electric submarines, and although these problem-plagued boats had been last on the wish list of Canadian submariners, this was the price we had to pay for being in an alliance. To save face and make this acquisition appear to be Canadian-inspired, a paragraph was hastily added to the 1994 White Paper on Defence that suggested Canada should explore the possibility of a lease-to-own arrangement with an allied navy to procure "four to six diesel-electric submarines." Not until 1998—five years later—did Canada formally admit that it was purchasing the Upholder class at the projected cost of $1 billion, but the deal was made on that December day in 1993.

The news that Canadian troops would remain in Croatia and Bosnia had a far more immediate impact, particularly as NATO was now threatening air strikes against Serbian positions in support of UN peacekeepers. In April 1994, I headed back into Croatia as tensions mounted. Since the Medak Pocket operation the previous September, the 1st Battalion of the Royal 22nd Regiment (the Van Doos) had replaced the 2nd Battalion of PPCLI. During the last six-month period, the front had remained relatively calm, albeit with the UN troops unable to deploy into an actual buffer zone between the Croatians and the Serbs in the Krajina. As a result, the Canadian battle group had remained positioned behind the Serbian front lines, ready to respond in the event of another Croatian offensive. This was not an ideal situation as the belligerents remained in close contact and continual conflict.

On April 4, literally as Lieutenant Colonel Mike Diakow's 1 PPCLI began its airlift from Calgary to Croatia, the United Nations brokered a new deal. The Croats agreed to pull back their

124

troops, and the Canadians were to move immediately into new positions and establish observation posts in the heretofore no man's land. For Diakow and his operations staff, this meant literally drafting a new plan on the flight over. During the handover period, the incoming battalion arrived in waves and usually had a brief familiarization period with the homeward-bound troops before assuming full duties. This often included the new arrivals receiving their helmets and flak jackets directly from the outgoing contingent due to the shortage of such protective gear in the Canadian supply system. On this rotation, the commander would have to work with a constantly changing mix of Patricias and Van Doos through a delicate operation that had to be conducted with haste in order to earn the trust of the belligerents. Beyond the language problem and inter-regimental rivalry, there was also a tremendous diversity in motivation between the Canadian units. The Van Doos were anxious to get home to their families, and the Patricias were keen, fresh and eager to see action.

I took a commercial flight into Zagreb and then hitched a lift with the 1 PPCLI vanguard when it drove down to Sector South, so I witnessed the chaotic circumstances and sense of urgency that prevailed among the Patricias. Immediately after signing for their armoured personnel carriers from the Van Doos, they had begun pushing patrols out into territory they had never seen before. It was only a matter of time before tragedy would strike.

At 9:45 AM on April 9, a Canadian M-113 armoured personnel carrier detonated an anti-tank mine, which critically injured the driver and one occupant. Although he was listed on the battalion's roster as the deputy commanding officer's driver, when the call had come down for volunteers to help establish the new observation posts, Private S.J. Bowen had been seconded to Delta Company to make good their manpower shortage.

Just forward of the main Serbian front line, Delta Company had been moving down a road that had been cleared by Serbian engineers. To prove that the route was clear of mines, the Serbian troops drove a car in front of Private Bowen's carrier. When the Serbian car skirted a mine crater, Bowen followed suit. However, the heavier weight of his vehicle triggered the sophisticated Croatian mine. In the ensuing explosion, young Bowen was hit by the main shock wave, which shattered his lower spine. Corporal D.K. Konchuk received a severe leg gash in the incident, while the crew commander, Sergeant Forsythe, survived unscathed. The overcast drizzle precluded an air evacuation, and the two wounded soldiers had to endure a fifty-five-minute ambulance drive back to the main Canadian base in Gracac.

The following morning I spoke to the female medic who had accompanied them in the ambulance. She was still in shock. With twelve years' experience in the Canadian army, Master Corporal Edna Strickland admitted that this had been her toughest challenge. The severity of Bowen's blood loss had made it impossible for her to administer any morphine to ease the pain. "I think what made it so disturbing was the fact that we were in the same convoy and we had witnessed the blast," said Strickland. "Usually we treat wounds and injuries when they're brought to us at a field hospital."

Corporal Konchuk was bandaged up and lucid despite his painkillers. He had only the highest praise for the medic, whom he credited with saving Bowen's life. However, he said, his torturous ambulance ride was the longest hour of his life. "Every time [Bowen] would come to, his screams would pierce right through you until he passed out again."

Bowen was flown to Zagreb for emergency surgery, but the medical doctors at the Canadian base in Gracac doubted he would ever walk again. This medical assessment ran in stark contrast to the official Canadian press release that cited Bowen's wounds as "slight."

Two days later, with barely half his battalion on the ground in Croatia's Sector South, Lieutenant Colonel Diakow was faced with a new challenge. There had been two NATO air strikes against Serbian positions in Bosnia. Although this was technically an entirely separate war—or, at least, a separate UN mission—the Serbs in the Krajina had informed Diakow that an attack against one Serb was an attack against all Serbs. As the entire Canadian battle group was now deployed inside the Serbian Krajina, such a threat could not be taken lightly.

I had attended a number of meetings between Diakow's Canadian commanders and the local Serbian officers where threats had been exchanged. On most of those occasions, the Serbs had extended the standard offer of strong plum brandy—regardless of the time of day. The Canadian soldiers were not allowed to drink on duty, and as the attendant civilian I had become the designated drinker. After four or five of these sessions, I usually had to beg off and locate a cot in order to sleep off the effects of the overproof alcohol.

To minimize my disruptive presence at a critical phase and to give me maximum flexibility to reconnoitre Sector South, Diakow had assigned me to Captain Mike Parker. I had been on the commando course with Parker and knew him well from our days in the 2nd Battalion. His job was to act as the liaison officer with the Jordanian battalion, which was technically under Canadian command. They occupied the Sector North, and this allowed us the opportunity to travel through the destroyed wasteland of the Medak Pocket. On our way, we also stopped to pay our final respects at Jim Decoste's crash site. On foot we visited some of

127

the front-line Serbian army positions in the Krajina. At one outpost, a half-dozen middle-aged Serbs were manning a small
bunker. They had dug in an armoured personnel carrier behind
their position. On close inspection, I realized that the battered
Soviet-style BRDM wheeled carrier was sitting in the open merely
as a show of strength. Some of its road wheels were missing, and
the heavy machine gun appeared rusted beyond use.

We were invited into the Serbs' small dugout, and I played
my role as the Canadian drinker. The latest news on CNN was
that following the NATO air strikes, Serbian President Slobodan
Milosevic was offering to relinquish Serbian claims in the Krajina
in exchange for some concessions to Serbs in Bosnia. In response
to this potential scenario, the Serbian soldiers spat in disgust and
asked me to show them what support they were receiving from
Belgrade and Milosevic. While the Serbian army of the Krajina
did possess a few tanks, the majority of those I had seen were old
T-34-85 models that dated back to the Second World War. Most of
the other armoured vehicles were either improvised or in short
supply of spare parts. The eldest Serb, who appeared to be the
section commander, made sure he had the translators' attention
before carefully stating, "If Belgrade [Milosevic] sells out the Krajina, then we will declare war on Belgrade too!" Half a bottle of
brandy earlier, this same chap had been intent on declaring war
on NATO. As we walked off into no man's land, I figured from the
state of their worn-out equipment that the Krajina Serbs would
have their hands full just holding back the ragtag Croatians.

CANADIAN SOLDIERS WERE not immune from the temptations of
the black market, which was evident from the number of Serbian troops who openly sported Canadian combat trousers in
the Krajina. At night, outside the barbed-wire perimeter of the

Canadian camp, elderly Serbian women came to peddle family heirlooms, wads of valueless dinars and even their young daughters. Basic items such as coffee and cigarettes became the market standard, as cash was of little use to these villagers—there were no functioning banks to exchange foreign currency.

At the same time that 1 PPCLI was deploying into southern Croatia, the Canadian contingent stationed in Bosnia was being rotated as well. The French-Canadian battle group based upon the 12e Régiment Blindé du Canada (12 RBC) was being replaced by another armoured regiment—the Lord Strathcona's Horse Regiment. When the Strathconas first took over their new responsibilities, they discovered that their predecessors had been engaged in some disreputable conduct—in particular, that of the company of Van Doo soldiers who had been tasked with protecting an abandoned mental hospital in the town of Bakovici. When Canadian troops had first discovered the plight of these Yugoslav inmates—left in no man's land to fend for themselves—it had been hailed as a major public relations coup. In the midst of all the damaging revelations coming out of the Somalia scandal, the tale of Canadian peacekeepers entering the facility, clearing away the filth and restoring order had been a godsend for the Department of National Defence. Now it was being alleged that the Van Doos left guarding the place had indulged heavily in the black market, traded fuel in exchange for sex with the nurses, sold off their ammunition and weapons for booze, and—in the case of one Van Doo officer—raped a mental patient in front of his troops.

The Strathconas had passed along this information to the 12 RBC commander, Lieutenant Colonel David Moore, who had just come through a particularly tense six-month tour, buried several of his men and averted a near disaster in the remote enclave of Srebrenica. Nevertheless, he passed along the information and requested a full investigation. Unbelievably, the National Defence's senior management had not yet learned the full lesson of the Somalia scandal and overturned Moore's request. The Bakovici hospital was to remain a positive news story—until it blossomed into its own full scandal three years later.

I was unaware of these developments as I made plans to visit the Strathcona battle group in Visoko, Bosnia, in June 1994. All I knew was that things were heating up around Sarajevo and that Canadians seemed to be in the thick of things.

BY THE SUMMER of 1994, Canada was maintaining three separate UN missions in the former Yugoslavia. In addition to a battle group in southern Croatia and another in central Bosnia, a logistic battalion—CANLOGBAT—had been set up outside the Adriatic port of Split to supply both the peacekeeping contingents. Since the situation in Bosnia was very fluid and increasingly dangerous, I felt that my best bet to assess the situation was to join a CANLOGBAT resupply convoy. This would not be without some risk; several of the Canadian convoys had been held hostage by Bosnian warlords, some for as many as several days.

As NATO stepped up air strikes against Serbian positions around Sarajevo, this type of retaliation against UN troops was becoming more common. Many of the locals—regardless of their ethnic faction—felt that the presence of UN blue helmets would increase their own safety, and quite often, civilians fearful of an enemy attack on their enclave detained the convoys.

Driving from Croatia into the Bosnian Muslim city of Mostar, our fourteen-truck convoy was often rerouted and delayed at innumerable checkpoints. It seemed that every village had its own warlord, and it was virtually impossible to get a clear delineation of who was fighting whom. In some areas, renegade Croatian commanders were actually allied with Bosnian Serbs. In the end, it took us more than nineteen hours to cover a route that would have required less than four hours before the war. Our destination was the Lord Strathcona's headquarters in the Bosnian city of Visoko. The camp looked like Fort Apache, with a three-metre-high perimeter wall constructed of gravel-filled gabions. There were barbed-wire obstacles and heavily protected observation towers at regular intervals. Inside the walls, the Strathcona's camp was a beehive of activity. The main building was an old brick factory that had been converted into offices and barracks; the outside yard had been transformed into parking lots and maintenance bays for armoured vehicles. The Lord Strathcona's, although technically an armoured regiment, was equipped with a combination of Cougar tank trainers and M-113 armoured personnel carriers. The operational tempo was taking its toll on both the soldiers and the army's inventory. The old Cougars, with a low-velocity 76-mm main cannon, may have looked impressive, but they were never actually intended to be used in a combat environment.

Lieutenant Colonel Ray Wlasichuk was the commanding officer, and he hosted me for dinner at the main mess hall that night. When I advised him that my visit was only going to be for a couple of days, he told me that my timing was fortuitous. They had been having a lot of sniper trouble on an exposed outpost known as Romeo One, and his unit had prepared a plan to put that threat to rest. It was agreed that I would sleep the night in the main camp and then head out to Romeo One for the rest of my story so that I could get an eyewitness account of the expected combat.

The following morning I tagged along with an armoured patrol that went first to the disputed bridge marking the boundary between Bosnian Serbian and Muslim positions. Visoko itself was a Muslim village that was situated north of the Serbian forces that encircled Sarajevo. The Bosnian Muslim forces were

131

essentially surrounding the Serbs, who in turn had surrounded the capital. We crossed the Muslim side of the bridge and dismounted near the Serbian bunkers. It was at this very spot that, just months earlier, a Serb had been killed and Canadian peacekeepers held hostage.

On this day the relationship between the Canadians and Serbs was far more cordial. After a preliminary round of plum brandy, the local Serbian brigade commander arrived with a handful of bodyguards. Major Jim Ellis, the Strathcona officer, knew the Serbian brigadier well—he was a friendly officer with a thick beard and a ready smile. The discussion centred on the fact that the Muslim sniper had been plaguing both the Serbs and the Canadians stationed on Romeo One, which sat on a ridge overlooking the bridge. The sniper's position was known to be located in an abandoned farmhouse on the far side of the valley. What made his elimination so problematic was that Romeo One was actually co-located within the Bosnian Muslim trenches. The Canadians and Serbs knew that the intention was to kill a peacekeeper and implicate the Serbian troops as the culprits. No one knew just how the Muslims would react to the Canadians garrisoned in Romeo One if they engaged and killed a Muslim. "Our detachment would be outnumbered twenty to one up there and in the middle of a hostile force," explained Ellis.

132

Without providing specific details, Ellis told the Serbian commander to be patient, because that night—July 3, 1994—they were going to kill the sniper. The Serb advised Ellis that he had brought up his own 40-mm cannon, and if the Canadians couldn't solve the problem within forty-eight hours, he would take care of it himself. A handshake and another round of brandy sealed the deal. I then headed off to Romeo One to watch the Canadians kill a sniper.

Sergeant Tom Hoppe, seven soldiers and two anti-tank armoured personnel carriers were all that constituted the call sign *Romeo One*. They had been up on the ridgeline for several days and had reported a number of the near-miss sniper rounds. Their two white-painted and clearly marked UN vehicles crested the ridgeline, while the Bosnian Muslim trenches and bunkers snaked down the forward face of the hill. We could see the bridge in the distance, and at about four hundred metres to our front were the Serbian positions An entire Bosnian rifle company was housed in the defensive positions around Romeo One and along the top of the ridge. Behind us, down the reverse slope, was the hamlet of Visoko and the long road that wound down through the narrow streets to the Canadian base camp. In the early evening, Hoppe was given his briefing, and the plan was unveiled.

Earlier that Sunday morning, Lieutenant Colonel Ray Wlasichuk had obtained permission from UN headquarters to fire illumination rounds from his 81-mm mortars. If the ceasefire was violated, the Canadian observers were to pinpoint the location, and then mortarmen were to shoot parachute flares directly over it. In theory, the UN's use of mortar flares would warn the perpetrators that they had been spotted, and if required, the next barrage of mortar shells could be high explosive. In reality, the Lord Strathcona's Horse believed that their sniper would be the first to open fire, and the powerful flares fired over his suspected position would allow Sergeant Tom Hoppe's section to aim and fire a TOW missile at him. The warhead on a TOW missile is intended to disable a tank, and the enormous blast was expected to kill the Muslim sniper if he were anywhere near his usual dugout. It would be like using a sledgehammer to kill a fly, but this particular fly had proven to be a deadly threat.

In case the Muslim troops turned on our position, we were

133

instructed to fight our way off the hill and link up with a squadron of armoured cars and an infantry platoon that were in place as a rapid-reaction force at the base of the hill. All we had to do was settle in, have a supper of hard rations, clean and check the weapons and wait for the show to begin. One of the officers who had given Hoppe his final briefing had had the foresight to hand me his pistol and two clips of ammunition. Hoppe added to my personal arsenal by handing me three hand grenades. I had never been able to hit much with a pistol—at any range—and the issuing of hand grenades reminded me that any combat on this night was going to be at extremely close quarters.

It was just about last light on a warm summer's night. An observer sat in each of the two Canadian vehicle turrets; the rest of the section were lounging near their tents, and Hoppe and I were having a coffee on the ridgeline. Suddenly a bright flash came from a Muslim trench no more than fifty metres from us, and we saw a jet of flame. We heard a hollow *fwwmp* and then felt the concussion shock wave. "Recoil-less rifle," explained Hoppe, and we strained our eyes to watch for the impact on the Serbian positions. Instead, we heard a dull thump come from behind us. The rocket had landed near the town of Visoko, exploding harmlessly in a farmer's empty field. In a flurry of radio messages back and forth to Wlasichuk's headquarters, Hoppe frantically tried to convince them that the Muslims had in fact fired on their own village. By now, both Muslim and Serbian troops were exchanging rifle and machine-gun fire. Sticking to the original plan, Wlasichuk ordered his mortars to fire flares directly over Hoppe's position to illuminate the Muslim rocket crew. We heard the distant thump from the Canadian mortars and knew that we had about twenty seconds before the whole landscape would be bathed in a brilliant phosphorescent light.

There was a bunker entrance into the Muslim positions immediately beside Hoppe's personnel carrier. I was positioned ten metres from the bunker's opening, along with a young militiaman armed with a C9 light machine gun. His weapon was on the full load—meaning he only had to pull the trigger to send a stream of 5.56 × 45 mm bullets into the bunker entrance. I bent straight the cotter pins on my grenades, at the ready to heave all three before racing to the ramp of the carrier. The militiaman was to cover my retreat. Presumably I would then use my pistol to cover his withdrawal to the vehicle.

By the time the first 81-mm flare popped in the sky above us, I was sweating profusely, and the machine gunner was nervously repeating the Lord's Prayer over and over again in a muffled monotone. In the first few moments that the ridgeline was lit up, everyone seemed completely confused. The firing stopped as both sides tried to figure out what the hell was going on.

The Muslims feared that this presaged an infantry assault by the Serbs, and they ordered a full stand-to. Heads of Muslim soldiers began popping up from foxholes to our front, and finally one of them noticed us—two Canadians standing at the ready at their bunker entrance. There was no defiance or alarm in the Bosnians' shout, only a curiosity about what we were up to. Somewhat sheepishly, but obviously relieved, my partner put his C9 back on safe, and I carefully bent the cotter pins on the grenade back into position. The sniper had not fired a shot, and therefore Hoppe had no provocation to fire his TOW missile; the flares had indeed created a temporary ceasefire. The Muslims stood down from their parapets, and it seemed like it was going to be quiet for the remainder of the night. Hoppe arranged a sentry detail, and the rest of us tried to get some sleep in the tent.

I was successful in that endeavour until I was startled awake

135

by heavy machine-gun fire at about 2:30 AM. This time the Serbs launched an intense fusillade of .50-calibre rounds that cracked the air just inches over our heads and threw up clods of earth all along the ridgeline. Hoppe's entire section quickly kitted up and took shelter either in or next to their armoured personnel carriers. This time Hoppe called in the co-ordinates to light up the Serbs. The parachute flares turned night into day for about ninety seconds as they gently floated to earth and then fizzled out. Each time that the landscape went black again, the Serbs would immediately resume their barrage.

Hoppe requested that a constant illumination be kept over our position until daylight. To emphasize the seriousness of the situation, he held the handset up in the air so that headquarters could hear the crackling of bullets around our position. Word came back from Wlasichuk that they had just fired the last of the parachute flare rounds they had stockpiled. "How soon can you get more?" asked Hoppe.

The radio operator replied, "Wait out."

When he came back on the air, he was dejected. "No resupply before first light," he said.

The last flare sputtered out, the world went black and then the air was ripped apart by machine-gun bullets. One ricocheted off a carrier, and then there was a flash directly in front of the second carrier. *Whoomp* came the deafening retort, and the entire second carrier lifted off the ground. "Holy fuck! That's an RPG! Get the fuck back off the crest—both call signs," Hoppe ordered his drivers, who were eager to pull back to safer ground.

Wlasichuk radioed Hoppe to tell him that a relief force was on its way. Four Cougars rumbled down the road from the Canadian main camp. Two hundred metres from the Muslim headquarters, the convoy came under accurate rifle fire. Master Corporal Frank

Canaco, the crew commander in the lead vehicle, was hit in the cheek by a ricochet. Under fire and with a soldier wounded, our would-be rescuers popped smoke grenades and hastily retreated back to base.

As Major Ellis had predicted, we were now sitting on top of belligerents who had just displayed hostile intent to Canadian troops, and we were outnumbered twenty to one. Wlasichuk was hastily organizing another relief force—this time, sixteen vehicles and one hundred soldiers—and the entire Canadian battle group was placed on full alert. It seemed that the Muslims were hoping to cause the Serbs to kill Hoppe's troops, by refusing to allow the Canadians off the embattled and exposed position. The Serb machine-gunners seemed intent on fulfilling that plan, and we knew that any attempt by the relief column would never get to us in time.

Hoppe attached trip flares to the tent and made ready to burn his code book and any sensitive equipment. His gunners were prepared to disable their missile launchers rather than allow them to be captured intact. It seemed crazy that we would have so much high-tech firepower and not be able to at least eliminate the Serb machine guns that were threatening our lives. The problem was that since the Canadian vehicles had pulled back, we could no longer observe the valley.

In the first few minutes of pulling back onto the crest, Hoppe's men would be exposed and unaware of the enemy location. I suggested going forward in the Muslim trenches to locate the machine-gun nest. Hoppe replied that UN troops were not permitted to observe from inside a combatant's bunker. This left the door open for me as I was technically just a civilian caught in a firefight. Leaving the grenades, I went into the bunker entrance, which just hours earlier I had been prepared to obliterate.

137

Inside the first dugout were a couple of bunks, some filthy bedding and a wide-eyed young Muslim soldier sitting behind the one candle that lit the tiny room. He spoke no English, and my few words of Serbo-Croat hardly mattered in this situation. Another burst of Serbian machine-gun fire sounded overhead, and I said, *"Chetnik, boom boom boom."*

He nodded understandingly. *"Kanatski rakete—whoosh, boom Chetnik gotovo,"* I said, making theatrical arm gestures and using my "Tarzan dialect" to inform him that the Canadians would fire a rocket and finish the Serbs.

I made a searching gesture with my hand shielding my eyes and turning my head from side to side; I then uplifted my palms and shrugged my shoulders in the universal sign of ignorance. *"Ah, Chetnik,"* exclaimed the Bosnian in sudden comprehension. He snatched up his Kalashnikov and beckoned me to follow him into the trenches. He ran fast at the crouch, well below the two-metre parapet. It was obvious that he was very familiar with his defensive position, whereas I was groping my way forward in the dark, trying to keep as low as possible. At a number of fire positions, my guide would stop to chat in a low whisper with his comrades and before proceeding forward, ever farther down the slope and every step closer to the Serb machine gun.

138   When we came to one Y junction in the trench system, my guide—I had named him "Eddie" because I could not pronounce his actual name—met up with his platoon commander. This young officer was initially pissed off to find a Canadian civilian roaming around inside his defensive position—with a pistol—in the middle of a firefight. When Eddie explained that I was trying to pinpoint the Serb machine gun so that the Canadians could destroy it with a TOW missile, his attitude changed. Smiling broadly, he extended his hand in greeting and then personally led

Eddie and me straight down the hill. The machine gun sounded very close when the lieutenant held up his hand and gestured off to his right. *Stoh metre* and *Chetnik* were the only words I understood, but I knew this meant that the Serbian bunker was only about one hundred metres away from our position.

As the lieutenant was whispering to me, Eddie stood up in the trench and began pushing dirt away from the parapet so that he could see over the top. Hearing his efforts, the lieutenant turned and in a single movement grabbed Eddie's legs and pulled him to the bottom of the trench. Within seconds, the Serbs were pounding extended bursts of heavy machine-gun rounds into the ground all around where Eddie had been spotted. Although the trench was at least two metres deep, the bullets were passing through the soil above us at an angle and thudding into the back wall. The air was thick with dirt, and at that close range we could feel the shock wave of each passing bullet. I kept my head pressed into the ground, gritting my teeth in anticipation of the next burst.

The Serbs probably fired only three or four bursts at us before turning their attention back to targets farther up the ridgeline. As we began brushing the dirt off our clothes, Eddie looked over at me with a goofy grin and said, *"Izvini"* (sorry).

I worked my way back up the hill. Clambering out of the Muslim trenches, I told Hoppe I had a rough fix on the Serbian bunker. From his map and range cards he plotted the position as being in the basement of or in a trench outside a burnt-out house on the valley floor. There was a faint light showing in the eastern sky, and Wlasichuk had promised Hoppe that "fast-air" (fighter jets) would be available to support us after dawn.

Rather than wait, Hoppe ordered one of his carriers to crest the ridgeline and align the TOW missile on the suspected Serbian

139

position. After a night under fire, the Canadians were anxious
for a chance to start shooting back. Almost immediately after
the Canadian armoured personnel carrier had moved forward,
the Serbs fired a short burst. It was not aimed at Hoppe's men,
but they now had a confirmed location: a basement window in
the burnt-out house. The TOW gunner laid his crosshairs on the
dark rectangle window frame, and Hoppe radioed Wlasichuk to
inform him that his detachment was about to fire a missile in
self-defence. The word came back from headquarters that the
next time the Serbs fired, Romeo One was to engage with the
TOW. Hoppe's troops began fighting over who would get the hon-
ours. I wanted to capture the moment on film.

Since I could not expose myself on the forward slope, I took
up a position in some dead ground next to the carrier. I thought
I would snap a shot of the missile firing and then move forward
to take a photograph of the destruction. It was not to be. A sudden roar sounded above, and two French fighter jets swept in low
across the valley. Everyone watched as they banked and came
back around for a second pass. At this stage in the use of air
strikes against belligerents, the accuracy achieved by NATO pilots
had been less than stellar. Just weeks earlier, during a training
mission a French pilot had bombed in error a corner of the Canadian camp. The presence of the jets skimming low overhead was
enough to cause everyone to stop shooting. Within an hour, the
previous night's crisis was over. The Muslims allowed Romeo One
to leave the ridge, and all sides agreed to renew the ceasefire.

I had Hoppe snap a photograph of me with my new friend
Eddie, and we packed up the vehicles. All along the ridge, soldiers brewed coffee, relieved themselves, cleaned weapons and
acted as though nothing had happened. When we drove back to
the front gates of the Canadian camp in Visoko, the guards gave

140

us a thumbs-up. The entire battle group had been up all night on full alert, anxiously following the fate of Romeo One over the battalion's radio network.

Waiting for us as we parked the vehicles was a group of civilian psychiatrists who were in Bosnia conducting a study on post-traumatic stress disorder. This was the first such survey done by the Canadian Forces into something that had never before been considered a priority. Armed with clipboards and pens, they eagerly approached Hoppe's troops and started asking a battery of questions. To his credit, Hoppe told them to "bugger off," that we didn't need psychoanalysis at this point; all we needed was a good breakfast and some sleep. After a mound of bacon and eggs, washed down with hot, strong coffee, I bid Hoppe farewell, turned in my pistol and grenades and caught a ride with an armoured convoy to Sarajevo.

I wrote up a news article during that drive and then faxed it to my office from the UN desk at the Sarajevo airport. I was lucky enough to get on board a British air force C-130 Hercules flying a supply shuttle to Split, Croatia. From there I used my UNPROFOR press pass to bluff my way into a seat on a UN Sea King helicopter back to Zagreb.

At the hotel that night I was informed by Julie Simoneau in Ottawa that the Sun newspapers had not published my story; they had a reporter in Yugoslavia already, and he had said that all had been quiet the previous night. The fact was that he was in Croatia and I was in Bosnia, but to the news desk Yugoslavia was just a dateline.

The next morning I showered and changed into a fresh suit. I was catching the early inter-city train to Linz, Austria, to meet with Mercedes-Benz officials regarding their military truck plant. I went directly to the café car, and as the train pulled out of the

Zagreb station it dawned on me that, just twenty-four hours earlier, I had been in a combat situation. The enormity of what I had been through began to sink in, and I started shaking like a leaf. I spilled my coffee all over the table and startled the other passengers, who no doubt feared I was entering some sort of seizure.

Had I stayed behind and spoken to the psychiatrists, I would have known that such a download of the nervous system is quite normal after an experience like the one I had just had. As it was, I had no idea what was happening to me. I rationalized to myself that I need not endanger myself in this manner any more. I was thirty-three years old, my wife was seven months pregnant with our first child, our business needed my full attention and now that I had been in combat, I had nothing more to prove. There and then I decided to retire from the risky business of war reporting.

The shaking stopped.

At the age of four months, in 1960, I am competing with a monkey and losing. On the left is my mother, Mary; my sister, Tracey, is holding the stuffed monkey she wishes were her real brother.

Vacationing at Wasaga Beach, Ontario, in the fall of 1962. It is already apparent that I see things differently than do those around me—in this case, Tracey.

On the boat sailing home to Canada from England in 1969, a crew member hams it up while my father, Raymond, supervises me at the helm. The notion of a life at sea once appealed to me, but my land-lubber's propensity for seasickness soon changed that.

Much to our neighbours' chagrin, the Taylor household served as the rehearsal hall for the Offenders. Playing the Toronto bar circuit at the height of the Punk Rock movement was a perfect fit for a student at the Ontario College of Art in 1980.

After graduating from battle school, I deployed to Germany as a member of the 2nd Battalion, Princess Patricia's Canadian Light Infantry. Here I am in Hammelburg, an urban warfare training centre, during a pause in the gruelling exercise in 1984.

After retiring from the army, I started working as the base's graphic artist in Baden-Soellingen while moonlighting as the art director for *Euroski* magazine. Here I am at my art desk in 1988.

Esprit de Corps began as an inflight magazine for air force passenger planes, and thus the editorial content was entirely vetted by "the brass." Despite these restrictions, I was able to perform as a real-life dummy for naval reservists in the summer of 1990.

On May 1, 1991, with as much fanfare as could be mustered, *Esprit de Corps* magazine was issued in its new independent monthly format. Here editor Jim Scott (*left*) and sales representative Eric Tate (*centre*) celebrate the event with me in Ottawa.

In the aftermath of the 1991 Gulf War, Canadian engineers were deployed into Kuwait to help clean up the battlefield. Here two Sappers examine a destroyed Iraqi tank on the "Highway of Death" outside Kuwait City. At that time, no one understood that the depleted-uranium rounds used against the Iraqis could lead to long-term health problems for allied soldiers.

In the spring of 1992, the United Nations mounted its biggest peacekeeping mission to date to stabilize and rebuild Cambodia in the wake of the genocidal Khmer Rouge regime. Here curious children gather outside the Canadian camp in Phnom Penh.

On the Croatian front lines in 1992, members of the 52nd Independent Battalion use a ripped-up Yugoslavian flag to clean their gun after a night of heavy fighting with Serbian forces.

Although the United Nations brokered a ceasefire in April 1992, peace-keepers were not immediately deployed. This Croatian tank in a hull-down position was just four hundred metres from the Serbian front lines. The destroyed houses illustrate the intensity of the fighting.

When I headed to Belgrade during the 1999 NATO bombing campaign, I told my four-year-old son, Kirk, that he would have to be the "man of the house" in my absence. When I returned home, it was apparent that Kirk was not prepared to relinquish the post.

6

CRIME AND CORRUPTION
IN THE CANADIAN MILITARY

You could feel the hatred of the rank and file—
it was like their eyes were burning holes in our
backs as we walked through the corridors.

A CANADIAN COLONEL

BY THE TIME I RETURNED to Canada I was in serious trouble—and
not just from a very pregnant Katherine, who was appalled at my
reckless disregard for my own safety in Bosnia. In April 1994,
Trooper Kyle Brown contacted me. His court martial for the torture and manslaughter of Shidane Arone had concluded the
month before, and he had been found guilty. Five other Airborne
soldiers had been charged in connection with this atrocity, but
Brown had been singled out by the military justice system and
the media as the primary scapegoat in this entire affair.

143

Brown wrote to me and said he felt that I, as an ex-soldier,
was the only journalist he could trust to tell his side of the story.
I agreed to interview him in the Edmonton jail, and his revelations were deeply disturbing. He did not know about the top-level

message traffic that we had compiled from access-to-information releases, but he did know that without his photographs thrown into the equation, the regiment had been prepared to cover up the whole murder. Now he was facing a five-year prison sentence for following orders to abuse the prisoner and then for coming clean with the evidence to implicate Master Corporal Clayton Matchee. Brown's new evidence—combined with the information we already had—led us to produce a fairly convincing argument that a top-level cover-up had been orchestrated from inside National Defence Headquarters.

I telephoned army commander Lieutenant General Gordon Reay with my allegations. Reay had been a regular contributor of inside information to *Esprit de Corps,* and he had often stopped by our office to pass along scuttlebutt. I considered him a friend, and I informed him that the questions we were going to ask would also implicate him. I offered him the chance to shed further light on who exactly had ordered the cover-up, but he politely declined. When I asked for his advice on how I should handle the informa-tion, Reay told me to follow my conscience.

I went for a long walk along the Ottawa River and mulled over the consequences that this might have for our business and for the Canadian Forces. In the end, I decided the truth had to come out. *Esprit de Corps* geared up for a special issue entitled "Scape-goat." Katherine painted a portrait of Kyle Brown for the cover, and two thirds of the editorial content was dedicated to the Somalia affair.

Just as our "Scapegoat" issue of *Esprit de Corps* was published, the Department of National Defence was quick to mount a coun-terattack. The mainstream media were very interested in the facts we had revealed, but we still had not unearthed the smok-ing gun, so there was very little with which they could move

144

forward. The senior brass understood the importance of the fact that people like Kyle Brown were starting to ask some unanswerable questions. A daily executive committee at National Defence headquarters decided to form a "tiger team" under the direction of the vice-chief of the defence staff to combat *Esprit de Corps*. National Defence was not about to start engaging the points that we had raised in public; instead, it intended to put our magazine out of business. Memos were sent to the CANEX military retail stores, ordering them to cease the sale of our publication; the copies we had donated through the Royal Canadian Legion were to be burned, according to the official directive from National Defence Headquarters and, most importantly, all our defence clients began calling to cancel their advertising contracts.

A number of those calling to pull even their prepaid ads told us that Defence had put out the word to cease all support of us. One advertising representative was flabbergasted when he called our office. "What did you do to General Reay?" he asked. "He just told me to cancel all my ads with you."

When I asked him what he was going to do, he replied, "I've got a $10 million order on the line. What do you think I'm going to do? Stop running our ads."

Supporters quietly faxed us copies of the more damning directives. We had no choice but to take our situation to the media, even if it meant frightening off our remaining advertisers and making shareholders nervous. A couple of the advertising representatives were so incensed by the attempt to muscle the press that they verbally confirmed the story to reporters.

As is usually the case with censorship attempts, this one backfired on the Department of National Defence. All of a sudden, everyone looked more closely at what it was about this little magazine that had frightened the brass enough to try something so desperate. The media spotlight may have been on us, but we were in serious trouble. We had taken the Somalia story as far as we could, all of our revenue had been stopped, and it was only a matter of time before we would have to admit the obvious and call it quits. What we needed was a miracle, and it was about to arrive in two separate pieces of correspondence.

The first was a faxed letter from a retired colonel, Michel Drapeau, who was writing to support our allegations of a top-level cover-up in our "Scapegoat" issue. While not adding any specifics, Drapeau mentioned his lifelong career in the army and his experience at the senior level of National Defence Headquarters as an officer and a civilian. In his opinion, we were not far off the mark, and he urged us to continue our quest for the truth. Editor Jim Scott and I flagged this for our letters section in what we figured would be the final issue of our magazine.

The next tipoff was an anonymous call from a National Defence bureaucrat working inside the executive secretariat. Jim Scott fielded the call and furiously scribbled some notes. As is often the case, the tipster was awfully cryptic with his information. He repeatedly told Jim that there was a case before the Federal Court that would help us discover the truth. Only when Jim read back the name on the docket—Colonel Michel Drapeau— did we realize that this was not the usual crackpot caller. Researching court documents was not something we had ever done before, but these were desperate times. Jim dutifully set off for the Federal Court to see if this lead were worth pursuing.

When he returned to our office at the end of the day, he was visibly shaking. "You're not going to believe what we've gotten involved with," he said. "We are in way over our heads on this."

Jim had brought back a copy of Drapeau's wrongful dismissal statement of claim against the Department of National Defence.

We pored over page after page of detailed allegations of corruption and wrongdoing. The absolute shocker was the fact that Denys Henrie, Drapeau's immediate predecessor as head of the executive secretariat in National Defence, had committed suicide. That in itself was alarming enough, but the fact that this good-looking, forty-year-old rising star of the civil service had named in his suicide note five of his colleagues as "responsible" for his death was intriguing. The fact that there had been no investigation or inquest into Henrie's dying allegation was frightening. That one of the five named was Deputy Minister Bob Fowler, Henrie's immediate boss and the man at the centre of the Somalia scandal, made it imperative for us to contact Drapeau.

When we first called him at his house in early August 1994, he was shocked to know that we had discovered his court documents. He reluctantly agreed to meet Jim and me, and he was insistent on providing us only with background information; he had no desire to go public as long as his case was before the courts. We drove out to Drapeau's suburban home in east Ottawa, and his wife, Nicole, very nervously let us in. It was obvious that she was extremely mistrustful of our intentions and very concerned about her husband's well-being. During the next few hours, Drapeau painted a picture of a completely dysfunctional senior command structure within the Department of National Defence, rife with corruption and driven by a culture of cover-up and abuse of authority. The best news of all was that Drapeau had made extensive use of the Access to Information Act to collect a staggering amount of detailed documentation to back up his allegations. He also had the experience of working inside the top offices, and he knew the personalities and power structure that existed in the empire created by Bob Fowler. We now had plenty of ammunition to resume our fight with National Defence, and a

147

new-found ally who knew where the bodies were buried because he had watched it happen. All we had to do now was make sure that the media could take this message to the public. In order to do that, *Esprit de Corps* had to survive.

WE KNEW THAT we had to bring Colonel Drapeau's information to the mainstream media in a manner that would propel the narrow focus on the Somalia scandal into a wider probe of a thoroughly mismanaged Defence department. To achieve this, we had to use all the contacts and tricks we had learned over the years. *Toronto Sun* editor emeritus Peter Worthington had been a friend, mentor and financial supporter since we had first contacted him in 1992. We had provided Peter with leads on a number of controversial issues and inside information that he had then put into much wider circulation through his columns. Peter had been an airman in the Second World War, an infantry officer in the Princess Pats in Korea, a natural journalist who had spent his entire career looking for—and finding—trouble and he was a kindred spirit.

Worthington met with Drapeau at our suggestion, and the two hit it off immediately. In Drapeau, Worthington saw a man of unimpeachable honour, and Drapeau saw a trustworthy journalist concerned more about fixing a once-proud institution than about inciting a sexy scandal.

To shore up our finances we held a shareholder meeting and explained the fight in which we were about to engage and what it would mean to the Canadian Forces if we were successful. Retired colonel Strome Galloway was one of our primary investors. Within military circles he was a living legend. Strome had fought with distinction in the Second World War, first as an exchange officer with the Royal Irish Regiment in North Africa and then with his

Royal Canadian Regiment through Sicily and Italy. As such, it was likely that he had spent more days in combat than had any soldier in Canadian history. A leader by example, a devout monarchist and an officer steeped in military tradition, Strome had served some sixty years in uniform, from boy soldier to honorary colonel. When we showed him what was transpiring in the upper echelons of National Defence, Strome eagerly enlisted to fight yet another battle. He and his wife, Jean, went so far as to purchase another share in our company, even though they knew the sort of economic battle we were going to have to endure.

Les Peate was instrumental in rounding up support for us from Cliff Chadderton, stalwart spokesman for veterans' rights. Chief executive officer of the War Amps and chairman of the National Council of Veterans Associations in Canada, Cliff would prove a valuable ally in the coming fight.

Les Peate was also instrumental in rallying support from the Korea Veterans Association of Canada. Most of these old soldiers were retired, but they were still looking to fight the good fight against a corrupt senior brass. Norm Shannon was the third member of our historical editorial team that we had affectionately named "The Old Guard." I had met Norm's wife, Jean, on a Boxing Day train trip to Toronto in 1992, and she had told me that her husband was a Second World War air force veteran with a passion for writing. Within a few weeks of our meeting, Jean had become a shareholder and Norm had established himself as a vital part of the magazine. Although his contributed articles to this point had been primarily historical features, Norm stepped up to add some of his own personal observations and provided sage advice in the current crisis.

To offset the loss of advertising revenue, we launched an appeal for our readers to take out a lifetime subscription at a one-time rate of $150. At this critical stage, *Esprit de Corps*'s life expectancy looked to be numbered in days, not years. Some key individuals stepped forward to assist us. Publicly voicing his displeasure at the Department of National Defence's attempts to silence our publication, recently retired major general Lewis MacKenzie, of Sarajevo fame, became one of our first lifetime subscribers. Hundreds more serving and retired soldiers followed his lead.

To ensure that the mainstream media would be made aware of Colonel Drapeau's damning revelations, we knew we needed some sort of novel approach. We were raising a trickle of money but not enough to allow us to attempt another mass printing and distribution. In fact, we could raise only enough cash to print five thousand copies of volume 4, issue 3. Every shot needed to count, so we went back to the fail-safe adage that "sex sells." As the "Scapegoat" issue had failed to garner widespread attention, we decided to bury the corruption hook inside the irresistibly juicy bait of a special report, "Sex in the Service." We cobbled together some of the choicest bits of tantalizing and titillating incidents we had uncovered over the years—lesbians on ships, prostitutes in uniform and orgies in the Arctic—and then fleshed the articles out with some studies and statistics on women in combat trades.

The big kicker was the cover photograph. We hired two strippers to pose in their lingerie, with my dogtags, an air force uniform jacket and a fistful of twenty-dollar bills as props. The dominant stance of the lead model over the submissive reclining form of the second girl plus the cash was meant to imply the purchase of girl-on-girl sex by a master corporal. This was certainly well outside our normal range of cover images. My old PPCLI comrade, Mark Lamontagne, agreed to do the photography session for free.

It was outrageously provocative, and our judgement of the media's response proved to be correct. Nobody wants to create this sort of image, but once it was in print, the media eagerly reported our "sex report" as news—complete with the cover photo. This was the first time *Esprit de Corps* had received so much nationwide coverage, and Jim and I were frantically fielding as many media calls as we could. Print, television and even radio were all over the admittedly non-story, and try as we might to interest our colleagues in the special eight-page report on corruption in Bob Fowler's empire, everyone remained fixated on the tits-and-ass photograph. In fact, the only news outlet that took a serious interest in the allegations against Bob Fowler was CTV's *Mike Duffy Live*. Jim Scott did the show live on Parliament Hill, and in that five-minute segment he outlined some of the more sensational examples of mismanagement, fraud and cover-up among the senior National Defence management team. Other outlets, such as the CBC's investigative news team and the *Ottawa Citizen*, took a more long-term interest in the revelations made by Drapeau. It was several months before they published their own damning exposés to corroborate the *Esprit de Corps* report.

We soon realized that instead of creating a massive public outcry that would have brought about a quick-fix solution—or at least launched a public inquiry—we were going to be in for a long, drawn-out fight with a resourceful, recalcitrant and vengeful foe.

In a hastily convened meeting, General John de Chastelain had his public affairs officers fabricate a letter of protest to our "Sex in the Service" report from a fictitious female sailor. In response to this phony plea for the chief of defence staff to set the record straight, de Chastelain then issued a Canadian Forces General Message denouncing *Esprit de Corps* for its unprofessional innuendo maligning the reputation of all serving personnel. This message was of course widely distributed to the media, along with the falsified letter of complaint. When we pointed out that our magazines would not even be on sale—or delivered in the mail to Halifax—for several days yet, the media asked on our behalf how the letter writer could have even seen the contentious issue. All requests to interview the offended sailor were refused as she was now "operationally deployed at sea" for at least six months. Meanwhile, Drapeau had filed an access-to-information request that would ultimately reveal that de Chastelain had orchestrated the whole thing.

In the short term, *Esprit de Corps* remained in perilous financial straits. We had no alternative but to begin cutting staff. Jim Scott was a full partner at that stage—he had been instrumental in shaping the magazine, and he was a valuable ally in the fight. He also had a wife and two young boys, and he knew that his salary—though modest—was more than we could continue to afford. It was a difficult meeting for both of us when he advised me of his intention to step aside. He would continue to assist us whenever and wherever he could, but from this point forward I would be alone at the helm of *Esprit de Corps*.

BY NOVEMBER 1994, the last of the courts martial into the murder of Shidane Arone had been conducted. As the verdicts of not guilty for officers began to contrast with Kyle Brown's five-year jail sentence, a groundswell of support grew for the young paratrooper who was now increasingly seen as the scapegoat for his superiors. In an attempt to stem the tide of suspicion and scrutiny and put the focus back on the lower ranks, the decision was made to release Clayton Matchee's trophy photographs for media publication. Technically, the photographs were the personal property of Brown, which he had voluntarily submitted to the court as evidence in a homicide, but National Defence decided to lift the publication ban on these photographs. Although largely unquestioned at the time, the rationale for doing so was based on the top brass's desire to have the public redirect its attention to the sordid events that had taken place in the bloody pit. The media bought this deliberate bait (in some cases, literally) and gave the graphic photographs front-page, top-of-the-news coverage.

Virtually every violent crime tried in civilian court, including homicide, is documented by photographic evidence of the victim's injuries; yet, the photographs are never released for publication. For the Department of National Defence, of all agencies, to suddenly and uncharacteristically have been so forthright with this material should not have gone unquestioned. That it did so testified to the talents of Deputy Minister Bob Fowler's hand-picked team.

The media, in fact, were almost lulled back to sleep following the explosive public outburst generated by the release of Brown's photos. The *Ottawa Sun* ran an editorial saying, in effect, that now the courts martial had concluded and we had seen the gory details, we could finally close the book on the Somalia scandal. Unfortunately for Fowler and his top officials, this single comment sparked Major Barry Armstrong to write a letter to the editor outlining how, as the surgeon in Somalia at the time, he had been ordered to destroy photographs and evidence by a senior officer and that the tale of the cover-up had yet to be unveiled. *Ottawa Sun* editor Rick Gibbons read the letter with disbelief, then contacted Armstrong directly. The cover-up story ran on the front page and was picked up by all of the networks and wire services. Over the next three days, public pressure mounted.

To add to that pressure, I secured a second interview with Kyle Brown at the military detention centre in Edmonton. The

Sun Media chain had agreed to give the story good play in all its papers. The actual interview was conducted late in the afternoon on a Saturday, and given the time difference, the weekend editors in Toronto were frantic for me to file my copy. They wanted a thousand-word story for the Sunday edition and a more in-depth, two-thousand-word feature for the Monday edition. It was a lot of pressure, and this was only exacerbated when they told me that the story was going on the front page on both days.

"Turkey Shoot" ran Sunday's banner headline, and the interview with Brown reinforced Major Armstrong's allegations that the March 4, 1993, shooting of looters had been a deliberate ambush. The second story brought to light for the first time the fact that, in the first seventy-two hours following the death of Shidane Arone, no statements or evidence had been collected. This was in sharp contrast to the message sent by Colonel Serge Labbé from Mogadishu to Ottawa, claiming that such information was going to be collected immediately. It became obvious that a cover-up had been initiated at the highest level.

On November 21 the government had no choice but to announce the commissioning of a full public inquiry into the Airborne Regiment's deployment into Somalia. *Esprit de Corps* had been instrumental in keeping this issue in the news. We had paid a steep price, but it seemed that vindication was close at hand. We could not have possibly foreseen that even before the Airborne Regiment could stand trial in the court of public opinion, the Liberal government would pass a death sentence on the accused.

"ARE YOU HAPPY now that you've killed the Airborne?" I was asked that question by several irate callers following Defence Minister David Collenette's announcement on January 23, 1995, that the elite regiment would be disbanded.

Coming from former and serving members, these words were understandably mixed with emotion, but the sting was harsh, nonetheless. The previous eight days had seen the media, fuelled by the release of two amateur videotapes, embark on a feeding frenzy that ripped the already tattered Airborne's reputation to shreds.

Yes, it had been my decison to release the first of the damning videotapes. The tape had been sent to me, and the source had intended for it to help convince the public that convicted Trooper Kyle Brown (as the lowest-ranking soldier involved) was being scapegoated by the military justice system. Brown had already served ten months of a five-year prison sentence for manslaughter and torture, despite the known fact that Master Corporal Clayton Matchee had been identified as the Somali victim's prime antagonist that night. However, Matchee's subsequent suicide attempt left him unfit to stand trial for his actions. Those who had given the order to abuse the prisoners and had attempted to dismiss the beating death as an "accident during apprehension" received reprimands or full acquittals.

The first videotape was a two-hour travelogue-cum-biographical sketch of the principal characters involved in the March 16, 1993, beating death of a Somali prisoner. To illustrate Brown's character, I wanted to use only one short segment from the tape. In the sequence, Brown was contrasted to his squad mates and came across as both introspective and reserved in comparison with the other soldiers, who postured for the camera and made morale-boosting statements in the form of racial slurs.

The inherent danger of releasing such material to the mainstream media was that they would do exactly as they did—focus upon the shocking and the sensational (someone in uniform saying the words *nignog* and *niggah*). However, arguments to defuse

155

the controversy when it blew up were readily available not only to me but also to the senior management of the Defence department. It was a two-year-old tape; the derogatory racial slurs used by the Airborne had been identified by the original board of inquiry and had been published as such in its Phase 1 report, tabled in August 1993; at that juncture, the media had put the regiment through the racism wringer, resulting in a zero-tolerance policy throughout the Canadian Forces. In April 1994, after personnel changes and "a detailed analysis of all the evidence," army commander Lieutenant General Gordon Reay had pronounced the Airborne fit for duty. Two months later, following his own inspection, Chief of Defence Staff John de Chastelain had concurred with General Reay and forwarded the regiment's clean bill of health to Defence Minister David Collenette.

Although the television images were disturbing, what we were seeing was old news that had already been discovered and rectified by the military authorities. I knew this because two months earlier I had been forwarded copies of the letters in which Reay and de Chastelain had urged Collenette to "clear the Airborne's name publicly" in order "to remove any lingering cloud of doubt."

My naïveté about the ways in which the media works was matched by a sense of the complete betrayal by senior military leaders once this story broke. By the second day of the Somalia videotape's extensive news coverage, most astute editors and viewers had begun to see past the obvious and ask, "Where were the leaders?" The complete absence of any officers in the footage gave one the sense that the soldiers in Somalia had been left to their own devices. The fact that not a single officer came forward to defend the regiment from the media onslaught made me realize that, once again, the Airborne was being completely abandoned.

The release of the second home videotape was unforeseen. Although it was unrelated to the regiment's professional conduct in Somalia, this tape had a force-multiplier effect when seen in tandem with the first. Cynthia Drummond from CFCF (a CTV affiliate) purchased the hazing tape from a disgruntled former Airborne member. It was only because I had been involved with the first tape (and due to the fact that defence officials declined the offer) that I was asked to view and then put this new initiation videotape into perspective.

Having served as a soldier in a combat arms unit for three and a half years and then reporting on military affairs full time for another six, I was prepared to see some vulgar but nonetheless harmless hijinks. Total shock and absolute revulsion was what I felt when I previewed the sixty minutes of graphic footage. I wasn't aware that human beings, let alone Canadian soldiers, did such things to one another. The brutal and dehumanizing hazing had obviously taken place at Canadian Forces Base Petawawa, in broad daylight, with at least sixty participants, several of whom were identified as senior non-commissioned officers.

It was plain to me that the airing of this second videotape was going to immediately cripple what was left of the Airborne Regiment's reputation. Despite my past differences with National Defence public affairs officials, there was no question that my loyalty in this situation had to be to the armed forces, not the media. Contrary to CTV's wishes and without their knowledge, I immediately tipped off both the brass at National Defence Headquarters and the senior Airborne Regiment officers about the contents of the damaging tape. Although this videotape was completely different from the first, I stressed that the same arguments—that it was two-and-a-half-year-old news and that the regiment was now clean—could be used if applied quickly and forcefully.

157

Instead, to my disappointment, Defence Minister Collenette simply decried it as an outrage and publicly ordered General de Chastelain to have a full report on his desk "by Monday morning!" There could be no justification for the behaviour of the troops involved in that depraved initiation ritual, but once again viewers and analysts quickly recovered from their initial shock and collectively asked, "Where are the leaders?"

Realizing that the senior commanders were not voluntarily rallying behind the regiment, I deliberately released the two letters from generals Reay and de Chastelain. I felt it was important for the public to know that the investigation Collenette had so hastily ordered had been completed six months earlier and that the report he demanded "by Monday morning" was already in his possession. It was my view that Defence officials were attempting to orchestrate a public relations sham.

Prime Minister Chrétien issued the Airborne's death warrant from the Caribbean island of Trinidad when he first uttered the word *disband* on January 19. His justification: "For the sake of the army's morale." In an attempt to save the Airborne, *Esprit de Corps* had put the professionalism and competence of de Chastelain and Reay on the public firing line by reminding the media and the public of the two 1994 reports, as both videotapes predated their recommendations to maintain the regiment.

As for Chrétien's "morale of the army" argument, we widely distributed to the media a November 1994 report prepared by Colonel George Oehring. This internal study stated that soldiers had "lost faith and confidence" in senior commanders and blamed it on "impotent military leadership." In other words, Canadian troops were saying exactly the same thing as the Canadian public: "Where are the leaders?"

Despite these facts, on January 23, 1995, at 3:10 PM, David Collenette announced the disbandment of the Canadian Airborne

158

Regiment. At his side sat a grim-faced General de Chastelain, his recommendations publicly rejected. With the regiment turfed, media and analysts immediately asked, "What about the leaders?"

Generals de Chastelain and Reay, who had previously pronounced themselves defenders of the Airborne, were quick to offer their services as pallbearers for the dismantled regiment, seemingly proving that honour is for suckers in a world of careerism. As for Prime Minister Chrétien's claim that this would improve morale, I suggested that he reread the definition of impotence and apply it to the military leadership. After all, soldiers do not respect self-preservation; they honour self-sacrifice.

In an attempt to restore credibility to the office of the chief of defence staff, the government issued a hastily drafted communiqué claiming that General de Chastelain had "tried" to resign but that Prime Minister Chrétien had refused to accept the offer. Unfortunately for all involved, this press release only further illustrated how out of the loop de Chastelain really was. The author of the document mistakenly referred to the disbanded unit as the Airborne *Division*, not *Regiment*, and anyone familiar with de Chastelain's penchant for details knew immediately that he would never have missed such an error if he had so much as glanced at the letter before its release.

159

WITH THE SOMALIA Commission of Inquiry due to begin its hearings and the Airborne Regiment already disbanded, it seemed as though *Esprit de Corps* had already set some serious changes in motion, and it was time for us to assess the damage we had suffered in the process. Katherine and I were both exhausted, and our financial status was worse than that.

In addition to this, we had cause for concern for our own personal safety. When the official word was given to disband the Airborne, Brigadier General Brian Vernon had told the emotional paratroopers not to forget that "Scott Taylor" had done this "to you." Sergeant Mark Boland, Kyle Brown's section commander in Somalia, had also been convicted for his involvement in the death of Arone. His sentence already served, he was in Petawawa when Vernon made that statement. He ran to a pay phone to warn me of the danger. It was a ridiculous statement to make to seven hundred enraged Airborne soldiers, and the fact that our address appeared in the phone book didn't help matters. We advised Colonel Michel Drapeau, who immediately sent a letter to Defence Minister Collenette. This missive outlined what Vernon had said and declared that the Department of National Defence would be responsible if any harm came to me or my family.

Nevertheless, this was not a stress that I felt I needed to endure any further. I arranged to have an off-the-record discussion with John Williston, personal assistant to Defence Minister Collenette. Drapeau accompanied me, and we said that I was prepared to throw in the towel and concede defeat. I proposed that if they could find a way to enable one of our competitors to purchase our subscription list, *Esprit de Corps* could simply disappear. The only thing we wanted at this point was to recoup the money owed to our shareholders, which was about $100,000. As I had no journalistic training, I would find a job in the graphics or publishing field.

Williston did not even take the time to consider the offer we were making. Stung by the wholesale embarrassment that we had been causing his boss, he revelled in our predicament. I do not remember his exact words, but they were to the effect that we could expect no quarter. There would be no deal, no way out for us, short of complete bankruptcy and ruin.

It was a decision they would regret. With no alternative but to continue fighting, Drapeau and I vowed to do just that. As long

160

as *Esprit de Corps* could keep the lights on and pay the rent, we would unleash a barrage of scandals, the likes of which could not have been conceived. For months on end, we fed as many as three stories a week to the mainstream media.

Publicly, military spokespersons desperately tried to downplay *Esprit de Corps* as nothing more than a soapbox for disgruntled corporals. Although it is true that our sources for information were often enlisted personnel directly affected by events, at the risk of revealing trade secrets I must confess that the most damaging revelations were forwarded to our offices by the generals themselves. In fact, it always amazed me that *Esprit de Corps*'s critics never questioned how our supposedly junior-ranking, non-commissioned whistleblowers were privy to such highly classified and sensitive policy papers. Even at the height of the Somalia scandal, when internal memos were circulating within the Canadian Forces to discredit *Esprit de Corps,* and defence contractors were being instructed by generals to cease their advertising contracts with our publication, other senior officers continued to frequent my office after working hours and to meet me for clandestine luncheons. Whether they were brigadiers, major generals or even lieutenant generals, all of our informants explained that, because their superiors were opposed to public disclosure, they themselves had no recourse but to make the information available to the media—via *Esprit de Corps.*

One of the safest ways for us to obtain copies of the original documents (and thereby protect our top-level sources) was to file access-to-information requests. This was a time-consuming process, and we often had to invent red herring requests to give National Defence officials the false impression that we were simply on a random fishing expedition with our access-to-information submissions. In the end, our patience paid a dividend:

161

by providing the mainstream media with the Department of National Defence's own damaging documents, our allegations of corruption were well supported and our credibility within the press corps grew rapidly.

In December 1995, I was about to start a relationship with yet another field of endeavour. Phil Nolan, a cameraman at Global Television, had worked with reporter Jacques Bourbeau on a documentary about the Airborne Regiment. Phil put me in contact with his father, Brian, whom he described as a retired teacher and an author of several history books. His most recent work, *Airborne,* was about the wartime exploits of the 1st Canadian Parachute Battalion. Brian agreed to run an excerpt from his book as our Second World War feature in the next issue in exchange for advertising. On my next visit to Toronto to shore up funding, I stopped at the office of Lester Publishing to pick up the original photographs we would need to illustrate the excerpt. Publisher Malcolm Lester took me aside and asked if I had ever thought of writing a book. The short answer was no because I was still pleasantly surprised whenever my op-eds were published in any publication outside of my own. "I can offer you a $10,000 advance" was all he needed to say to seal the deal. In fact, I needed the first third of that to make my Christmas payroll.

162   "Where do I sign, and when do you need it complete?" I asked.

Things would not be that simple, and I soon got bogged down in the massive project. When I submitted the first few chapters to Malcolm, his disappointment could not be disguised. "How would you feel if we added a co-author to your book?" he asked. Knowing I was in over my head and thinking that I could perhaps dictate the direction while the other sucker actually wrote the material, I eagerly agreed.

Malcolm's choice was Brian Nolan. At that point, Brian was undergoing treatment for prostate cancer, and he seemed to be in a perpetually foul mood. He threw out half of what I had written to date, completely restructured the chapters and provided a new outline. Over time I learned of Brian's own incredible lifetime career in the media and as a professor of journalism. The relationship started as that of teacher-student, but it soon developed into a genuine mutual friendship. More slowly than anticipated, but better than expected, the massive collection of internal memos, travel claims and expense accounts that we had amassed with Drapeau's assistance became the 1996 bestseller *Tarnished Brass: Crime and Corruption in the Canadian Military*.

Although many of the scandals and wrongdoings recounted in *Tarnished Brass* had already been revealed in the mainstream press as isolated news items, the combined effect presented in a single work set off a renewed media storm. While Defence spokespersons tried to downplay *Tarnished Brass*, the book's contents were supported by a unique source. In his 1996 annual report, Auditor General Denis Desautels cited *Tarnished Brass* as having made "skilful use" of the Access to Information Act. No doubt the lawyers at Lester Publishing were thankful as well. Despite Canada having one of the most stringent libel laws in the world, the allegations in *Tarnished Brass* were so well substantiated with access-to-information documents that not a single lawsuit was filed in protest. This is not to say that *Tarnished Brass* did not have an impact on the Defence department. In fact, historians David Bercuson and Jack Granatstein have both mentioned the pivotal role played by *Esprit de Corps*, and by *Tarnished Brass* in particular, in forcing the Canadian military to undergo a series of drastic reforms in the mid-1990s.

At that time, and perhaps still to this day, the Defence department denied that the revelations made by *Esprit de Corps* had any bearing whatsoever on their policy changes. The standard press line of the day was to impress upon journalists that a department with a $10 billion budget and 100,000 personnel didn't need to worry about "a little independent publication." As documents tabled at the public inquiry into the Somalia scandal would later reveal, however, the top offices of the Department of National Defence were very much consumed with whatever *Esprit de Corps* was up to. Colonel Geoff Haswell, the former head of public affairs, testified before the Somalia Inquiry that any questions asked by *Esprit de Corps* were to be relayed immediately to Deputy Minister Bob Fowler.

As for the impact of the continuous stream of scandals on morale within the military, I learned of this first-hand from a Canadian military attaché whom I met at a cocktail party. Although this colonel had never been mentioned in either *Esprit de Corps* or *Tarnished Brass,* he nevertheless felt the need to challenge me on behalf of his fellow senior officers. According to him, I had made life for the top brass miserable at National Defence Headquarters. "You could feel the hatred of the rank and file—it was like their eyes were burning holes in our backs as we walked through the corridors," he said. Following the longstanding modus operandi of shooting the messenger, he accused me of single-handedly "breaking down the basic trust between the officer corps and the enlisted personnel."

164   In my own defence, I asked him what those officers involved in the various scandals did to contribute to that breach of trust. By us revealing that air force generals were conducting million-dollar fishing camps in Labrador and planning "Operation Palm Tree" as an annual golf vacation in Florida, were we not simply showing the troops how the other half lived? Of course, when these stories were aired alongside tales in the media of soldiers lining up at food banks and delivering pizza in their off-duty hours just to support their families, it certainly made the generals appear

to be callous, self-serving careerists. Similarly, stories about how young soldiers making just $22,000 a year could barely pay the rent on their rundown 1950s-era military housing units were offset by the revelation that many generals making six-figure salaries were living rent free in their publicly funded commander's residences. Naturally, the rank and file would begin to question the sincerity of those senior officers who were nominally responsible for the welfare of the troops.

I reminded the attaché that the worst example of Canadian military leadership occurred during the public hearings of the Somalia Inquiry throughout the summer of 1996. Although many of the officers who testified acquitted themselves admirably, then chief of defence staff Jean Boyle was a different story altogether. Called to appear before the commission in regard to his involvement in his staff's tampering with some key documents, General Boyle quickly blamed the whole mess on his subordinates. "They failed me," was Boyle's response to direct questions about his immediate staff's actions in altering the press releases in question (this despite the fact that Boyle's own signature appeared on the documents). It did not take long for the Somalia Inquiry commissioners to pounce on Boyle's delegation of responsibility, and the media soon followed suit. For days, Boyle was pilloried in the press from coast to coast, and within six weeks of his controversial testimony he was terminated from the post of chief of defence staff. At least in that instance, there was a price to be paid for failing to demonstrate reciprocal loyalty to the troops.

I admit that I raised the example of Lieutenant General Armand Roy deliberately to the attaché, knowing it to be a sore point among the brass, and once again it struck the mark. As much as the officer corps want to believe that they are the victims of media persecution, the case of Armand Roy is a clear

165

example to the contrary. It was not journalists who invented the allegations of fraud; in fact, it was none other than the auditor general who first began investigating Roy in June 1995. Whistle-blowers on Roy's staff had forwarded the damaging evidence to the auditor general when they learned that he was claiming unauthorized residence allowances to the tune of $3,000 a month. Although the auditor general notified the military's chief of review services about this matter, at that time Armand Roy was serving as the deputy chief of defence staff. In that capacity, all internal police investigations ultimately came under his overall control. Needless to say, little emphasis was placed on the Roy investigation. Once the details of Roy's alleged transgressions were published in *Tarnished Brass,* however, the military could no longer ignore the situation.

By December 1996, enough evidence had been collected to publicly pronounce Lieutenant General Roy guilty of fraud. In a quiet press release issued between Christmas and New Year's Eve, it was announced that he had been fired and that he would be making restitution to the Crown of some $100,000 in fudged expenses. Incredibly, the judge advocate general's office claimed they did not have enough evidence to lay criminal charges in the case. Despite this admission, Roy never once proclaimed himself to be innocent, nor did he contest the firing or his obligation to pay restitution to the Crown.

It was at about this time that a sergeant based at Canadian Forces Base Petawawa was court martialled for having embezzled about $900 from his unit's canteen fund. Upon being found guilty, the sergeant was sentenced to three months in the detention centre and discharged from the military. As is the norm in such cases, he also forfeited any pension other than a return of contributions.

It was difficult for the media not to draw comparisons between the two cases. For the rank and file, it clearly showed that once again there existed an obvious double standard in the military justice system. Despite the internal backlash created by his lenient punishment, Armand Roy remained unrepentant. Even after he had been publicly fired from his position, Roy contrived to use his government cellular phone. Between January and May 1997, the disgraced general used more than $3,000 in long-distance service (mostly Florida and Caribbean numbers) on his "expired" Defence account. It was not until late in 1997 that *Esprit de Corps* discovered this irregularity in accounting through an access-to-information release. Although some clever Defence department officials had tried to conceal Roy's continued unauthorized privileges by altering his rank to major and jumbling all the phone records out of sequence, our persistence paid off in the end.

Once all the documents had been properly collated, we forwarded our findings to the opposition party's defence critic, and the issue was raised in Parliament. The defence minister, Art Eggleton, stated that an investigation would be conducted and that, if necessary, Armand Roy would be required to repay the $3,000 phone bill. After months of internal investigation, it was concluded that Roy had not done anything wrong by continuing to charge for his personal long distance calls—it was the fault of the Defence department's clerks for failing to cancel the account. Case closed. Needless to say, such an absolution of Roy's command responsibility did not resonate positively among those who were virtually powerless to curb a superior's transgressions in the top-down autocracy of a military environment. It had always been presumed that in order to administer strict discipline, those in top command positions had to possess the moral authority to punish those who committed criminal or service offences.

By failing to deal severely with one of their own in the Roy case, the brass collectively lost credibility and were regarded as an old boys' club.

To drive this point home, along came the bizarre case of Colonel Reno Vanier. In the summer of 1997, with the military senior leadership still reeling from the fallout of the Somalia scandal, came the report that Colonel Vanier had gone missing from his home in Ottawa. The colonel had been the executive assistant to the army commander in Saint-Hubert, Quebec, and had just returned from commanding the Canadian contingent in Haiti. Having served in two relatively high-profile positions, Vanier was fairly well known to a number of journalists, and his strange disappearance was soon noticed by the national media. As the public curiosity about this case intensified, an anonymous caller informed *Esprit de Corps* that prior to his going absent without leave (AWOL), Vanier had been questioned by the military police in connection with a fraud case. The Ottawa-Carleton police had already started their manhunt, so we forwarded this information to their liaison officer. Apparently, no one at the Department of National Defence had thought that Vanier being a suspect in a criminal investigation would be of any significance. The Ottawa-Carleton police were furious about not having been informed of this from the outset. In response, National Defence dropped the pretence that this was a missing-person case and put out a nationwide arrest warrant for Vanier.

Soon the Vanier story became a major national mystery. The media simply had to speculate about whatever information the Defence department had and would not divulge. Admittedly, there was no shortage of bizarre angles, one of which was Vanier's wife arriving in Ottawa from Montreal. For some reason, she was convinced that her husband's body had been dumped in the

168

Rideau Canal close to National Defence Headquarters. No one ever asked why she was convinced of this, but as she spent her days pacing the canal's banks, looking forlorn, and with no other solid leads to follow, it was announced that police divers would search the waterway. On day twelve of Vanier's disappearance, all media attention was directed to the Rideau Canal, where just past midday a startling announcement was made. Colonel Reno Vanier had been found, floating in the Rideau River (not the canal) and, incredibly, he was still alive. A rehabilitated drug addict had spotted Vanier in the river and pulled him to safety. According to his rescuers, when they found him, he was "bab bling in Creole."

Vanier was taken immediately to the hospital and placed under military police "protection," and the media could gain no further insight into his curious twelve-day ordeal. In addition to the obvious questions like "How could someone simply float around unnoticed on a river in the middle of the city for twelve days?" the speculation only increased when the military announced that it would not be charging Vanier for having been AWOL. Every soldier knows that an AWOL charge is pretty much a foregone conclusion in such a situation. Obviously Vanier was not at his post, and just as obviously, given the nationwide arrest warrant, he did not have official permission to be absent. If mental health were an issue, it would be tabled by the defending attorney, not factored into the equation by the prosecution. Nevertheless, once Vanier had recovered from his ordeal and had returned to duty at National Defence Headquarters, he was indeed charged and convicted of fraud. In addition to paying a small fine, Vanier was demoted one rung, to lieutenant colonel.

While many soldiers and media analysts were wondering how Vanier could have received such a mild slap on the wrist and yet

169

continued to serve as a commissioned officer, the best was yet to come. Again as the result of an insider tipoff, *Esprit de Corps* was able to learn that in 1997, despite all his trials, tribulations, ultimate conviction and demotion, Vanier still received the $4,000 performance bonus issued to all National Defence executives.

BY THE TIME I had finished recounting the Reno Vanier affair, the military attaché conceded that there were "a few bad apples" within the senior ranks of the military and that Armand Roys and "floating colonels" were the exception rather than the rule. On this point I hastened to agree. Most of the senior officers I have encountered over the years have been honest and dedicated professionals. When, however, these cases had popped up in the media and solid leadership was required to deal with them, bad choices had been made. A clear message could have been sent with the Armand Roy affair had the brass been willing to apply the full extent of military justice to their own colleague. Unfortunately, in being lenient and failing to press charges, they inadvertently institutionalized the corruption—when they might have cut loose an individual who had disgraced his rank. Loyalty is a wonderful trait, provided that it is earned and reciprocated. It is something that must flow two ways in a military system, and in the Roy case the brass collectively forfeited their moral authority by failing to hold him accountable to at least the same standard of conduct as that demanded of the average soldier.

While I did emphasize to the attaché that many a good officer had been unjustly tarred with the brush of corruption in various scandals, I reminded him of the basic principle taught to all military recruits from the outset of their careers: how they conduct themselves in public will reflect upon all those who wear the uniform. This holds true whether one is simply drunk and

170

disorderly in a Canadian establishment or one finds oneself in life-threatening situations where it is necessary to build trust with belligerent factions. Leadership requires more than simply spouting guidelines. Military commanders must be living examples of a martial code of honour. To tell soldiers that they will be judged collectively, the brass must realize that the same rule will apply to themselves and that they must take the necessary steps to ensure that their colleagues are held to the highest level of scrutiny.

THE PERSONAL RESPONSIBILITY of leadership in the private sector was an ongoing lesson for me throughout the financial crunch we faced during the protracted battle with the Defence department. Ironically, the production of *Tarnished Brass,* which ultimately saved us, nearly killed us in the process. My focus on the writing and the day-to-day media issues, coupled with the ongoing embargo of advertisers, meant that the publication of *Esprit de Corps* was sporadic at best. In 1996 we managed to produce only four issues, and as a result we were not even able to attract our regular subscription-renewal revenue.

In late August 1997, I met with *Globe and Mail* editor William Thorsell to ask for some publicity for our magazine's struggle to survive. Ironically, during the following week it was the *Globe and Mail*'s collections department that served us with a legal claim for an unpaid bill. We had placed an insert in the newspaper five months earlier, and they were no longer accepting our excuses and payment promises. We were staving off a multitude of creditors, and the minute that this claim was requested in the courts, it would trigger an avalanche of similar liens. I called up Thorsell and explained the situation, prompting him to run a front-page story on *Esprit de Corps*'s imminent demise. This article initiated a flurry of calls from frightened shareholders, worried suppliers and sympathetic media. We took the last of our cash and paid Julie Simoneau and Cathy Hingley their two last weeks' pay, and I called up a friend at VIA Rail to scrounge a free ticket to Toronto.

Peter Worthington had arranged for me to open discussions with Conrad Black for a last-ditch bailout. We were prepared to offer Black a controlling interest in the company in exchange for the cash we needed to survive. Before departing, Julie had compiled all the numbers and statements that illustrated the potential of our magazine when we had not been boycotted by the Defence department. Although the potential was evident, the present situation was not attractive, and we were relying on Black's being a military enthusiast. His media empire was at its zenith, and it would require a relative pittance for him to acquire what was then one of the most influential publications in Canada.

At least, that was what I had intended to convey to Black as I walked up the front steps of the Hollinger building. I was ushered into a boardroom, where I was greeted by David Radler and one of his accountants. Black would not be joining the meeting, and Radler very quickly informed me that Hollinger would not be getting involved with *Esprit de Corps* in any way. He excused himself after introducing the accountant. Since I had come all this way, Radler generously offered me this man's services to help outline the administrative process of declaring bankruptcy. The accountant spoke to me for about half an hour, but I didn't hear a word he said. All I could think of was the phone call I would have to make to Katherine to tell her that there was no relief on the way.

I tried to retain my composure as I made the long walk back down the hallway, but I'm sure I didn't fool anybody. When I did call the office, it was a strange voice that answered. Dianne St.

Germain had read the *Globe and Mail* article and contacted us to see how she could help. Dianne had been a long-time administrator at CBC Radio, and although she could not help us financially, she offered to volunteer her services. For that crucial week, she and Katherine held down the fort in Ottawa as I went on a desperation-inspired crusade to raise the remaining money in Toronto.

Staying at my in-laws' place and with our accounts and credit cards maxed out, I had nothing left to lose, aside from my train ticket home. The car payments had already lapsed, and the leasing company was threatening repossession. As owners of *Esprit de Corps*, Katherine and I would not even be entitled to unemployment insurance. We would have to apply for social assistance until we found other jobs. Armed with that knowledge, I set out each morning and began banging on millionaires' doors to ask for donations. The media interview requests kept coming in, and the raised profile of our predicament helped to open some of those doors.

One of the messages passed along to me by Dianne was that I should call the CBC Radio outlet in Windsor, Ontario. When I contacted them, I was told it was not regarding an on-air interview. "You are this year's winner of the Quill Award." My silence prompted them to add, "It's awarded annually to a Canadian who has made a significant achievement in the field of communications."

I believe my first question was, "Is there any cash attached to that?"

There was a nervous laugh, followed by the explanation that this was a very prestigious award that had previously been presented to the likes of Mordecai Richler, Peter Gzowski and Robert Fulford. When I was told I would get an all-expenses-paid trip to the black-tie award dinner in November, I advised them that this might prove problematic: "You do realize I'll probably be work-ing the burger bar at Harvey's by then."

The laughter at the other end of the line told me that they had no idea how desperate I was. It was a bittersweet moment to learn that I was being honoured by a journalism community of which, it seemed, I would never become a part. As fate would have it, that phone call proved to be the turning point in our for-tunes. I had lunch the same day with former defence minister Paul Hellyer, who agreed to contribute to the cause. As he had been the architect of the controversial unification of the Cana-dian Forces in 1968, many critics over the years had heaped the current woes of the Defence department at his doorstep. In the past, *Esprit de Corps* had been one of the voices that were quick to point the finger of blame at Hellyer, but our discussion proved very enlightening. He too had faced a recalcitrant senior brass and a bureaucracy that had worked against the successful imple-mentation of his policies, rather than adapting to them.

Hellyer's support was soon matched by other donations from foundations of families such as the Westons, Donners and Molsons. As some cash began to pour in, a number of our major creditors agreed to lump-sum payments at fifty cents on the dollar. By the time I boarded the train back to Ottawa on the Friday afternoon, our financial position, adding forgiveness of debt to charitable gifts, amounted to more than $100,000. *Esprit de Corps* would sur-vive. Julie and Cathy returned to work, and the battle continued.

FURTHER BUOYED BY the sales success of *Tarnished Brass*—fourteen thousand hardcover copies were sold, followed by a mass-market paperback edition released in 1997—Brian Nolan and I decided to write a sequel. This time we wanted to focus on the unsung exploits of our soldiers, and we titled it *Tested Mettle: Canada's*

Peacekeepers at War. Although it covered every operation from the Korean War to present battles, the majority of the combat incidents had occurred while Canadian Forces were deployed in the former Yugoslavia. We had requested the military's significant-incident reports using the Access to Information Act, plotted all the casualties incurred, studied the after-action reports and made notes of all the commendations for valour that had been issued. Assembling all this data on a massive timeline, Nolan and I then set out to interview as many of the participants as possible. Katherine was commissioned to produce a dozen paintings to chronicle the more dramatic, and virtually unknown, actions that we were researching.

I was also finally able to find an outlet for the story of 1st Combat Engineer Regiment's Lost Boys and the American ammunition-dump explosion in Kuwait in 1991, which resulted in a commendation for Captain Fred Kaustinen. To help publicize the book—which we chose to publish ourselves as the inaugural imprint of Esprit de Corps Books—I fed the Lost Boys' story to David Pugliese at the *Ottawa Citizen*. David was one of the very few reporters in Canada who was dedicated solely to the defence beat. As such, he had an in-depth knowledge of the Canadian Forces and was able to put many of our leads into wider circulation. The Defence department could not explain why this heroic action by our soldiers had never been reported.

When *Tested Mettle* was released in November 1998, there were a lot more untold stories that the Department of National Defence had trouble trying to deflect. In particular, the plight and suffering of soldiers wounded—either physically or mentally—while on operations sparked public outrage. There were horror stories of neglected veterans being denied pensions, veterans having wheelchairs taken away from them simply because of bureaucratic procedures, wounded reservists having their pay stopped as soon as they were admitted to hospital, soldiers suffering from a multitude of illnesses they believed were a direct result of exposure to toxins while they were on deployment, medical files being purged to limit the Defence department's legal liability and one case of a general officer's neglectful administration that led to the bodies of two Canadian troopers rotting in their caskets before being transported home.

Nolan and I also focused on the relatively new phenomenon known as post-traumatic stress disorder, or PTSD. Sergeant Tom Hoppe had endured combat situations while at Romeo One and had received two decorations for valour during his tour in Bosnia—the most medals earned by a Canadian soldier since the Korean War. However, when his unit was due to redeploy in 1995, Hoppe could not face the prospect. This hero suffering from PTSD made a very compelling case for us, and having Hoppe—along with another half-dozen of the key people mentioned in *Tested Mettle*—present at the launch served to ram home our point with the media in attendance.

The news stories about neglected casualties helped kick off our promotion. We followed this with a series of excerpts in weekend Sun newspapers across the country. The first passage chosen was the account of the Croatian attack and ethnic cleansing in the Medak Pocket. Although David Pugliese had broken this story in 1997, it was still news to most Canadians. The follow-up excerpt was the tragedy that had occurred in Knin, in the very same corner of Croatia, in the summer of 1995. On this occasion, the soldiers of the Royal 22nd Regiment had not fired at the Croatians, as 2 PPCLI had done. Instead, they were forced to watch impotently as the Croatian forces launched Operation Storm, the ethnic cleansing of nearly 250,000 Serbs in the Krajina and in

Bosnia. At that time Brigadier General Alain Forand, the UN commander of Sector South, had radioed to the advancing Croatian forces that all Serbian soldiers had fled the town of Knin and that the streets were crowded with throngs of refugees. Despite Forand's pleadings, the Croatian artillery commander launched a deadly barrage against the Serbs. It was estimated that more than five hundred innocent civilians were killed in a matter of hours. To the horror and amazement of the Canadian UN observers, Croatian troops then came with trucks to pick up the corpses, street cleaners to wash away the blood and even glass to replace the shattered storefront windows before the media arrived. The massacre had been planned down to the finest detail.

Despite the strong Canadian military involvement in recording it, there had been virtually no coverage of this ugly incident in the Canadian media at the time. After the excerpt was published, I began receiving all sorts of cards and letters from Serbian Canadians thanking me for telling the story of their plight. That had never been my intention. I was simply recording the experience and observations of our soldiers.

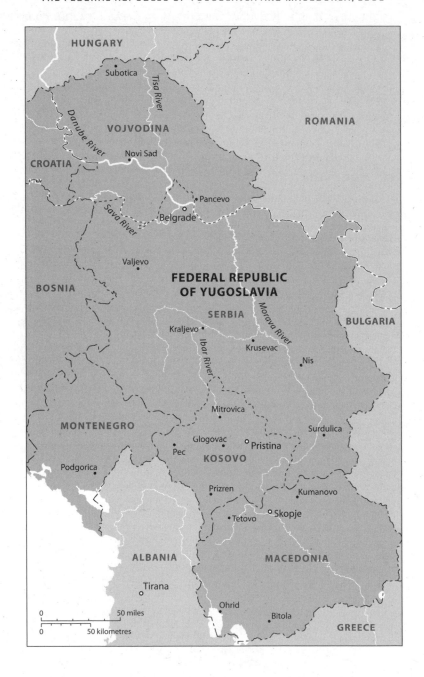

HUNGARY

Subotica

Tisa River

VOJVODINA

ROMANIA

Danube River

Novi Sad

CROATIA

Sava River

Pancevo

Belgrade

Valjevo

FEDERAL REPUBLIC
OF YUGOSLAVIA

BOSNIA

SERBIA

Morava River

BULGARIA

Kraljevo

Krusevac

Ibar River

Nis

Mitrovica

MONTENEGRO

Surdulica

Glogovac

Pec

Pristina

KOSOVO

Podgorica

Prizren

Kumanovo

Tetovo

Skopje

ALBANIA

MACEDONIA

Tirana

Ohrid

Bitola

GREECE

0   50 miles

0   50 kilometres

7

BACK TO THE BALKANS

You cannot be a NATO spy. No one in
intelligence would be so stupid as to pick
a code name such as *Skot*.

BEBA UGARKOVIC

BY LATE 1998, VIOLENCE IN the Balkans was again in the headlines. This time it was flaring up in the Serbian province of
Kosovo, where Serbian military forces were engaging Albanian
separatists known as the Kosovo Liberation Army (UCK, also
known as the KLA). Although the KLA had been listed as a terrorist organization by the U.S. State Department until just a few
months earlier, Bill Clinton's White House had decided that this
group could prove a useful ally in the destabilization of Slobodan Milosevic's Republic of Yugoslavia. The western media began
yet another round of demonizing the Serbs and pumping out
sympathetic prose in support of the Albanian cause in Kosovo. I
did not have a deep understanding of the historical roots of this
conflict, but what I did know was that something was seriously
amiss in January 1999 when NATO announced the appointment
of a new commander for the KLA guerrillas.

After resigning his post with the Croatian army, Agim Ceku
was going home to Kosovo to lead his Albanian followers in a

179

guerrilla war. Not only was Ceku the butcher of the Medak Pocket, but he had also been the artillery commander during Operation Storm. Canadian soldiers had witnessed his barbaric cruelty and had tabled evidence of his war crimes with The Hague's International Criminal Tribunal for both the Medak Pocket massacre and the slaughter of hundreds of civilians in Knin. Instead of forcing Ceku to face justice in a criminal court, the United States and NATO were sending him into the erupting conflict in Kosovo—and this time they intended to provide Ceku with the full support of their allied air force.

That NATO should be involved in determining the leadership of a foreign rebel force was curious enough, but that they had selected such a candidate was even more questionable. Infuriated by the jingoistic media coverage that was unquestioningly beating the pro-war drum, I revisited my 1994 decision to retire from front-line reporting. By the time the first NATO air strikes had begun on the night of March 23, 1999, I was convinced that the U.S. State Department had been instrumental in forcing the hand of the Yugoslav government into a position of defiance, thus making the war inevitable. As the trickle of Albanian refugees fleeing out of Kosovo into neighbouring Macedonia became a human flood, NATO spokespersons cleverly seized upon this humanitarian crisis as justification for the military intervention. That the bombing had triggered the exodus mattered not at all; what was important was that we had to keep bombing Serbia and Serbian military forces to prevent the Albanians from suffering any further.

The western media turned to the flood of refugees to provide the only glimpse of what was happening inside Kosovo. Unable to enter the embattled province, journalists set up shop in neighbouring Macedonia and began pumping out third-hand, uncorroborated accounts of atrocities committed by Serbs. There

180

was no clear picture emerging from the Serbian side, and the vacuum allowed NATO to rule the airwaves.

One night after catching me once more yelling at the television, Katherine finally lost her temper too and told me to either shut up or do something about it. Believing that to be a green light to return to war reporting, I went to the Yugoslav embassy in Ottawa and applied for an entry visa. The staff dutifully explained that there was a tremendous backlog of applications for journalists and that because Canada was a belligerent country, there were very few spots available.

Retired general Lewis MacKenzie, who had also been strongly opposed to Canada's participation in the war, had been reporting for CTV from Belgrade. No one had expected the bombing campaign to last more than a few days, and no one at the Yugoslav embassy expected me to maintain daily pressure on them to process my visa. I enlisted the aid of every Serb I knew in Canada and found an excuse to contact the embassy staff as often as three times a day.

By May 22, with no let-up in the bombing campaign, no wavering of the Serbian resolve to resist and NATO commanders claiming they were prepared to launch a ground assault, my visa was finally approved. I hastily booked a flight and made my travel plans. It wasn't until I was waiting in the Toronto airport lounge for my connecting flight that the magnitude of this venture hit fully home. I had no return ticket and no way of knowing how things would work out.

IT WAS SUNDAY afternoon, May 24, and the trip had so far gone without a hitch. Since there were no international flights to Belgrade (other than NATO bombers), I had to fly to Budapest first and then secure passage on a Yugoslavia-bound minibus.

Apologizing for the rush, an agent at the Budapest airport

explained that all the drivers had to be en route to Yugoslavia before three o'clock in order to complete the six-hour trek before dark. Although NATO had begun launching daylight air strikes, the majority of the attacks still took place at night, and main roads were favourite targets.

I managed to secure a seat on the last scheduled vehicle. At the border we found a considerable amount of traffic already backlogged in the four-hundred-metre neutral zone that separated Yugoslavia from Hungary. However, the actual queue through the Yugoslav customs and police checkpoint was moving quickly since most travellers seemed intent on patronizing the six large duty-free shops that occupied the short stretch of neutral ground.

Knowing that I had a valid visa—along with a recommendation from the Yugoslav embassy in Ottawa—I felt no trepidation as we approached the Serbian border police. My confidence quickly vanished when a thick finger pointed at me through the driver's window. Although the officer spoke in Serbian, his thumb-jerking motion left no doubt as to his meaning. By the time I got inside the customs building, the bus driver had unloaded my bags at the curbside and was speeding off towards Belgrade.

A Serbian captain explained to me that I did not have a stamp in my passport signifying that I had been registered by the police. I asked how I could acquire such a stamp. He replied, "It can be done only in Belgrade, at police headquarters." Naturally, my next question was, "How does one get to Belgrade to get a border clearance without first clearing the border?" Shrugging his shoulders, he replied, "That's your problem."

For the next six hours I alternately sat in the police waiting room and strolled about the duty-free area. As dusk approached, the traffic all but disappeared. At 9:30 PM, the duty-free shops

182

closed, the sales staff departed and the police changed shifts. With not much else to occupy them, the new crew of police turned its attention to me. One sergeant decided to search through my luggage, presumably looking for contraband. He discovered a number of letters written in Serbian. These notes of introduction had been prepared for me by Bora Dragasevic, the Toronto-based president of the Serbian National Shield Society of Canada. In these letters, Dragasevic explained, among other things, that as a journalist I had helped publicize the Croatian massacre of Serbs in the Krajina.

After reading this correspondence, the police sergeant explained that he had been a resident of the Krajina until his expulsion in 1995. From that moment on, he became my personal advocate. A few calls were made, my passport was stamped and my luggage returned. The only thing left to arrange was a means of transport. At 11:45 PM this was resolved by the unexpected appearance of a minibus crossing over from the Hungarian checkpoint. My new-found protector spoke briefly with the driver, then waved me over to the van. I was on my way.

As the minibus hurtled along the pitch-black highway, I had an eerie feeling. There were no other cars on the road, and we were often required to detour around poorly marked bomb craters. All too frequently, a filtered red light would wave up ahead, indicating yet another military checkpoint manned by roving patrols of well-armed soldiers. The ranking officer would quickly check the driver's identification papers and ask a few questions. Once satisfied, the patrol would melt back into the darkness and we would proceed towards Belgrade. Invariably, our driver would be questioned on the sanity of driving after dark—with headlights on high beam while NATO aircraft roamed the night skies.

The experience appeared to be equally unnerving for my fellow passengers, who began to pass around a large jug of duty-free cognac. As the miles and hours rolled by, the cheap alcohol took effect. Two of the six travellers spoke some English, and soon everyone wanted their war story or political opinion told to the *Kanadski novinar* (Canadian journalist). The icebreaker was the revelation of my first name—*skot* means "jerk" or "lowlife" in Serbian. "You cannot be a NATO spy," said Beba Ugarkovic, one of the passengers. "No one in intelligence would be so stupid as to pick a code name such as *Skot*." The bus erupted in drunken laughter.

As we approached the city of Novi Sad, we could hear the distant thumps of anti-aircraft fire. Flashes on the horizon indicated bomb explosions. At the next checkpoint a young lieutenant informed us that there had just been at least three heavy attacks. About five kilometres away, we could see a large building burning brightly. For the next few minutes, with jets droning overhead, we rode in silence. Our nerves began to get the better of us. Then, softly, Beba began to sing a Serbian folk song. The others soon joined in, their collective voices steadily rising in strength. Throughout the remaining two hours of the trip, our little bus resonated with a seemingly endless stream of spirit-lifting ballads. All fears were lost in the cognac and song.

184

I awoke the next morning in my room at the landmark Hotel Moskva in Belgrade with a booming headache and a slight sense of panic. Since I had been unable to contact the Kopric family, my delay at the Yugoslavian border had caused a fair measure of concern in Belgrade. Before I had left Canada, Bora Dragasevic had arranged for the Koprics to assist me upon my arrival. Vlada, a twenty-two-year-old university student, spoke fluent English and had access to a wealth of computer equipment. His father, Zlatan, had spent his youth in the Yugoslav marines, and in the late

1960s had served as one of Josip Broz Tito's personal bodyguards. He, too, spoke excellent English and had turned his innovative computer skills into a successful business. In addition, Vlada's mother, Radmila, worked as a reporter for Vesti, the Yugoslavian international news agency. Such a collection of talents and contacts made the Kopric family a powerful asset.

They agreed to provide me with translation services, transportation (they owned a Ford Escort and had a good source of black market fuel) and computer resources (including my own e-mail address). The rate we settled on was less than half of what a foreign journalist could expect to pay simply to charter a driver and a car. Further proof that this new partnership was of a more "personal" nature was apparent in the Koprics' insistence on bringing me home and feeding me lunch. Although I was anxious to get officially registered with the Yugoslav army press centre, their hospitality was not to be denied.

The mounds of sausages and fried potatoes they served up belied reports of chronic food shortages. As we ate, the air raid sirens suddenly sounded—the first that I'd heard and Belgrade came under a daylight air attack. Nobody at the table paid any heed. Despite my growing unease, I too remained seated. Several minutes later, there was a loud explosion followed by a concussing shock wave. Without even going to their window, Vlada and Zlatan nonchalantly debated which district the bomb had hit.

Andjelka, Zlatan's eighty-one-year-old mother, lived in the small apartment with them. Since the war began, she had been intently following the Yugoslav state news broadcasts. After the all-clear had sounded, she burst into the kitchen and excitedly proclaimed that the Serbian air defence had just shot down two more NATO planes. She then caught herself and (through Vlada) added apologetically, "I hope they weren't Canadians."

IT WAS BARELY dusk when the bombers struck and a massive explosion rocked the downtown core of Belgrade. Less than a minute later, a second blast in New Belgrade knocked out the city's power grid. Following the attack, several Hotel Moskva employees rushed into the lobby bar to announce that the Hyatt Hotel had been hit. Everyone ran out into the street to watch a giant column of black smoke spiral skywards from the far bank of the Sava River. In the dim light it was impossible to determine whether the burning target was, indeed, the Hyatt, home to most of the foreign reporters in Belgrade. The Moskva's bellhops and desk clerks were visibly dismayed when a maid yelled from an upstairs window that the Hyatt was still intact; the billowing smoke was coming from the district of Zemun. Like most Belgraders, the Moskva staff believed that the NATO air raids would stop immediately because of a massive international public backlash that would occur if collateral damage were inflicted on the foreign press corps.

A more immediate and personal concern was the power outage, which meant that I now had to rely upon my translator's laptop computer to input and file my story. Unfortunately, Vlada's portable computer had only enough battery power to compose the article. I would have to find another method to send it to Ottawa. After obtaining permission from the Hotel Moskva's manager to use its generator, Vlada and Zlatan disassembled their computer equipment by candlelight. Carefully negotiating the pitch-black roads, they transported the gear to the Moskva, only to have the hotel generator sputter and die promptly after their arrival. The night manager was apologetic, saying he just couldn't understand the problem. "In twenty-six years, that generator has never failed, and it's never needed any maintenance. Why would it break down now?" he wondered.

186

As my press deadline loomed nearer, I had no option but to telephone the *Ottawa Citizen* and dictate my story line by line, reading my scrawled notes by candlelight.

Shortly past midnight, power was briefly restored to the downtown sector. With their computer gear still sitting in my tiny hotel room, Vlada and Zlatan decided to have a go at transmitting photographs via e-mail. Before the blackout we had scanned three photographs, which I hoped to send to the *Citizen* to illustrate my copy.

It was stiflingly hot, and our work was hampered by the continuing air raids that constantly threatened to (and twice did) cut the power again. The excessive bomb damage made the telephone exchanges unreliable. Several times, in the middle of sending files, we were knocked off line. Finally, at 2:45 AM, our persistence paid off. When the report came back that the photographs had been successfully received by the *Citizen,* we cracked open a bottle of wine. For the next hour we drank lukewarm Chardonnay and quietly watched the fireworks as wave after wave of jets pounded the Obrenovac district.

News agencies covering NATO seemed to have no such difficulty in getting their message into Yugoslavia. BBC World Report and CNN News were broadcast via satellite, using powerful transmitters based in Bosnia, so new developments were known almost immediately inside Belgrade. On the morning of May 27, the major story on all the networks was the announcement by The Hague's International Criminal Tribunal that indictments had been issued against Yugoslav President Slobodan Milosevic and four of his top officials.

At a hastily convened press conference Yugoslav officials formally rejected the indictments, claiming they were a "U.S. propaganda ploy, aimed at sabotaging the latest peace initiatives."

Goran Matic, the Yugoslavian minister of information, stated that the entire UN judicial process was tainted. "The Hague Tribunal is, in reality, an inquisition which the U.S. is using to deny sovereign rights to any government which does not comply to their wishes," he added. When asked whether Milosevic and the four other Serbian officials would submit to the tribunal voluntarily, Matic replied, "Yes, but only after President Clinton, General [Wesley] Clark, Tony Blair, Robin Cook and other top NATO officials are similarly indicted."

Throughout Belgrade, public reaction to the UN's announcement was studied indifference. For the past several weeks NATO planes had been dropping propaganda leaflets urging the Serbs to overthrow Milosevic. Many Belgraders felt that the war crime charges were part of the same public relations campaign.

"The UN and NATO have no credibility," said university student Slavica Angarkovic, an ardent anti-Milosevic activist. "Where was the U.S. support in 1997, when we were protesting in the streets? They were backing Milosevic! Now they are bombing us and asking for our help at the same time?"

Following Matic's press conference, foreign journalists were taken to a bomb site just south of Belgrade, where a bomb had fallen in a rural village that contained no industrial—let alone military—targets. The projectile had struck a Serbian family, killing their two children (aged eight and four) and seriously injuring both parents. Tragically, the family had moved there from Belgrade only two weeks earlier because they were convinced their children would be safer in the countryside.

As we surveyed the grisly scene, one reporter took the opportunity to ask residents for their reaction to the UN's indictment of Milosevic. In an emotional outburst an elderly Serb made a sweeping gesture towards the blood-spattered rubble and said, "The people who ordered this, they are the real war criminals!"

188

Vlada's mother, Radmila, had followed the fate of this family and suggested that we attend the funeral. It was a mournful procession that wound its way through the Bezanija cemetery in suburban New Belgrade. Hundreds of grieving mourners stopped at the fountain to wash their hands before leaving the burial ground. In the Serbian Orthodox religion, this custom is meant to cleanse away the sorrow so that it may be left behind at the cemetery. However, with air raid sirens wailing once again in the distance, the tear-stained faces of those leaving the ceremony showed little sign of having put the recent loss to rest. Two young children—eight-year-old Stefan Pavlovic and his four-year-old sister, Dijana—had been killed by a NATO bomb three days earlier. Both parents had been seriously wounded in the countryside attack. Such a tragic loss of young life is never easily accepted, not even in wartime.

With the mourners' emotions running high, I was a little concerned about their reaction if they were to discover I was from a NATO country that had participated in the air strikes. When one man did approach me, he politely thanked me for making the effort to attend the funeral. He explained, "The people of Canada must see this. They must know what the bombing is doing."

MOST OF BELGRADE'S downtown restaurants and clubs closed their doors at around seven o'clock to allow patrons and employees the time to get home before darkness brought the next round of air strikes. One notable exception to this practice was the elegant Writers Club, which catered to an exclusive late-supper clientele. Equipped with generators, the Writers Club remained unaffected by power outages, its kitchen still churning out gourmet dishes. On hot summer nights most of the diners preferred to take their meals on the candlelit patio where they could watch the anti-aircraft display during the raids.

It was nearly ten o'clock by the time I had finished filing my story on the Pavlovic funeral. With few other options for a late meal, I agreed to join some media colleagues at the Writers Club. Seated at a table nearby was the notorious Serbian gangster-cum-war criminal known to the western world as "Arkan." Since the beginning of the NATO bombing campaign, it had been widely reported that Zeljko Raznatovic (also known as Arkan) had reconstituted his infamous Tigers, a nationalist Serbian paramilitary unit that had fought in both Croatia and Bosnia. The alleged deployment of Arkan and his ruthless killers into Kosovo was being proclaimed by NATO as proof that Milosevic was engaging in a campaign of genocide.

On this night, we could attest that the much-feared Arkan was nowhere near the disputed regions of Kosovo. Sporting a slight paunch, the middle-aged, cherubic-faced Arkan did not appear to be at all martial or menacing. The only visible evidence of his violent legacy was a couple of tough-looking security types lounging by the garden door. They kept a close eye on their boss as he dined in the company of a very young, attractive blonde.

A trio of guitar players, bedecked in sombreros, was serenading the Writers Club patrons with Mexican music when the air raid sirens sounded. Even as air defence cannons lit up the sky, the musicians continued to stroll about the patio, strumming their instruments and singing love ballads.

My second outing from Belgrade was an escorted tour of the central Serbian city of Valjevo. The first stop for our group of foreign reporters was the hospital. As we entered a ward, Slavoljub Simic struggled to sit upright in his hospital bed and painfully told his story. He described how he had been loading a truck at the nearby Krusik factory when NATO had struck. Over forty-three projectiles exploded on the two-acre grounds of the manufacturing plant. Simic described the effect as "horrific." An initial blast threw him from his truck, and throughout the bombardment he "was flung bodily about amidst the concrete debris so many times [he] lost count."

It was only when he talked of his rescuers being unable to remove a large slab from his arm that I noticed that his right pyjama sleeve was hanging limp. Simic explained that his amputated stump had become infected with gangrene but that the doctors were hopeful they had caught it in time.

Lying in the bed next to Simic was Dragoljub Tesic, who had been at his home near the Krusik factory on May 2 when NATO jets pulverized the plant and surrounding area. Tesic's spine had been badly damaged by the blasts, and his right leg shattered. Doctors said he would remain partially paralyzed and confined to a wheelchair for life. Nevertheless, Tesic still displayed his defiant patriotism by flashing the Serbian national hand signal.

With no peace deal to end the suffering caused by NATO's two-month bombing campaign, one would think that the Serbs would be resentful. That did not, however, appear to be the case. When asked for his opinion on the war, Tesic angrily denounced any peace agreement as "capitulation," and several of his ward mates concurred. Crammed into the crowded Valjevo hospital were hundreds of local citizens, only thirty-two of whom had been injured by NATO air strikes. All of them, though, had been affected by the attacks.

With shattered windows and collapsed ceilings and after experiencing several near misses, two of the hospital's six storeys had been evacuated. As a result, patients could no longer be segregated by age or sex. In open wards of eight to ten beds, teenage girls awaiting surgery shared the same room as elderly men waiting to die. Only the maternity unit and the pediatrics department remained separate. Children resided in the basement of the hospital, where they were safest from the bombs.

On the night of June 1, I was still writing up my Valjevo stories when my translator showed up at the Hotel Moskva in a state of panic. An hour earlier, Vlada Kopric had gone to the army press centre for an update on developments. The senior press relations officer—a burly colonel named Velickovic—had ordered him to surrender his media credentials, insisting that Vlada had aided me in producing pro-NATO propaganda. This allegation stemmed from a brief incident earlier in the day.

While inspecting a NATO bomb site, a destroyed residential district, Vlada and I had spotted several children playing in the wreckage. Being a novice photographer who relied heavily on the camera's automatic light sensor, I had Vlada ask the young trio (who were scampering in the shadows) if they could move into the sunlight ten metres to their left. The children eagerly complied, and I shot several photographs. At this point, other cameramen and photographers decided kids-on-rubble was an interesting shot, and they too crowded around, snapping furiously.

One little boy, about five years of age, was carrying a crudely made wooden rifle. Finding himself to be the centre of all this attention, he began to ham it up. Just as the female army major who was chaperoning our tour arrived, the little boy aimed his toy gun at the cluster of photographers. Several sharp orders in Serbian were barked at the children, and the major quickly herded the media back to their cars. Nothing more was said.

When terminating Vlada's credentials, however, his accuser (the escorting major) explained her concerns. She claimed that I (with Vlada's help) had staged the shot of a toy-gun-wielding child for the purpose of further diminishing the world's negative opinion of Serbs.

I had learned that questioning the authority of Yugoslav officials generally compounded the difficulties, but this unfounded

192

allegation could not go unchallenged. It took nearly three hours of heated debate to convince the colonel that the accusations against us were without merit. The clincher was my developed photographs, which simply showed children clambering atop the ruins of their home. In the end, Colonel Velickovic barked out an apology of sorts, threw Vlada's press pass onto the table and strode from his office without looking back. We could continue.

IT WAS JUST after one o'clock in the afternoon of June 3 that the Yugoslav parliament adjourned in Belgrade, after voting to accept NATO's proposed peace plan. Journalists raced back to the army press centre to relay the news that peace had broken out in the Balkans. Less than an hour later, the air raid sirens began to wail and, once again, warplanes pounded Belgrade. Throughout that afternoon, six attacks were launched against the Yugoslav capital.

Even as details of the peace agreement spread across the city, the only reaction from the citizenry was abject skepticism. There were neither spontaneous celebrations nor protests As they had done throughout the bombing campaign, people continued to ignore the threat of air raids and displayed a business-as-usual attitude.

At around 4:30 AM on June 6, a cruise missile landed quite close to the Hotel Moskva. The force of the explosion shook the building, and the concussive shock wave was strong enough to fling open my window. Startled awake, my heart racing, I awaited the sounds that followed each near miss. The jolt set off every car alarm in the vicinity, and every dog in Belgrade went berserk and began howling at an unseen intruder—or perhaps felt compelled to announce to all that they had survived the blast.

According to the peace deal announced on June 3, this was to be the last day of the NATO bombing campaign. The Kosovo with-drawal-implementation talks had already begun in Macedonia, with Yugoslav army officials meeting their NATO counterparts in an armed camp. Everyone in Belgrade braced for a final mad min-ute of bombing during the run-up to the midnight ceasefire.

The first of the heavy daylight raids began at around 9:30 AM; the target was the nearby government district. I heard the explosions from the street in front of the Moskva, where I was watching the Belgrade fire department fight a raging chimney fire in the bakery next door. There was no real danger of the fire spreading, but the choking clouds of black smoke made for an impressive display. About thirty minutes after the bombing, Vlada and his father breathlessly arrived on the scene, relieved to find the hotel unscathed.

Power and telephone lines had been knocked out across the city, and all of Belgrade believed that the Moskva had been hit. No doubt the staff and foreign press patrons at the Hyatt Hotel were disappointed when they learned the truth.

Around 7:00 AM on June 7, air raid sirens sounded once again across Belgrade. After seventy-five days of constant attacks, the citizens were not normally upset by the piercing sound, but this time it was different. "Why?" asked the startled hotel clerk, her eyes wide with disbelief. "The war is over." Dull thumps from exploding bombs in New Belgrade and the pounding of anti-air-craft cannon indicated otherwise.

Radmila Vukovic, like most Yugoslavs, was unaware that peace talks in Macedonia had broken off the previous evening and that NATO was threatening to intensify the air campaign. Vukovic had spent her summer Sunday in the traditional Serbian manner—at a family barbecue followed by an outing in the park. That evening's television newscasts had given no indication that the peace talks had stalled, and everyone had expected the proposed ceasefire to come into effect at midnight.

Following the shocking air attack, word of the war's resumption spread quickly across the city. For the first time I detected a crack in the resilience of the Serbs. Gathered around their radios and pumping foreign journalists for the latest news, the Moskva staff were visibly rattled by the latest setback. Their initial reaction was fear. The June 3 diplomatic deal was widely considered to be NATO's last and final offer. Most Yugoslavs felt that if their government did not accept the proposal, they would face a renewed military campaign aimed at the total obliteration of Serbia.

This sustained pressure by NATO was seen by many as further proof of the alliance's intention to prolong the conflict, regardless of the cost to the Serbian people. However, within hours the fear had disappeared and had been replaced by stoic practicality. In anticipation of NATO planes mounting a major offensive during the night, fresh candles and matches were distributed throughout the hotel, buckets of fresh water were hauled to all the rooms and bathtubs in the vacant suites were again filled to capacity—as they were anytime the water supply was up and running.

The crowd at the noon-hour concert in the central square was larger than usual, and the atmosphere was sombre. The feature performers were a traditional dance troupe in ceremonial Serbian costume. I was mesmerized as the large crowd linked arms and, step for step, followed the dancers on stage. Hundreds of people aged five to eighty-five raised their voices and sang out their national folk songs, effectively drowning out the air raid sirens.

It wasn't until three o'clock the following afternoon that Nebojsa Vujovic, the Yugoslavian foreign ministry spokesman, could convene a press conference to explain the Serbian version of the breakdown in the peace process. He had been forced to drive the six hundred kilometres from Macedonia because NATO had denied the Yugoslav delegation access to the international press. The story being broadcast on CNN and the BBC was that the Serbs had made new demands and then walked out of the discussions concerning the Yugoslavian army's withdrawal from Kosovo. It was alleged that the Serbs were once again acting in bad faith and that NATO had "no choice" but to resume the bombing campaign—which, in fact, had never been interrupted.

What Vujovic wished to convey to the press was that, contrary to NATO's claim, the Yugoslav negotiators were still locked inside the armed camp that housed the peace talks. He categorically refuted the allegation that new demands had been tabled.

On Sunday evening, when the talks broke down, the official NATO position had been that, after two days of fruitless negotiations, there would be no third day. However, it was reassuring to learn that, even as the bombing intensified, the two sides were still actively negotiating. Before climbing into his car for the long drive back to the Macedonian summit, Vujovic said, "It is time for the language of war to be abandoned. It is time for peace and harmony."

The following evening, thousands of bomb-weary Yugoslavs poured into the streets in an emotional outpouring of relief. Shortly after eleven o'clock, word spread that the stroke of a pen in a camouflaged army tent on the Macedonian border had transformed a week of phoney peace into reality.

After seventy-seven long nights of NATO bombardment, the residents of this battered capital abandoned their air raid shelters and threw off their inhibitions in a wild party that lasted until the first rays of dawn. Arm in arm, they danced and sang patriotic Serbian songs, flooding Republike Square and the streets of the downtown core. It was a scene reminiscent of Britain and the

196

United States in 1945 when Londoners and New Yorkers flocked to Trafalgar and Times squares to celebrate the defeat of Hitler and the Nazis. But while Yugoslav television was proclaiming victory, most Serbs were more pragmatic.

"It is good that my children will no longer spend nights in shelters, but the bad thing is that all this is not for celebration but for weeping," said one reveller.

"Victory?" laughed another partygoer. "No, we're just glad that it's over and we survived. That's why we're happy tonight."

Many Belgraders flocked to the city bridge that in the early days of the bombing had been a favourite gathering point for thousands of anti-war protestors who had the trademark target insignia pinned to their chests. They paraded through the streets waving Serbian flags from their cars as drivers leaned on their horns.

The fusillade of gunfire would have convinced any observer that the war was still raging. Revellers were pumping enough celebratory lead into the air to deter any NATO pilot, firing anything with a trigger—from automatic rifles to handguns and ancient shotguns.

In the euphoria of the ceasefire, a communications overload restricted the city's contact with the outside world. Phone lines were swamped, and even computer e-mail services became overwhelmed. Clubs and cafés that normally would have been closed quickly opened their doors to the overjoyed throng, and a spontaneous rock concert was soon underway.

Who won or lost the war didn't matter anymore. That it was finally over was more than enough. One young man expressed the relief that many Belgraders felt. "I could not wait for the end," he said. "I was sick of all this."

BARELY THIRTY-SIX HOURS after the bombing had ceased, and with an ominous rumble, a convoy of Serbian armoured vehicles raced down the narrow roadways in Nis. From the sidewalks small children and elderly couples tossed flowers and cheered as the column of retreating Yugoslav army troops headed home from Kosovo. From atop their vehicles the soldiers responded by waving flags, firing their rifles in the air and flashing the Serbian hand signal. One could have mistaken the jubilant procession for a victory parade rather than the retreat of a defeated army from the battlefield.

We were witnessing the vanguard of the Serbian withdrawal, their air defence weapons pulling back into Serbia as agreed in the peace plan. It was these gunners who had engaged the NATO attackers nightly, and they, in turn, had borne the brunt of many air strikes. For the Serbian citizens, these troops symbolized the Yugoslav defiance of NATO; hence they deserved a hero's welcome.

For the next two hours, as part of the foreign media convoy crawling into Kosovo, we fought against traffic and struggled past numerous road obstacles created by the seventy-eight-day bombing campaign. As for independently confirming the withdrawal of their military forces, the Yugoslav army officials put on quite a show for us. In navigating our way from Serbia into the Kosovo capital of Pristina, we passed eighty-two anti-aircraft artillery pieces and more than forty surface-to-air missile launchers. In addition, three separate radar command posts were scattered among the dusty columns of armoured anti-aircraft artillery vehicles.

Taking into account both the numbers and composition of these units and drawing on my intelligence training of Soviet-style weapons and formations, I estimated that this represented three virtually intact air defence regiments. In some cases, where the canvas muzzle covers had not been attached, the baked-on carbon stains—indicating heavy recent firing—were visible. Many of the surface-to-air rocket launchers still had empty missile racks, further evidence of the fighting that had taken place. The soldiers themselves seemed in excellent spirits, perhaps because their long ordeal was over. They looked neither shell shocked nor defeated.

The mood was entirely different among the long lines of Serbian refugees who had begun to flee Kosovo in anticipation of Albanian reprisals and attacks by the Kosovo Liberation Army. Thousands of Serbs packed their belongings and clogged the roads alongside the withdrawing Yugoslav forces. It was a scene all too reminiscent of the many previous Balkan ethnic cleansings: forlorn-looking families clinging to overloaded tractors and broken-down Yugos.

The reason for the refugees' fears became apparent shortly after we crossed into Kosovo. Fires were burning in most villages, all of which appeared to be deserted. Nearly 50 per cent of the dwellings had been destroyed, most by arson, some by NATO bombs. After the army pulled out, lawlessness took over and ethnic violence ensued. Serbian extremists were said to be taking a last opportunity to send the Albanians a message, while ethnic Albanians set homes recently vacated by the fleeing Serbs on fire. Roughly 20 per cent of the latter chose to remain in Kosovo throughout the conflict, despite fears of violence. (Ironically, it wasn't the Serbian soldiers they feared but rather the ultra-nationalist extremists who were expected to step up their activity after the withdrawal of the Yugoslav army.)

Irmeli Seipagarvi, a Finnish television reporter who was also travelling to Pristina as part of the large delegation of foreign media, had spent several weeks in Macedonia covering the refugee crisis before her arrival in Belgrade. In the camps she had met a number of Albanians and developed several close contacts.

199

One had provided the name and address of his brother who had chosen to remain in Pristina. Through a roundabout phone connection (via Finland), Irmeli had managed to advise the brother in Pristina of our arrival. When our hodgepodge media convoy arrived in front of the Grand Hotel at around three o'clock on June 11, Sylejman Bucaj was waiting with a Welcome Irmeli sign. Bucaj and the translator who accompanied him did not attract even the slightest notice from the Yugoslav soldiers or police units. Arrangements were quickly made for Irmeli, the Swedish journalist Nils Horner and me to lodge with the Bucaj family.

Due to the pressing deadlines facing my two European colleagues, and thanks to the six-hour time difference between Kosovo and Ottawa, I was the one chosen to accompany Bucaj to his home to assess the accommodations. His apartment block was at least two kilometres—straight uphill—from the Grand Hotel. The translator explained that the reason this sector of Pristina had not been gutted or vacated was because it housed roughly a fifty-fifty mix of Serbs and Albanians. Unlike the eerily empty, horribly vandalized suburbs we had seen upon entering Pristina, Bucaj's neighbourhood appeared unaffected by the war. However, many graffiti slogans had been painted prominently on every available wall space. Both Kosovar factions had posted statements of nationalistic fervour and ethnic hatred. Interestingly, all these messages were scrawled in English, presumably for the convenience of the foreign press rather than any domestic audience.

Given the horror stories of conditions in Pristina, the Bucaj household was surprisingly plush and well stocked. As Sylejman Bucaj proudly presented his wife and three children, it became evident that adding three journalists to the two-bedroom apartment might make things a bit crowded. Bucaj explained that his wife and two sons would bunk with a neighbour, while he and his eldest daughter, Arta, would stay to cater to their new guests. It was an extremely hospitable gesture and, given the danger of last-minute ethnic violence before NATO's arrival, a courageous one. Four Serbian tenants lived in the Bucajs' six-unit apartment building, including a soldier and a Yugoslav policeman.

We realized that three foreign journalists being billeted by an Albanian might cause some resentment on the part of the Serbs. Thankfully, our fears proved unfounded. Over the course of the four days we spent at his home, Sylejman Bucaj was able to tell me of his own family's experience during the air campaign.

A quiet, gentle man, Bucaj had been a high school geography teacher before the hostilities. He had been directly involved in the political movement of the Kosovo Liberation Army (KLA) and had helped solicit funds for their cause. The happiest day of Bucaj's life had been March 24, the day NATO began the bombing. When the Pristina Yugoslav army barracks was carpet bombed, Bucaj and his friends celebrated.

The Serbian reprisals did not begin until six days after the fall of the first NATO bombs. According to Bucaj, on March 30, Serbian police forces approached the predominantly Albanian Kodra e Trimave (Hill of the Brave) suburbs. At approximately seven o'clock in the morning, the Serbian police, in armoured personnel carriers, opened fire on the upper floors of the houses, using heavy machine guns. After a few bursts they withdrew.

There were no casualties because all the residents were sheltering in their basements. Asked why the Serbs didn't simply enter the Kodra e Trimave district to evict people at gunpoint, Bucaj laughed and replied, "Because they are terrified of the KLA."

Following the machine-gun attack, the Bucaj family piled up their belongings and joined the columns of refugees fleeing Pristina. Their destination was not the camps in Montenegro or

201

Macedonia but rather the southern Kosovo town of Prellez. Since the civil war in 1998, this region, as well as 40 per cent of the disputed province, had been under the control of the KLA. Bucaj and his family spent just twelve days in Prellez before deciding to take their chances and return to their home in Pristina.

For the Bucaj family, that homecoming proved to be harrowing. After the mass exodus of Albanians from the Kodra e Trimave district, many of the houses had been occupied by Serbian soldiers. The family discovered that an anti-aircraft detachment had dug in a 23-mm cannon on their front lawn.

Unable to live in their house, Bucaj and his family joined about a dozen other Albanians in a basement shelter. For the next two weeks they alternately hid out from Serbian soldiers or took refuge from the NATO bombings. On April 12, sixteen-year-old Arta Bucaj was caught in the garden by a trio of Serbian paramilitary policemen. Hearing his daughter's screams, Sylejman raced to the scene. A young captain in charge of the Serbs arrived at the same moment, and orders were given to release the terrified girl. Bucaj was infuriated at the rough treatment his daughter had received, and he appealed to the officer to discipline his men.

"What is this?" screamed Bucaj. "Under normal circumstances I would come to the police looking for help, and now it is you who are attacking my family!"

In response, the captain, who spoke fluent Albanian, retorted, "You are absolutely right, but these are not normal times. I have told my men that they cannot have your daughter, but I'm allowing them to loot your home. Be thankful!"

Even as the paramilitary police unit began emptying his house of its contents, Bucaj was once again packing up his family and heading to a safer locale, his cousin's home in the southeastern suburbs. His cousin had fled for Macedonia in early April but had left her apartment well provisioned. It was here that Bucaj hosted us.

The first NATO troops were due to arrive in Pristina on June 11, but Russia's sudden and unexpected move of sending troops to Kosovo threw a wrench into the works. One American television reporter panicked upon hearing of the Russian column's advance and began shouting, "It's going to be World War Three—and we're at ground zero!"

NATO had consistently tried to retain sole control of the operation, only grudgingly accepting a token Russian presence. Through this rapid deployment, the Russians had one-upped NATO and now threatened to steal its thunder. After word got to the Serbs in Pristina that Russian troops were to arrive at 10:00 PM on June 11, more than seven thousand people congregated in the plaza across from the Grand Hotel.

There was shouting, flag waving and fireworks, and shots were fired into the air as thousands of people crowded the city's main street to greet the soldiers, who arrived shortly after midnight, aboard trucks and troop transports. When the Russian soldiers—cheered as liberators by a large crowd of Serbs—entered Kosovo's capital during the wee hours of the morning, it was a huge morale boost for all Yugoslavs. They took a measure of joy in the knowledge that their leader had publicly embarrassed NATO.

By mid-morning, however, the international gamesmanship and political power-plays meant little to the citizenry of Pristina. Instead, everyone focused on the painfully slow (and, in view of the circumstances, almost laughable) advance of the British army towards the city. During the previous evening fifty carloads of foreign press had raced two abreast down that same highway to Macedonia so as not to miss the historic photo opportunity—NATO's first penetration into Yugoslavia. With the

Russian soldiers already drinking coffee at Pristina's airport, it was amazing to watch the drama that the BBC and CNN were trying to create around the British troops' overly cautious approach. Some defence analysts spoke gravely of the dangers lurking on the road ahead and suggested that troops might have to fight their way into Pristina airport. One BBC commentator went so far as to suggest that this would be a magnificent battle honour for the British 5th Parachute Brigade.

Sitting at the vortex of all this swirling speculation, I decided to go for a long jog around Pristina to get a sense of the city's mood. Through the issuance of specific approval forms, the Yugoslav army press officials had, so far, tried to regulate media access. Having staged their last-minute public relations coup on NATO by bringing in two hundred foreign media to record the Russian arrival, the officials now completely lifted any press controls. "Go anywhere you want," said Vesna Jukic, formerly the press centre's most strident warden. "KFOR is in control now," she added, referring to the contingent of two hundred Russians.

During my tour I spoke first with an assembly of nearly two hundred Serbs who were preparing to leave Kosovo for sanctuary in Serbia. Soldiers and police were evident amid the crowd of crying women and young children. Vehicles were anything that had wheels and a motor, and all overflowed with clothes and furniture. Some of the women were preparing food for the long trip. (Given the state of the cars and tractors, it appeared that few would successfully complete the gruelling trek.)

The leader of this convoy was former tailor Vladimir Djecic, who explained that these people were afraid of Albanian retaliation and gave little credence to NATO's promises to protect them. "They bomb us for two and a half months, they give arms to the KLA to attack us, and now we are to trust them as protectors?" he asked.

Serbian police and soldiers staying behind were saying good-bye to their families. The security escort for Djecic's convoy would be provided by teenage boys and old men—all of whom were armed with AK-47s. With the KLA stepping up its attacks along the main Pristina–Belgrade route, even Yugoslav police units feared the prospect of pulling out at night. According to the peace agreement, all Serbian army and security forces were to be out of Kosovo within eleven days.

"Tequila" was the only name that a young Serb policeman said he went by, but he became talkative once he learned I was from Canada, because he hoped, eventually, to live in Toronto with his brother. He was guarding a motley collection of twenty-nine ancient armoured personnel carriers that were to be transported back to Belgrade. Over the past eighteen months, his police force had lost five such vehicles to mines placed by the KLA, but none had been hit by the NATO air strikes. "Do you think we'd be crazy enough to drive around in these things during the air campaign?" he asked. Instead, like most of the Yugoslav army's heavy equipment, the vehicles had remained hidden. Tequila and his colleagues, all from Kosovo, were to be expelled from their homes as per the peace agreement, and unemployed as well.

Tequila planned to take off his uniform the next day and attempt to join the refugee column with his wife and six-month-old daughter. Others in his unit apparently had the same idea; all of the armoured vehicles had been packed with bedding and other household items.

As we spoke, police officials were burning a mountain of files. Across the street at the army headquarters, a similar blaze was fed by a constant stream of administrative clerks. These fires, behind the Pristina media centre, continued all day, but the foreign press were too engrossed in the snail-like advance of the NATO column to notice.

Throughout the day, Yugoslav anti-aircraft units continued to retreat through Pristina. Their irregular, and often bizarre, head-gear (Rambo headscarves were common, and a sombrero and top hat were spotted) served as evidence that their spirits were still high. Administrative units had also begun pulling field kitchens and mobile laundry units through town. The Yugoslav army had apparently suffered fewer losses than NATO claimed.

Another startling example of the discrepancy in NATO's claims was the sudden appearance of six MiG-29 jet fighters over Pristina. The Yugoslav air force pilots flew a low-level formation overhead, tipped their wings in farewell and then headed north to Serbia. Very early in the bombing campaign, NATO spokesman Jamie Shea had told the world that all such fighter planes had been destroyed. In fact, throughout the war, the MiGs remained hidden in bunkers. They had survived unscathed, while NATO planes were tricked into bombing museum pieces placed around airfields.

Once again, this gesture of smug defiance raised Serbian morale. The Serbs who chose to remain in their homes and the soldiers awaiting repatriation orders appeared to be in denial. They crowded into the few cafés that remained open and filled the outdoor market. In the lobby of Pristina's Grand Hotel, Serbian soldiers lounged with their lemonades, watching BBC's coverage of the British advance. Seeing the heavily laden NATO troops sweltering in the heat, the Serbs laughed and asked what all the fuss was about.

By mid-morning on June 13, the British 5th Airborne Brigade's tanks and armoured vehicles were rolling down the war-ravaged streets of the Kosovo capital. Aiming their gun turrets menacingly, these combat vehicles made an impressive show of force that was intended to quash any outbreak of ethnic violence. By

206

late afternoon the Brits had finally arrived at the Pristina airport, only to find the Russians already well entrenched. However, as NATO planners soon realized, hatreds in the region ran deep.

As darkness fell around the city, Serbian soldiers shot their rifles randomly into the air, and a number of fires burned fiercely. As Vladimir Djecic had predicted to me, fleeing Serb civilians were burning their own homes in order to deprive the Albanians of the satisfaction.

With Serbian forces continuing their withdrawal and their police units being demobilized, the KLA became bolder. Although small armoured patrols of Yugoslavs still maintained a presence alongside allied Kosovo-Force (KFOR) troops, the KLA could see that the Serbs were quickly losing control.

At noon on June 13, the KLA opened its Pristina headquarters. Thirty minutes later, one of its members shot and killed twenty-five-year-old Slavisa Isteric from an upstairs window of the converted schoolhouse. Although Isteric was in his uniform, he wasn't a soldier; he was just a trombone player in the Pristina militia band.

Rade Hrnic was driving a red Opel Ascona when he and Isteric were ambushed. Only slightly injured, Hrnic left his friend for dead and fled on foot to a nearby Yugoslav army installation. Here, less than an hour later, I, along with Nils Horner, the Swedish reporter, stumbled on the story. By the time we arrived at the ambush site, armed with a detailed account from Hrnic and accompanied by a petrified Serbian civilian guide from the checkpoint, three KFOR armoured vehicles had arrived. A huge crowd of Albanian Kosovars had formed, bedecking the peacekeepers with flowers and chanting "U-C-K! NATO!"

Mistakenly believing that British officers must be inside the schoolhouse investigating the shooting, I strode purposefully into

207

the KLA headquarters. They were surprisingly cordial, given that both Horner and I were wearing Yugoslav army press passes. Bahri Goshi, the twenty-five-year-old deputy commander of the Pristina district KLA, agreed to grant us an interview. Goshi commanded the "Red Patch" unit, named for the distinctive arm bands worn by his soldiers. The group was widely feared by the Serbian security forces because of its bold hit-and-run attacks. Asked how he felt about the Russian troop presence in Kosovo, Goshi replied, "They have no place here." However, after some coaxing from the translator, he recanted, saying: "It is up to NATO."

Goshi was indifferent to the plight of fleeing Serb refugees. "If they committed crimes, then they are correct to be afraid. For those who are criminals and remain, they will be punished." The interpreter hastily added, "At The Hague Tribunals."

During the interview Goshi repeatedly stated that there were no weapons at Red Patch headquarters. However, when we finally got around to the shooting of Slavisa Isteric, his answers became contradictory. "They were people looking to do harm to innocent Albanian citizens. They got what was coming to them," he said. "Why do you care so much about two Serbs who ran away? What about the one and a half million Albanians who were forced to flee?"

208 Throughout our conversation the KLA entourage filling the small office took turns videotaping Horner and me, which was rather unnerving—especially after they presented us with our own Red Patch arm bands.

After leaving the KLA headquarters, we again sought out the British detachment commander to report on the killing of Slavisa Isteric. After hearing our tale, the young lieutenant dismissed Horner and me with a flippant wave of his hand. "We're not here to go chasing down unsubstantiated rumours," he said. "We're here to provide a secure environment." The platoon sergeant, who had overheard the conversation, piped up, "The murdering Serb bastard probably had it coming to him." By this time, the cheering crowd of Albanians had completely covered the British vehicles with flowers.

If NATO's stated intention of providing, through KFOR, a safe environment for all Kosovars were to be believed, the actions and attitudes of the soldiers on the ground would have to change. Virtually sanctioning a guerrilla headquarters on the outskirts of Pristina was not the message KFOR should have been conveying.

The flood of Albanian refugees returning to Kosovo had already begun, the Yugoslav army was still in the middle of its retreat, and the situation remained a powder keg.

TWO YOUNG GIRLS began pounding on the bus window, yelling and waving to a group of Yugoslav soldiers at a roadside outpost. Recognizing them, one of the Serbian militiamen raced to the curbside, shouting their names and running alongside the bus. Tears were streaming down his face; both girls were weeping. After he had disappeared from sight, the elder of the two sisters, Yvonne Jukic, explained to me that the soldier was their father. She and her sister were heading to the town of Krusevac, inside Serbia, to escape the ethnic violence that was once again consuming Kosovo.

Their father was a member of the Yugoslav army reserves and was due to be demobilized as per the peace agreement signed on June 4, 1999. He would then try to join his family and, they hoped, eventually resettle in Belgrade. In the meantime, he remained at his post, providing security along the main Pristina–Belgrade route, which was increasingly subject to violent KLA guerrilla attacks. The Yugoslav army's ongoing withdrawal from

209

Kosovo had sparked a marked increase in military operations by the KLA—despite the arrival of KFOR peacekeeping forces. The situation had deteriorated so badly that Serbian military officials had to request an armed convoy escort from KFOR troops in order to provide safe passage to foreign journalists wishing to return to Belgrade.

For the thousands of Serbian citizens fleeing Kosovo, the Yugoslav army made no such arrangement. Citizens either took their chances with an escort of young boys and old men or put their faith in what was left of the Serbian militia. Even with thousands of NATO-accredited journalists running around the streets of Pristina, the story that remained largely untold was that of the retreating army and the attendant flood of refugees.

On the morning of June 15, I didn't think the best vantage point for covering this would be a KFOR-escorted convoy, so I had bought a ticket on the local bus. It had been a long wait, but I had finally secured a standing-room-only spot among young families, soldiers and a few elderly couples. By the time we departed, sixty-seven people and their worldly possessions were crammed into a forty-four-passenger bus. The British troops stationed at the bombed-out Pristina terminal came out to gawk and laugh at our vehicle.

210 Things worsened as we approached the main turnoff towards Belgrade, where approximately six hundred Albanian residents had set up a gauntlet to jeer and stone withdrawing Serbs. Thankfully, no windows were broken in the hail of projectiles, but it was an unnerving experience. Once outside the city limits, everyone became visibly apprehensive each time the bus came to a stop. With the massive load restricting visibility, people would shout frantic questions to those in the front seats concerning what had caused the halt. The soldiers aboard were particularly

tense because they were unarmed but still in uniform. Between the panic-filled stops, there was silence, except for babies crying. After safely crossing into Serbia, everyone seemed to relax, and we became aware of the scale of the human exodus from Kosovo.

The first large convoy we overtook was a column of Yugo-slav T-72 and T-64 main battle tanks. An impressive string of sixty-seven of these armoured behemoths lined the roadside. Most surprised by the large formation of mint-condition tanks were the Serbian soldiers aboard the bus. At first they thought it was a Russian battalion, but when they saw the red-white-and-blue Yugoslavian flags fluttering from the antennae, they asked, "Where the hell have they been hiding?"

Once again it would appear that, in the final tally, NATO's bombing campaign success had been grossly exaggerated. Just ahead of the tanks we entered the small village of Kursumlija, the first Serbian settlement outside Kosovo. Judging from the number of tractor-pulled wagons and the volume of refugees, one widely circulated rumour appeared to be confirmed: the Yugo-slav government was turning back Serb refugees to keep a visible post-war Serbian demographic in Albania. However, as we continued slowly along the hot, dusty side road littered with the debris of a retreating army, it became obvious that Kursumlija was just a staging area for the fleeing Serbs. Roads remained clogged with tractors, trucks and horse-drawn carts.

Since NATO bombs had destroyed most bridges and overpasses, our trek involved many lengthy detours. It took more than ten hours to cover less than two hundred kilometres. In the 30°C heat, the bus became almost unbearable; young children suffered the most. But as we passed forlorn families standing next to vehicles that had broken down or simply run out of fuel, the passengers considered themselves lucky.

211

AFTER ARRIVING AT the Hotel Moskva in Belgrade, I began making hurried plans for my return to Canada. In the few hours before my departure I had to write and file two stories, obtain an exit visa from police headquarters and make a final trip to replenish my dwindling cash reserves. Squeezed into that schedule were several interviews with Canadian radio and television stations. Naturally, my Kosovo update included my experience on the outward-bound bus. Off-air, one producer commented that the Serbs who were fleeing and being stoned by Albanians were "probably war criminals anyway." I took the time to explain that the majority of my fellow passengers on the bus had been terrified elderly couples and mothers with small children. "Well," the radio producer replied, "you've got to understand the Albanians' position. These Serbs did nothing to prevent the atrocities from taking place."

I answered him by asking, "You mean in the same way our NATO soldiers stood at the Albanian gauntlet and did nothing to stop the stoning of the Serbs?"

His response? "Boy, do you ever need to get home and be deprogrammed."

BY THE TIME I did return home, the wheels were already beginning to fall off the mainstream media's propaganda bandwagon. When the horde of journalists finally descended upon Kosovo, reporters weren't interested in Albanian revenge killings of Serbs—they were on a collective race to uncover the first "mass graves," discover the "rape camps" and portray the shattered remains of the Serbian army.

What they found was evidence of a war very different from the one they had just spent the past three months reporting. The mass gravesites proved to be elusive. Despite much-repeated

212

eyewitness accounts of the execution of 700 Albanians at the Trepca mines, for example, not a single body was found. The biggest find was seven corpses exhumed at Ljubenic, a site that had purportedly been the burial ground of more than 350 Kosovars. After five months of searching, UN forensic teams uncovered a total of 670 bodies. Keeping in mind that this tally included Albanian, Serbian and Gypsy civilians plus suspected combatants, the numbers did not justify the careless use of the word *genocide* and was a far cry from NATO spokesman Jamie Shea's wildly exaggerated claims.

As the last of the Yugoslav army and police columns withdrew, journalists were equally hard pressed to locate the burnt-out hulks of vehicles that Shea had promised them. In his daily press briefings he had kept a running tally of destroyed Serbian weapon systems, boasting that NATO air power had effectively created "a ring of death around Kosovo."

The truth was sobering. Despite NATO's dropping more than US$15 billion worth of ordnance, only thirteen Serbian tanks had been destroyed in seventy-eight days of bombing, and five of these were credited to KLA land mines.

Claims of mass rape also failed to stand up to scrutiny. At the height of the fighting, the Canadian Broadcasting Corporation had produced a short documentary, profiling a female fighter in the Kosovo Liberation Army. Her heart-rending story was that she had taken up arms after being forced to watch as Serbian police raped, then killed, her sister. When a television news crew tracked her down for a follow-up homecoming piece, they found her sister very much alive—and unmolested. When the CBC aired what amounted to a retraction of the original story, she was unrepentant. "We did what we had to do," she said. "We could not beat the Serbs ourselves."

Journalists are loath to admit they've been duped, and as a result, retractions or corrections rarely receive the same prominence as the original stories—and once public opinion has been shaped, it is difficult to shift it. Since news reports are considered the first rough draft of history, books based on this one-sided coverage of the conflict exacerbate the original distortions.

In *Virtual War: Kosovo and Beyond,* Canadian author and Balkan analyst Michael Ignatieff perpetuated many of the misunderstandings that had been generated to justify NATO's intervention. Although it can be gleaned from the anecdotes he used that only one side of the conflict was being presented, Ignatieff gave the impression that he was telling the whole story. His interviews with U.S. envoy Richard Holbrooke, chief prosecutor of war crimes for The Hague's International Criminal Tribunal Louise Arbour and U.S. General Wesley Clark were not offset with the views of the Serbian leadership. Much of *Virtual War* was written during the air campaign and was based only on information available at the time. Consequently, Ignatieff's supporting arguments for the campaign were based on the same two "galvanizing incidents" used by NATO spokesmen to justify their actions: the January 1999 massacre of Albanian civilians by Serbian police at Racak, and Operation Horseshoe, the plan for Yugoslavia to ethnically cleanse Kosovo.

By the time *Virtual War* was published in 2000, German intelligence had confessed to having fabricated the Operation Horseshoe documents, and a UN forensic team had concluded that "no massacre" had taken place at Racak. Despite the importance of these findings, Ignatieff chose to ignore them rather than rethink his basic premise.

Likewise, veteran CBC journalist Carol Off failed to note that Racak was a hoax. In her book *The Lion, the Fox and the Eagle: A*

Story of Generals and Justice in Rwanda and Yugoslavia, Off devoted a third of the book to The Hague prosecutor Louise Arbour ("the Eagle"), but no mention was made of this new evidence.

Arbour's indictment of Milosevic as a war criminal on the basis of the Racak massacre during the NATO air campaign had served the U.S. State Department's propaganda interests. However, by proceeding with this indictment without corroborating forensic evidence, Arbour undermined not only the credibility of The Hague Tribunal but also her professional reputation as an impartial prosecutor.

In March 2000, I compiled my observations into a book entitled *Inat: Images of Serbia and the Kosovo Conflict. Inat* is a Serbian noun that does not translate directly into English, but roughly it means "regardless of the consequences." Far from being a simple word, *inat* is best described as a spirit that is embodied in the psyche of the Serbian people. Had NATO planners understood *inat,* they never would have predicted that with just five days of air strikes they could overcome the Serbian will to resist.

Included in this book were my experiences of returning to Serbia and Kosovo in November 1999. The war-weary Serbs were still reeling from the destruction of their country's infrastructure, the embargo was still in full effect, the black market was thriving, hundreds of thousands of refugees from Kosovo were hosted in temporary shelters and Milosevic was still in power.

After the book was released, I received an invitation from former U.S. attorney general Ramsey Clark to participate in a mock war crime tribunal in New York City. Clark was taking the audacious step of putting the U.S. government and NATO on public trial for the bombing of Serbia. It was a low-budget affair, organized by various peace groups, and those of us witnesses who presented during the event came from diverse backgrounds. It

215

was here that I met Ben Works, an American military analyst,
and Rollie Keith, a former Canadian major and UN observer. As I
had to share a hotel room with Keith, I soon became very familiar
with his experiences at the outset of the bombing. This former
officer had been reporting on the provocations launched by the
KLA against Serbian police checkpoints when the international
observers were ordered to pull out of Kosovo. Contrary to the propaganda, the Serbs did not order them out; they were withdrawn
by the UN. Keith was also adamant that the exodus of refugees
began only after NATO started to bomb—not as a result of a Serbian police-organized expulsion.

Also present at the tribunal was George Bogdanich, a Serbian-
American filmmaker who was then directing his award-winning
documentary *Yugoslavia: The Avoidable War*. Bogdanich found
all sorts of invaluable input at the conference, and I agreed to
contribute my information regarding the still-unindicted commander of the KLA, Agim Ceku.

In May 2000, I again returned to the Serbian capital to attend
a conference for foreign journalists. At that same time Alexandre
"Sacha" Trudeau was in Belgrade making a documentary entitled
Among the Serbs. I had met Sacha before he left Canada and had
arranged to interview him in Serbia. I was impressed with the
fact that he was anxious to see things for himself and that, as the
son of a former prime minister, he knew enough to look beyond
the spin offered as fact by spokespersons and the mainstream
media. On this particular visit I also made my first contact with a
new movement called Otpor, an underground political coalition
gearing up to oust Milosevic from power.

I was brought to a secret club in Zemun, where many of
the Serbian intelligentsia, politicians and artists gathered to
exchange their views. Taking me into their confidence, the Otpor

leaders told me that the fledgling movement was about to make its mark on the Serbian political scene. To get Milosevic's attention they were planning to assassinate some of his key officials. I kept the names and locations out of my story but reported that Otpor was planning to kill top cabinet ministers. Within weeks at least six of Milosevic's senior aides had been gunned down.

The situation came to a climactic showdown following the much-anticipated September 24, 2000, federal election in Serbia. Milosevic's Socialist Party had faced a unified opposition in the form of Vojislav Kostunica's Democratic Opposition of Serbia. When the initial votes were tabulated, no clear-cut winner was announced, and Milosevic claimed that a second election would be required. The opposition supporters cried foul and demanded an immediate end to Milosevic's rule. Daily demonstrations grew in size and number until October 5, when an estimated one million Serbs converged on the parliament building in protest.

The police fired some tear gas, but after only token resistance most security forces joined the crowds of protesters. By the next day Milosevic had conceded defeat and stepped aside. A new era was about to dawn on Serbia, and a new wave of violence was about to hit the Balkans. This time it would be in the heretofore quiet republic of Macedonia.

MY AUSTRIAN AIRLINES flight on August 3, 2001, had been delayed for over three hours in Vienna, and we did not touch down in Belgrade until after 5:30 PM. Since my last trip to Yugoslavia in December 2000, there had been a number of significant developments. In early February 2001, President Vojislav Kostunica had formally ratified Yugoslavia's previously disputed border with the Republic of Macedonia. Although Macedonia had peacefully seceded from the Federal Republic in 1991, then-president Slobodan Milosevic had refused to define the border. However, with Albanian guerrillas now occupying territory in southern Serbia and threatening action inside northern Macedonia, Kostunica's government felt it only prudent to clearly set out areas of military responsibility. Within days of the agreement being signed, Albanian KLA guerrillas had crossed into Macedonia from Kosovo and launched a major offensive.

In March, the international media turned its attention to this latest round of inter-ethnic Balkan fighting, particularly in the northwestern Macedonian city of Tetovo, which had been the scene of several clashes between the KLA and Macedonian security forces.

This little-known city was thrust into the world news spotlight with the release of some graphically violent footage. Macedonian television crews at a security checkpoint had captured the killing of two KLA members on tape. The incident began when a Macedonian policeman stopped the Albanians and one of them pulled out a hand grenade. As the startled policeman ran away from the car, shouting a warning, his comrade opened fire. The Albanian with the grenade was hit but, despite his wounds, managed to throw it. The Macedonians unleashed a deadly barrage, killing him and his companion.

218   Albanian media outlets claimed that the two men were innocent civilians murdered by Macedonian security forces and that the grenade had in fact been a cellphone. Rade Lesko, a former soldier, was one of the Macedonian cameramen who had filmed the incident. In this footage, the Albanian is clearly shown tossing a grenade, which came to rest against a curb with the safety pin still attached.

At the end of March, it was reported that the KLA guerrillas had withdrawn back to their bases inside Kosovo. International envoys—Javier Solana, secretary-general of the Western European Union, and George Robertson, secretary-general of NATO, in particular—made several trips to Macedonia to try to hammer out a peaceful solution. Many analysts believed that further violence could be avoided and that a peace proposal could be formalized by mid-June.

On April 1, the media focus shifted back to Belgrade when Yugoslav authorities stormed Milosevic's villa A month earlier, federal prosecutors had announced that they were launching an investigation into allegations of corruption by the deposed Yugoslav president. On March 29, Milosevic was charged and then released following police questioning. This set in motion a comic-opera police raid on his home. For twenty-six hours Milosevic's bodyguards returned fire with the police tactical squad as a herd of journalists surrounded his walled estate. At one point Milosevic issued a statement to the press that he would not be taken alive, but in the end this proved not to be true.

Immediately after Milosevic's anti-climactic surrender on April 3, Colin Powell, the U.S. secretary of state, promised to provide Yugoslavia with US$50 million in "reward" money. Although the country desperately needed the cash, the American statement undermined political support for the new regime. To many, it appeared as if Serbian President Zoran Djindjic, and to a lesser extent federal Yugoslav President Vojislav Kostunica, had sold out to American interests.

Even though the original charges were for corruption within Yugoslavia, The Hague's International Criminal Tribunal wasted little time in demanding Milosevic's immediate extradition. The chief prosecutor, Carla Del Ponte, submitted a warrant to the Yugoslav authorities on April 5. A few days later, the U.S. State Department dangled a financial carrot of US$1.3 billion in foreign aid, but the release of these funds was predicated upon the handing over of Milosevic to the tribunal. Such temptations would prove irresistible to the new Serbian government.

AS THE AUSTRIAN Airlines flight touched down at Belgrade airport in August, I was reminded of the plot of the movie *Groundhog Day*, in which the character played by Bill Murray becomes trapped time and time again—interminably.

Once again I was arriving late on a Friday afternoon, leaving me little time to accomplish anything. During my two-month absence from the Balkans much had happened. My assignment was to write some contextual backgrounders on these events before the dust completely settled on their newsworthiness.

Although my flight arrived on schedule, this time my attempts to make final arrangements for interviews were hampered by the calendar. I soon learned that during the hot summer months Belgraders practically abandoned their city for beaches and cooler climes. When its government offices, schools and major industries shut down, it was estimated that less than 30 per cent of Belgrade's population remained at home.

My first objective was to assess the political fallout in Yugoslavia from the handover of Slobodan Milosevic to The Hague's International Criminal Tribunal. In June, this issue had been of major international media interest. The internal political power struggle between Serbian President Zoran Djindjic and Yugoslav President Vojislav Kostunica had centred on the fate of the deposed dictator.

Kostunica remained adamant that Milosevic would be tried in Yugoslavia for the crimes he had allegedly committed against the Serbian people. This stand was popular with the nationalists, many of who believed that the war crimes tribunal was a tool of NATO. On the other side of the equation, Djindjic's supporters were lured by the promise of substantial foreign aid in exchange for their compliance with Milosevic's extradition. To effect this, an international donors' conference had been scheduled to take place in Zurich, Switzerland, at the end of June. With the talks faltering, the U.S. State Department threatened to pull out of the conference. Their message was clear: no Milosevic, no money.

On June 23, an emergency session of the Serbian parliament had voted to approve a decree that paved the way for Milosevic's handover. Three days later, more than ten thousand Serbs took to the streets of Belgrade to protest the "sellout" to western demands. Kostunica calmed the crowds with assurances that Milosevic would remain in Yugoslavia.

On June 28—the Serbian national religious holiday of Vidovdan—Djindjic acted in direct defiance of Kostunica's federal authority. Not knowing whether the Yugoslav army would interfere to prevent Milosevic's removal, Djindjic and his officials carried out an elaborate abduction plot. With decoy cars dispatched to confuse pursuers, Milosevic was transported from the Belgrade prison to the Republika Srpska in Bosnia. There he was turned over to NATO authorities and whisked away by helicopter to arraignment hearings at the International Court of Justice in The Hague.

Upon learning of the handover, thousands took to the streets to vent their anger at being betrayed. Even the subsequent announcement that US$1.3 billion in economic aid had been pledged at the donors' conference in Switzerland did little to diminish public outrage.

IN EARLY 2002, I once again compiled my experiences and reports into a book, entitled *Diary of an Uncivil War: The Violent Aftermath of the Kosovo Conflict*. By one of the few western reporters to have covered the Balkans extensively for nearly a decade, my books have been translated into Serbian, Macedonian and even Japanese. *Diary of an Uncivil War* was written in the immediate aftermath of September 11, 2001, and to keep the links in the spotlight, one chapter was entitled "Osama Bin Laden's Balkan Connections."

Fortunately, the Serbian and Macedonian expatriate communities around the world were keen to promote the book, and I travelled extensively on speaking tours that included stops in Australia, Sweden, Germany, Austria, the United Kingdom and the United States. However, with the new "war on terror" garnering the headlines, events in the Balkans were relegated to the back burner.

That would remain the case until I received a phone call in July 2004. It was an invitation to travel to The Hague to be interviewed by an accused war criminal. When I learned the identity of my interviewer, I knew I could not turn down the opportunity. I accepted the invitation and went to The Hague to meet him.

"How would you like your coffee?" he asked.

Even as I answered, I realized the situation was surreal. Here was Slobodan Milosevic, former president of Serbia and an indicted war criminal, preparing instant coffee in a plastic cup for me. While I had been reporting on the Balkan wars for the past twelve years, Milosevic had always been somewhat larger than life for me—whether he was loved by the million-plus crowd who chanted "Slobo! Slobo!" in June 1989 or whether he was hated by the similar-sized angry mob who ousted him from power in October 2000.

Now I was suddenly face to face with the man in a prison cell. The experience was surprisingly casual. It was definitely unnerving, almost like seeing the curtain pulled back on the Wizard of Oz. But this time I was not there to interview Milosevic; rather, I was the one being questioned.

222

Under the terms of his incarceration, the former Serbian president was not allowed to meet with media or make public statements. For me to have access, I had to sign a strict non-disclosure agreement that prevented me from describing any aspect of the actual facility in which Milosevic was being detained. Furthermore, I must not speak of "the health of the accused, including his mental health and physical appearance."

While I still cannot describe in detail the security measures at the detention facility, I will say that any future witness should be sure to wear clean underwear on the day of the visit. While not intrusive, the searches are thorough.

As for Milosevic, he wore a plaid shirt, buttoned to the top, and casual slacks. Another rule forbade me from disclosing "any other information relating to . . . any detainee other than the accused." I do not think it would be a violation of these guidelines, however, to point out that when Milosevic came into contact with other Serbian prisoners, he was greeted cordially as "Slobo" and was introduced respectfully to their visiting family members.

I also do not think I am violating the spirit of the signed agreement by stating that Milosevic spoke excellent if somewhat accented English. The only confusion we had during our conversation occurred when he discussed his indictment on May 26, 1999, by Canadian Justice Louise Arbour. I mentioned that at that time I was in Belgrade reporting on the NATO air strikes. As chief prosecutor for the newly formed war crimes tribunal, Arbour had startled the world with her surprise mid-war announcement of the Serbian president's indictment. "That was funny," I heard him say. But when I questioned his response, Milosevic corrected himself. "Phoney," he said, and after a moment's hesitation he added, "and funny, too."

There is also a strict guideline whereby The Hague's International Criminal Tribunal can deny access to a visitor if they

223

believe the visitor's purpose to be "to obtain information which may be subsequently only reported in the media." However, I was not prevented from discussing my personal experience and potential testimony, which was the reason for my visit to The Hague.

This trip had begun with a call from Branko Rakic, who identified himself as a legal assistant to Slobodan Milosevic. He advised me that three of my books—*Tested Mettle, Inat* and *Diary of an Uncivil War*—had been obtained by the defence team and submitted to The Hague's International Criminal Tribunal for the Former Yugoslavia as evidence. Rakic also told me that Milosevic wished to interview me as a potential witness, and I was told up front that I would not be compelled to testify. My co-operation would have to be voluntary. I had reservations about appearing before such a tribunal, particularly because I have frequently questioned the impartiality and legitimacy of such a post-war judicial process—established and funded by the victors to determine the guilt of the defeated. From the perspective of a journalist and an author, though, who had spent so many years covering the complex Balkan conflict, the prospect of meeting one of the central figures was too powerful a lure to decline.

The entire administrative process of becoming a tribunal witness was also fascinating. Following the formal request by Milosevic's team for an interview, the travel arrangements were then processed by the tribunal's Witness and Victims Section. Approximately thirty-four clerks and field workers were assigned to facilitate such visits to The Hague. While the cloak-and-dagger precautions—from the coded sign held by the airport guide to the anonymous hotel registration—seemed somewhat excessive, they served to remind me of the magnitude of the crimes committed and of the far-reaching power of many of the accused. Several witnesses actually appear under the condition of tribunal protection.

Although this option was offered to me, I declined because my books are public documents.

As the tribunal was technically in recess throughout August, I happened to be the only witness called during this seventy-two-hour period. When cases are being heard, the Witness and Victims Section handles as many as forty individuals a day. For privacy and security reasons, witnesses are housed in a number of different hotels located throughout the city.

My hotel happened to be situated very close to the detention centre and only metres from The Hague's beaches at Scheveningen, one of northern Europe's most popular seaside resorts. Thousands of topless bathers were making the most of the midsummer heat wave just half a kilometre from the war crimes prison. Perhaps fortunately for the inmates, the packed beaches cannot be seen over the red-brick walls of their confines.

Judging from the volumes of documents and books cluttering his desk and bookshelves, Milosevic would have little time for such distractions. He had only until August 31, 2004, to prepare and finalize his defence, and he planned to call several hundred witnesses. Included in his wish list were a number of potentially hostile witnesses such as Bill Clinton, Tony Blair and former NATO spokesman Jamie Shea. Although there was little chance that any of them would willingly agree to testify, the request to compel their attendance would be a difficult challenge for the prosecutors. Not that there was any shortage of legal expertise arrayed to contest such a challenge: the lawyers and researchers on the prosecution team were estimated to total several hundred personnel, a large percentage of whom were Canadians.

Milosevic was representing himself in this case and was assisted by a small team of legal supporters and researchers who operated with a minimum of financial assistance from the tribunal. Most of their financial support came from private donations—primarily from Serbian expatriates, including several Canadians.

Researcher Cathrin Schütz accompanied me during my meeting with Milosevic. The thirty-three-year-old German political science graduate commuted by train from her hometown near Frankfurt—a five-hour trip to The Hague—to process potential witnesses. "We operate on a shoestring budget," she explained, "but we believe that everything must be done to try and achieve a fair trial."

One of the most disconcerting things to the small defence team at that stage was that the tribunal was once again trying to impose its own legal counsel. "They say it is for health reasons, but that is not true," said Schütz. "They told him ten days before his defence was supposed to begin that the trial was being postponed. He stopped his preparations on their orders, but the tribunal did not inform the media," she continued. "Instead, they allowed foreign journalists to register, and then brought Mr. Milosevic to the trial chamber on the original date. When he explained that he was not prepared because of the health restriction, the tribunal used this as further proof that they must impose counsel on him. It was courtroom theatrics."

226 In addition, members of his defence team alleged that events were being orchestrated to deliberately isolate Milosevic, with the aim of heightening his stress levels. "Following the indictment of Mira [Markovic, Milosevic's wife] in Serbia last year, Slobodan has not been allowed to see her," said Schütz. "This only further isolated him and denied him personal support."

Most published accounts of the Milosevics described them as "inseparable" and "soulmates." Although Mira conducted her own political career, her Yugoslav Left party was always seen as an extension of her husband's Socialists. When Slobodan was first handed over to the tribunal, Mira made frequent trips to visit him in jail and to attend the hearings.

The evidence cited from my books concerned a number of issues pertaining to the atrocities witnessed by Canadian troops serving in Bosnia and Croatia between 1992 and 1995. One incident of particular interest to Milosevic was the September 1993 confrontation in the Medak Pocket. Although Canadian soldiers had engaged Croatian troops and officially recorded the atrocities that the Croatians had committed against Serbian villagers, many of the key participants had never been brought to justice before the tribunal.

Furthermore, Agim Ceku, an Albanian commander and one of those responsible for the massacre, ended up playing a lead role—with NATO's blessing—in the 1999 conflict in Kosovo. The Milosevic defence team recognized my role (with David Pugliese of the *Ottawa Citizen*) in first breaking the previously untold story of the Medak in the fall of 1996.

At the end of our six hours together, Slobodan Milosevic asked me if I was still prepared to take the stand to defend an alleged war criminal. When I discovered the nature of my intended testimony, I realized that I would simply be defending the stories I had already written. I told him I believed it would undermine any journalist's credibility to refuse to stand by his or her reports under such circumstances.

When I was finally ushered out of the detention centre at the conclusion of our meeting, Milosevic was taken by the guards back to his private cell. In addition to making coffee for his witnesses, the ex-president was apparently also responsible for preparing his own meals.

His final words were for me to be careful on my upcoming trips. I assured him that I would be safe. Ignoring his advice, three weeks later I set off for wartorn Iraq.

227

IRAQ FOLLOWING THE U.S. INTERVENTION, JUNE 2003

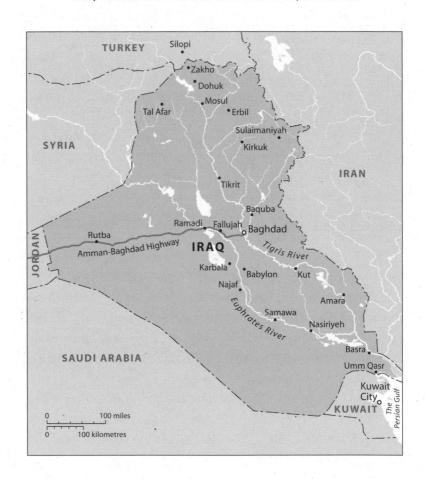

8

SADDAM'S IRAQ

We've got plenty of gas up at our air base.
Hell, we'll probably have to start drinking the
stuff now that we've run out of places to put it.

STAFF SERGEANT AL TIFTON

MAKING THE LEAP FROM COVERING the Balkans to my first foray
into Iraq began in May 2000 when the first consul at the Yugoslav embassy in Ottawa invited me out for a special lunch. I had
met with Ljiljana Milojevic-Borovcanin on many occasions, and
she had been instrumental in approving my travel visas. Since
Milojevic-Borovcanin was not a member of the Communist Party
and was active in Serbia's underground opposition movement,
she had introduced me to many of the top Serbian democratic
leaders.

229

The lunch Milojevic-Borovcanin arranged took place at La
Favorita in Ottawa. The restaurant's proprietor, Najeeb Shallal, an Iraqi-Canadian who had set up shop in the city in 1985,
had studied cooking at the University of Belgrade after emigrat-
ing from Iraq. Najeeb spoke fluent Serbian, and many of his staff
were recent Yugoslav immigrants, so he had no trouble preparing a special off-menu Serbian feast for us.

Instantly likable, Najeeb was a generous host who wore his heart on his sleeve. Having spent so much time living in Belgrade, he had followed the war in Kosovo closely and was genuinely interested in my book *Inat*. When he asked why I wasn't exposing the same sort of lies about Iraq, I explained that as a reporter I wrote about events as they happened and not about issues that had long since been resolved. Although an abortive showdown had taken place between Iraq and the United States in 1998, the issue of Iraq's readmission of UN weapons inspectors had subsequently disappeared from the news.

"Old news?" Najeeb sputtered incredulously. "They are bombing Iraq every day!"

Sensing that I found it amazing that a war could be underway without anyone in the western media reporting it, Najeeb disappeared into his office. He returned, brandishing a number of wire reports and e-mail messages detailing the ongoing U.S. and British air strikes. I was immediately intrigued, and I pledged to visit Iraq if Najeeb could help with arranging a travel visa.

This proved to be a major stumbling block. One of the first requests from the Iraqi embassy was that I submit all the articles I had written about the Gulf War and Iraq. In 1991, I had made four trips to the Persian Gulf theatre. Operation Desert Storm was the first war I had ever covered. In reporting for *Esprit de Corps,* my coverage of both the buildup for war and the actual combat had been naive and heavy on the rah-rah. It was only after I had visited 1st Combat Engineer Regiment's Lost Boys in June 1991 that I had started to observe some U.S. duplicity in its Iraq policy—particularly when I was informed of the uncontested retrieval of abandoned Silkworm missiles by Iraqi troops inside Kuwaiti territory.

While I was perplexed at the time as to why the United States would have openly allowed Saddam Hussein to re-equip his

230

battered army, I was thoroughly incensed nineteen months later.
On January 13, 1993, following George Bush Sr.'s November 1992
election defeat—but before Bill Clinton's taking office—the Americans launched a punitive round of air strikes against Iraq. Four
days later, on the second anniversary of the start of the Gulf War
and with just seventy-two hours remaining in his stint as American commander-in-chief, Bush ordered another military strike
against Iraq. About fifty cruise missiles smashed into Baghdad,
including one that hit a conference room where Saddam was
supposed to be making a speech. The explanation given by Pentagon officials was that they had caught Saddam's operatives inside
Kuwait attempting to recover military hardware.

Furious at the hypocrisy, I fired off an immediate press
release accusing the United States of staging a propaganda ploy. I
included the information about the Silkworm missiles and stated
that either the U.S. wanted to get rid of Saddam Hussein or this
attack was a last hurrah by outgoing President Bush. The rearm-
ing of Iraq's army was old news and certainly not the real reason
for these attacks.

Several Canadian media outlets picked up the story and called
the Pentagon for a response. "We respect [Scott Taylor's] opinion,
but we do not share it," replied spokesman Colonel Dave Garner.
"U.S. President George Bush has given his reasons for the action,
and those words stand on their own."

This was the first time that I had challenged the Pentagon.
Neglecting to include my early Gulf War articles with my visa
request to the Iraqi embassy in Ottawa, I forwarded only the
press clips associated with the 1992 propaganda ploy. On the
strength of Najeeb's recommendation and my deliberately thin
resumé of reports on Iraq, my credentials were approved. There
certainly wasn't a lot of North American media interest in Iraq,
but by using the ten-year anniversary of the Kuwait invasion as

a hook—and given that it was the dog days of summer—I was able to persuade news editor Bruce Garvey at the *Ottawa Citizen* to publish a four-part series. With little money for expenses, my best hope was to break even on the trip. But the more I began to research Iraq and its people, the more I felt that this was a story that needed to be told.

FROM THE JORDANIAN capital of Amman, one had to charter a taxi—or take a chance on a bus—to make the gruelling thousand-kilometre trek across the Syrian Desert. Daytime temperatures at this time of year averaged 55°C. Depending on the make of vehicle and its condition, the one-way trip could take up to twenty-two hours. Although drivers preferred to make the crossing at night, competition for a fare meant they worked virtually around the clock. Those who drove the few modern Chevrolet Suburbans available were in great demand as they could make two ten-hour crossings every day with a mere four hours' downtime between trips.

For reasons known only to airline schedulers, flights from Europe to Jordan always seemed to arrive in the middle of the night. For the uninitiated like me, arriving at a strange airport, exhausted and without any means of arranging transportation in advance, the situation was a little intimidating. Although Iraqi shuttle drivers were not permitted direct access to the airport, there was no shortage of Jordanian taxis willing to take me to one of the depots for transport to Baghdad.

Because of the economic embargo against Iraq, no financial transactions could be conducted after crossing the border. There would be no way of using a credit card or traveller's cheques, or even of picking up a wire transfer. With no access to any banking services whatsoever in Iraq, there was no alternative but to travel with large quantities of cash. (Ironically, the only foreign currency accepted in Iraq at that time was the U.S. dollar.) For most travellers, the thought of carrying a large amount of cash is not reassuring, and in this case, anyone aware of my destination would also presume that I must be carrying all of my travel funds on me—in U.S. dollars.

Late in the night of August 1, 2000, while making my way by Jordanian taxi to the transport depot with a driver who spoke no English, my apprehension heightened as we drove for more than thirty minutes across nothing but empty desert. When we finally pulled into the shuttle depot, a variety of vehicles were parked in the lot. From battered old Chevrolet Coupes to brand new Suburbans, all were painted in the distinctive orange-and-white pattern that I would soon learn denoted Iraqi taxis.

Inside a small cement building, about a dozen drivers were sleeping on floor mats. My 3:00 AM arrival caused a commotion. From the back of the room, Mooky, the foreman, clapped his hands and yelled at the drivers to rouse themselves and clear a passage to his desk. As the drivers gathered around Mooky's desk, a tray of chai tea was brought in from a small anteroom. I had been told by Iraqi-Canadian acquaintances that a one-way passage to Baghdad should cost no more than US$100. Mooky's price, however, was five times that. With my Jordanian cabbie having already left, I found myself alone in the middle of nowhere, surrounded by a sullen-looking crowd—hardly a strong bargaining position. Since I was on an extremely tight budget and had no way of knowing what costs to expect over the course of my two-week trip, I bartered as best I could.

During the protracted negotiations the tousle-haired Mooky revealed that he had been educated in Belgrade and had fled Yugoslavia at the start of the 1999 air strikes. When I told him I had reported from inside Serbia and Kosovo during the NATO campaign, Mooky's attitude softened. We eventually agreed that

233

I would make the trip in an old Crown Victoria rather than a Suburban and that I would pay US$250 upfront for return passage.

As it turned out, my designated driver was the only one still sleeping on the office floor. Mooky had to prod him with his foot several times before he woke up. Unshaven and completely exhausted, the youngster was angered by the manner in which he had been awoken. He nevertheless accepted his assignment, and a beaming Mooky assured me that Mohammed was fit to make the twelve-hour drive.

There were still roughly three hours until dawn when we finally set out towards the Iraqi border. Mohammed spoke no English, but by using hand signals he repeatedly indicated I should climb into the back seat and go to sleep. Despite my own exhaustion, I had serious concerns about Mohammed's fatigue. More importantly, I still feared that I might end up robbed and murdered somewhere on that barren stretch of roadway.

The desert highway into Baghdad was like a scene from an old *Mad Max* movie. Strewn about the barren landscape were numerous hulks of vehicles that had either broken down or been damaged beyond repair in collisions presumably caused by driver fatigue. Passing motorists had stripped anything usable from the wrecks, often leaving nothing more than a skeletal chassis.

234

On a road running parallel to the eerily empty four-lane highway, a continual stream of petrol trucks hurtled along in both directions. At intervals, robed drivers would park their tankers in a cluster to create a brief, shady respite from the sun, scorching even in these mid-morning hours. Their colleagues, meanwhile, continued to rumble by in dust-raising columns that stretched across the horizon. For Iraq, this "rolling pipeline" constituted a precious link: in exchange for selling vast quantities of oil to Jordan at below-market prices, Iraq was able to trade for the essential goods prohibited under restrictive UN sanctions.

Ever since the invasion of Kuwait on August 2, 1990, the UN had imposed severe trade sanctions against Iraq. Following the military success of the Gulf War, the UN embargo had been tightened in an effort to destabilize Saddam Hussein's regime. Ten years later, although these measures had taken a terrible toll on the Iraqi people, Saddam remained firmly in control.

The crippling combined effects of the sanctions and the massive destruction caused by allied bombers during Operation Desert Storm were evident. Rotating power failures regularly blacked out entire districts of Baghdad for two-hour periods twice a day. With a bomb-damaged power grid and a shortage of spare turbine parts, the Iraqis had no choice but to tightly curb their use of electricity. In rural areas many people had been without power since 1991.

Rampant inflation had caused the devaluation of the Iraqi dinar (IQD) by an astounding 7,000 per cent. (In 1990, one IQD was the equivalent of US$3.60; by August 2000, 2,000 IQD were worth US$1.) Although aware of the exchange rate, I was shocked the first time I exchanged a US$100 bill into dinars at my hotel. With the largest denomination being a 250 IQD note, the teller handed me several four-inch-thick wads of cash. The money more than filled my briefcase, and the remaining bills made unsightly bulges in my pant pockets.

As a result of the complete ban on automobile imports, the streets of Baghdad were clogged with ancient relics—the newest cars were 1990 models. And thanks to ten years of sanctions, modern technology had bypassed Iraq. Cellphones were non-existent, and the Internet was a closely controlled, almost inaccessible resource. Use of the only Internet café in Baghdad required prior photo registration and security clearance from the Mukhabarat, Iraq's secret police.

After my safe arrival in Baghdad it did not take long for the

235

Mukhābarāt to find me. Although ostensibly working for the foreign ministry, Jabar Abu Marwan was actually a senior officer with Iraqi intelligence who had been assigned to be my "guide" during my stay. Short and slightly built, Jabar was hardly intimidating, yet his mere presence provoked fear in the average Iraqi. Like the rest of the population, he drove a broken-down old car that had no air conditioning. As a result of having spent several years as a diplomat at the Iraqi embassy in Ottawa, however, he had been able to procure several modern electronic goods for himself, not the least of which was a portable computer.

Although computers were banned by the embargo, spare parts were not. As a result, enterprising entrepreneurs had begun acquiring all the parts and then assembling them in Baghdad. It was a laborious process, but Iraqi merchants boasted that their finished products cost less and worked better than the few preassembled models available in Iraq.

In one decade, what was once a progressive, emerging middle-class society had been transformed into an impoverished and often desperate population. Immediately after the first Gulf War, hard-pressed Iraqis had been forced to find new ways to simply feed their families. Children were pulled from schools to help sell goods on the streets. To raise money, many families had no choice but to sell their heirlooms and prized furniture. Virtually overnight, Baghdad abounded with new auction houses, where desperate Iraqis would accept minimal bids on cherished belongings.

This situation was brought home to me one evening at a dinner party. My host was the older brother of my friend Najeeb. Najeeb had instructed Sami to look out for me while I was in Baghdad. The Shallals were Christian, and Jabar, my guide, was eager to accompany me to their home. Although he was a Shiite Muslim, Jabar had developed a taste for whisky during his stay

236

in Canada. The extended Shallal family was in attendance that evening, all of them eager to gawk at the Westerner, to try their limited English and to hear news of relatives in Canada.

Following an enormous feast, Sami's eldest son arrived—with dinner. Jabar politely explained that the first course had been a mere appetizer. When I told him I couldn't possibly eat another bite, Jabar dropped his voice to a whisper. "You had better make an attempt because this family sold a coffee table to buy you this food," he explained.

A former nuclear scientist, Sami had lost his career when the Israeli air force had attacked and destroyed Iraq's Tammuz reactors in a 1981 air strike. Although his family still lived in an upper-middle-class neighbourhood, Sami now operated a small stationery store. To make ends meet, the Shallals also relied on occasional donations from relatives living abroad. Seeing the extent to which this family would go to make me, a total stranger, feel welcome was enough to inspire me to eat another helping.

ONE OF MY first guided tours was to Baghdad's Saddam Central Teaching Hospital for Children, where I was surprised to meet a small delegation of British peace activists. We had not yet entered the cancer ward when a series of mournful cries filled the corridor. Slumped on the floor, an Iraqi woman wept inconsolably as a young orderly brushed past, carrying the lifeless form of her twelve-year-old son. Ravaged by leukemia for the past fourteen months, the boy's tiny body appeared grotesquely disfigured and frail.

I recognized a vulnerability in myself then that I had not previously known. Seeing that grief-stricken mother holding on to the orderly's leg as though trying to will back the life of her child, I was overcome. Although I knew I should record this image on camera, I simply couldn't. I froze. I could not bring

237

myself to take a photograph, and I was suddenly very aware that our little group was invading the privacy of this woman at a very painful moment. I could all too clearly envision Katherine and our son Kirk interposed in that scene, and it was overwhelming. As nurses and some of the British women in the group rushed to console the mother, I moved farther away. A team of orderlies entered the room and began to strip the sheets from the boy's bed, making room for the next patient.

Looking at the now-vacant bed were five other young patients and their mothers, all of whom seemed more apprehensive than upset by the boy's death. "They are waiting to see if they will be moved to the bed beside the door," said Dr. Basim al-Abili, chief of residents at the hospital. "They know the worst cases are moved there and that they are usually the next to die."

Thin and gaunt, the twenty-seven-year-old Doctor al-Abili looked at least a dozen years older. The stress of providing care on this death row for children had clearly taken a toll on him. Before the 1991 Gulf War, leukemia had been virtually non-existent in Iraq. By the summer of 2000, it was reaching alarming proportions: more than fifteen hundred cases had been diagnosed in children. "We have no modern technology to conduct bone marrow transplants or transfusions," Doctor al-Abili explained.

238 With access to such treatments, the remission rate for leukemia in developed countries is 60 to 80 per cent. For Iraqi doctors, the situation was difficult to accept. During the mid-1980s, Iraq's health care system had been one of the best in the Middle East. Unfortunately, the machines it needed were banned under the decade-long UN trade sanctions. Since the UN Security Council considered anything that produced radiation as potentially dual purpose (it might be used to make a weapon of mass destruction), radiation units were forbidden.

Tragically, there was mounting evidence that the coalition bombardment, including large quantities of depleted-uranium warheads used during Operation Desert Storm, may have caused widespread cancer. In a report issued in July 2000, the World Health Organization confirmed that the United States and Britain had, in fact, employed depleted-uranium shells against Iraq, and noted a potential link to the increased incidence of leukemia, in particular.

The UN's ban on dual-purpose items also applied to a large number of vaccines considered to be potential biological weapon agents. One direct result of the embargo on vaccines was the 1999 outbreak of polio, a disease that had been all but eliminated in the late 1980s. In a report issued by the UN Humanitarian Mission in Baghdad, the blame for the outbreak was placed squarely on UN Security Council sanctions.

Before the Gulf War, Iraq's pharmaceutical plants had produced and exported antibiotics throughout the Middle East. However, in the 1990s, Iraqi doctors were often unable to prevent routine ailments from becoming fatal.

Pregnant women were hard hit by the food shortages. The overcrowded wards of the neonatal intensive care unit at the Baghdad children's hospital were filled with premature babies and malnourished newborns. With no air conditioning (a result of the UN's ban on essential spare parts), the heat was almost unbearable. Still, because of the chronic shortage of nurses, all mothers were in attendance to watch over and fan their tiny babies.

In the room next to the neonatal unit, a husband tried to comfort his sobbing wife as she clutched the motionless body of their doll-sized infant. An orderly holding a blanket stood by patiently, waiting to wrap up the tiny corpse and take it away. Doctor al-Abili said that his staff used to cry with the families,

239

"but now we lose an average of three children a day. After a while, you are just numb."

The 1999 UNICEF child and maternal mortality survey revealed the scope of this humanitarian crisis. The incidence of malnutrition had doubled since 1989, while the mortality rate for children under the age of five had more than doubled to 131 per 1,000. "That amounts to nearly 500,000 children lost over the past ten years," explained Nasra al-Sadoon, editor of the *Baghdad Observer*. "In a population of 22 million, that means every family has suffered a loss."

Although al-Sadoon's comments to me were filled with anti-American rhetoric, the numbers she quoted were backed by independent UN reports. Incredibly, the U.S. State Department never questioned the death toll, nor did any representative ever publicly challenge the UN assertion that this was directly attributable to ongoing sanctions. In late 1995, when asked on the U.S. news program *60 Minutes* whether the U.S. policy towards Iraq could possibly justify the death of 500,000 children, Secretary of State Madeleine Albright didn't hesitate: "We think the price is worth it."

Children were not the only ones suffering under the sanctions and the war's aftermath. An estimated 1.5 million Iraqis had died in the 1990s as a direct result of the Gulf War and the ensuing embargo. In addition, many of the Iraqi soldiers who had fought in the Kuwait campaign were diagnosed with a variety of illnesses similar to those afflicting the Canadian and U.S. soldiers who were suffering from what has been termed Gulf War Syndrome.

Gulf War Syndrome was another primary motivation for my trip to Iraq. With everyone speculating that the soldiers' illnesses had been caused by the experimental anthrax vaccine they had received or by exposure to depleted uranium, it seemed that no one in the West had thought to ask how the Iraqis had fared.

Given that Iraq had not issued any anthrax vaccines and that its soldiers had fallen ill as well, it was obvious that the experimental drug was not the sole culprit.

At the end of my three-week fact-finding trip I filed my reports and thankfully headed back across the desert to Amman, Jordan.

WITH THE WORLD'S attention shifting from the aftermath of war in Afghanistan to the prospect of war in Iraq, in April 2002 I gladly accepted an invitation to attend the annual conference sponsored by the Baytol Hikma (House of Wisdom) in Baghdad. Although the theme was globalization and its effect on world economies—something outside my normal field of study—it was an opportunity to return to Iraq.

On the third day of the conference, a Mukhābarāt agent sought me out. "Your interview with the foreign minister has been cancelled," Ahmed said. "You are to come with me instead." Unwilling to leave the conference with this complete stranger, I insisted on being told our destination. "You are to dine with General Hasan, the head of the Mukhābarāt, and we are already late."

Still a little perturbed, I asked, "Do I have a choice?" Ahmed looked me in the eye and said flatly, "No."

Lunch had been arranged in a private room at the prestigious Hunting Club. General Majid Hasan al-Majid arrived in the company of a nervous-looking Mukhābarāt agent, Sami, clearly uncomfortable in the presence of his boss. Hasan, on the other hand, seemed relaxed. Wearing a brightly coloured Hawaiian shirt and a gold necklace, and sporting the typical Iraqi jet-black hair and moustache dye jobs, Hasan appeared harmless, even comical. Short and rather stout, the fifty-something head of intelligence had spent time in Washington, and his English was excellent.

Throughout the four-course meal only the general and I spoke, while Ahmed and Sami silently took notes. Surprisingly, Hasan

241

seemed to have a good grasp of the Canadian political scene and asked a number of questions about newly appointed Foreign Affairs Minister Bill Graham.

After the table had been cleared, Hasan lit a cigar, sat back in his chair and said matter-of-factly, "Iraq's army is fucked if the Americans attack. There is no way we can stop them. You have seen our troops, so you know what I'm saying is true."

While I understood perfectly, I could not believe the general's candour, particularly in front of subordinates who solemnly nodded in agreement. All of the Iraqi officials I had met to date had sputtered the party line that ultimate victory would be attained through loyal sacrifice and so on. However, when I asked Hasan if he would be prepared to go on record with his comments, he smiled and said, "I will deny I ever met you."

I soon learned, however, that the purpose of our meeting was for Hasan to convey to me Iraq's novel plan for victory through defeat. The idea was to create a humanitarian crisis of such magnitude that the world would be compelled to intervene, bringing any U.S. military intervention to a halt. Hasan proudly described the tactic as a copycat of the Albanian strategy in Kosovo. "There are nearly eight million inhabitants in Baghdad. If we keep only males of military age inside the city limits, we could push six million non-combatant refugees into the path of the Americans," he explained. "Even the U.S. military could not supply enough food and shelter for so many and still feed their own soldiers."

The Iraqis believed that Saddam Hussein could keep the moral high ground by claiming that the exodus was initiated to prevent civilians from becoming collateral damage. As the Americans struggled to feed so many displaced persons, the presence of foreign journalists would make the plight known the world over, further fuelling anti-war sentiment.

242

This plan to deliberately jeopardize the lives of so many of their own people indicated just how desperate Iraq's situation had become. However, I could not imagine how the United States could cope with such a strategic manoeuvre as the massive flow of refugees and the global backlash.

Throughout our discussion Hasan occasionally directed his underlings to pass along certain orders to various cabinet ministers. Curious to learn where exactly he fit into the command structure, I asked Hasan to explain his level of authority. Amused by the question, Ahmed and Sami listened as the general replied, "Let's just say I can get things accomplished."

From then on I could easily identify General Hasan in the televised images of Saddam's Revolutionary Command Council; more often than not, the head of Iraqi intelligence sat right next to the president.

IN EARLY AUGUST 2002, the U.S. Joint Chiefs of Staff announced that they had formally approved a war plan for intervention in Iraq. Discussion in the western media shifted decisively from *if* to *when* a second Gulf War would begin, and President George W. Bush made it clear that his administration was intent on enforcing a regime change in Iraq. In fact, he said the buildup of U.S. forces in the Persian Gulf was already underway.

World opinion, it seemed, mattered little to this Bush administration. When the United States failed to put forward a strong enough case for intervention, France, China and Russia all said they would use their Security Council vetoes to prevent the United States and Britain from obtaining a UN mandate for the attack. To give the appearance of continued diplomacy, the United States and Britain publicly maintained that by refusing to readmit the UN weapons inspectors, Iraq was in violation of the

1991 ceasefire agreement. The two superpowers urged that a new resolution be passed, authorizing the use of military force.

Neither the European Union nor NATO would lend their support to a U.S.-led attack on Iraq. Even the Arab countries that had been long considered staunch supporters of America, such as Saudi Arabia, were unwilling to back Bush. This limited the buildup of U.S. forces in the Persian Gulf to Kuwait and Qatar. Nevertheless, the U.S. president was determined to wage war on Iraq—with or without allies.

Although I knew that September would be too hot for the launch of a ground invasion in Iraq, I had a hunch that Bush might use the first anniversary of September 11, 2001, to send Saddam a message. While many journalists headed to New York City to cover commemorative ceremonies, I booked a flight to Baghdad. By the pool at the Al-Rasheed Hotel I bumped into Toby Dodge, a British academic expert on Middle Eastern affairs whom I had met at the previous year's Baytol Hikma conference. He was finalizing research for his book and hoped my premonition of a September 11 air attack would prove false.

However, at 10:30 that evening, as Iraqi air defences began pounding tracer fire into the air in the western suburbs of Baghdad, it appeared as though the United States would beat the anniversary by four days. Hearing the distant thumping of cannons, Dodge brought a bottle of whisky to my room and invited me to "enjoy the fireworks." Over the next thirty minutes the gunners concentrated their fire on one unseen target after another. But there were no explosions or bomb blasts to indicate that the Iraqi capital had actually come under attack. Since air raid sirens had not sounded in the downtown core of the city, most residents appeared unperturbed.

From my balcony Dodge and I watched four bikini-clad Russian prostitutes cavorting in the pool below as rockets and tracers arced skyward in the distance. The women were part of a rotating harem kept by Saddam Hussein's eldest son, Uday, and their semi-clad poolside antics had become the gossip du jour for foreign correspondents staying at the Al-Rasheed. As for the half-hour of anti-aircraft fire, either jittery gunners were shooting at shadows or, more likely, the United States was conducting a test of the Iraqi air defence system by using unarmed drone aircraft.

Whatever was going on in the airspace over Baghdad, it was not the first raid in George Bush's promised war. On that same night, up to one hundred American and British warplanes pounded Iraqi military installations in the isolated village of Rutba, sixty kilometres southwest of Baghdad. There were reports of serious damage and an undisclosed number of casualties. With the war of words mounting between Washington and Baghdad, allied air strikes inside the southern no-fly zone had become an almost daily occurrence. The number of planes involved in this raid, however, was said to be the largest in a single attack since Operation Desert Storm.

Rutba was also close to the Jordanian border, and a large number of American ground troops were already in Jordan conducting desert warfare training. Although the Jordanian government maintained that the U.S. manoeuvres were a routine annual exercise and not part of a buildup to an invasion of Iraq, Sami and Mohammed claimed to have proof that the Americans were using this deployment to conduct reconnaissance and to establish special forces bases inside western Iraq.

As the military action intensified, it seemed that Iraqi efforts to resolve the crisis diplomatically were floundering. A hoped-for intervention by Russia at the end of August failed to materialize, and a crucial summit between U.S. President George W. Bush and British Prime Minister Tony Blair took place a few days after the Rutba attack. At this meeting Blair brought forward British intelligence's dossier on Iraq's weapons programs while Bush shared the CIA's files. Despite this deliberate showboating for the public, it seemed that only the timing of the intervention was still in question. Nevertheless, some Iraqi officials remained optimistic that armed conflict could be avoided.

"I don't believe that the Iraqis understand the urgency of the matter and realize how high the stakes have gotten," said Dodge, who had spent the previous week conducting frustrating discussions with top officials from Iraq's Ministry of Foreign Affairs. "The time for diplomacy has almost expired. This is no time for Iraq to begin bargaining for a better position."

Tariq Aziz, Iraq's deputy prime minister, had just tabled a new proposal with UN Secretary General Kofi Annan, stating that the country would submit to further weapons inspections but only after nineteen preconditions had been met by the United Nations. In addition to the lifting of the eleven-year-old economic sanctions and the setting of a time limit on inspections, Iraq demanded financial compensation for the war damage it had suffered in 1991.

As one of several top European academics in Baghdad, Dodge was trying to help broker a peaceful resolution while there was still time. "In my opinion, the only option is for Iraq to submit to weapons inspections with a security guarantee from a third party, such as Russia or France," he said. "Unfortunately, no one seems to be listening."

The Iraqi media and government spokesmen had played up reports of international anti-war protests and, in particular, anti-U.S. protests. Unfortunately, those responsible for broadcasting the propaganda had apparently started believing their own fabrications. "The people of the world are not so stupid," said Director General Uday al-Tai, the Iraqi government's senior press relations officer. "They know that the U.S. is not justified in attacking Iraq, and that is why you see so many American flags being burned and trampled all over the globe."

Tall, thin and immaculately dressed, al-Tai cut a dapper figure, and he was eager to conduct interviews with the foreign press. There were some forty international journalists registered in Iraq, but when you discounted camera crews and producers, only a dozen reporters were in place. Officials from the Ministry of Information had deluded themselves into believing that their messages were being heard around the world. Later, when I spoke privately with al-Tai, I didn't have the heart to tell him that more than three thousand journalists were converging on New York City to commemorate the first anniversary of September 11.

A number of international delegations had also come to Baghdad in early September to help boost morale. One of the most politically significant was a contingent of Turkish politicians. Bringing their own entourage of journalists, the Turks wanted to publicly demonstrate their opposition to a U.S.-led war. This was significant, not only because Turkey was a member of NATO, but because this country's shared border with Iraq was considered one of the few "friendly" invasion routes for coalition troops into the country.

Should this wave of international support fail to achieve a last-minute diplomatic solution, Baghdad authorities were now more willing than ever to fight. In a public address Saddam Hussein said, "While we pray that war will never happen . . . if the U.S. attacks Iraq, then the Iraqis will fight in an extraordinary manner to ensure their defeat."

AS AMERICAN AND British governments tried to convince the world that Saddam's weapons programs posed "a clear and

247

present danger" to global security, the last thing they needed was former UN weapons inspector Scott Ritter undermining their arguments.

Since resigning in protest from his UN position in 1998, the former marine lieutenant colonel had embarked on a one-man international crusade to educate the world about the suffering of Iraqis under the sanctions. Although he had returned to Baghdad on several occasions, this trip was special: it would be the first time a foreigner had ever made a presentation to the Iraqi National Assembly.

Although we had spoken on the phone and exchanged e-mails, our first meeting was in the lobby of the Al-Rasheed Hotel. Ritter was on his way to the parliamentary building to deliver his speech, and tall and muscular, he still looked the part of the all-American marine. His comments, however, were bluntly critical of the Bush administration's push for war. "Given the situation today, it is impossible to conjure up any scenario that would justify military action against Iraq," he said in his opening remarks. "The United States' case for a war is based on fear and rhetoric, rather than facts and truth."

In addition to the two-hundred-plus Iraqi politicians in attendance, all the Baghdad-based journalists, including the Turkish contingent, were on hand to record Ritter's comments. Ritter made it clear that he was making his address to the Iraqi National Assembly as a private citizen and not as a formal U.S. representative. Despite his harsh criticism of the American policy towards Iraq, Ritter made it clear that he was proud of his country's Bill of Rights, which allowed him to make such public statements.

Ritter told parliamentary officials that the Iraqi flag and poster of Saddam would have to be removed from behind the podium where he would speak. At first the Iraqis refused, but when the assembled press corps pressed for an explanation of the delay, they acquiesced. From the outset Ritter made it evident that although he disagreed with U.S. policy, he was not in Baghdad to side with the Iraqi leadership.

Convinced that the United States was "poised on the brink of making a historical mistake," Ritter said he could not sit idly by "as my country behaves in this fashion." Noting that the first anniversary of September 11 was just days away, he asked the Iraqi leaders to understand how fear was clouding the average American's judgement. "This fear has fuelled a war fever, and it has been exploited by those with a dangerous agenda."

Acknowledging that his inspection team had conducted the "most intrusive" searches ever performed in a country, Ritter stated that Iraq's weapons programs had been "90 to 95 per cent decommissioned" when the inspectors were withdrawn in December 1998. Of the remaining capacity, he explained that the material was strictly "technical, and in no way posed a threat . . . Since there is no proof that Iraq possesses weapons of mass destruction, and because there is no evidence linking Iraq to terror attacks against America," he continued, "the rationale behind a U.S. military strike remains based purely on speculation. And there is no basis in international law for a country to go to war based on speculation." The former marine added that should evidence be subsequently uncovered that showed Iraq posed "a clear and present danger to America, [he] would volunteer [his] services to counter that threat." On issues of the past, Ritter said there "was blame enough for everyone—including the Iraqis." Such previous violations as the gassing of Kurdish rebels and the 1990 invasion of Kuwait made it easy for "the average American to now believe every allegation they hear pertaining to Iraq, whether or not it can be backed up by hard fact."

249

The loudest objections expressed by the Iraqi National Assembly came when Ritter tabled his recommendation for resolving the current crisis by having Iraq "submit itself immediately to unconditional and unfettered resumption of the UN weapons inspections." This was the only way that it could "eliminate the remaining doubts of Americans, which the fearmongers are manipulating," he noted.

Ritter's second recommendation was that the Iraqis should "embrace the U.S. suffering [from September 11] and make it clear to the world that although they are a Muslim country, Iraq in no way sponsors such terrorist activity." Acknowledging that Iraq had suffered the loss of 1.5 million people over the past decade, Ritter urged Iraqis, nonetheless, to extend their empathy to the families of the 2,700 Americans who had perished in the World Trade Center attack. Noting that Iraq had long since been engaged in suppressing the very same Islamic fundamentalists that had attacked the United States, Ritter urged the assembly to let the world know "that Iraq stands shoulder to shoulder with them in the fight against terror." Adopting a defensive posture and preparing for a possible war allowed "U.S. warmongers to distort [this] defiance into aggressive intent," he advised the Iraqis.

His most controversial remark was that Iraq must be prepared to accept a negotiated solution to the Palestinian question. (Saddam had remained a steadfast supporter of the Palestinian cause, and Iraq still refused to recognize the state of Israel.) "It is time that you stop being more Palestinian than the Palestinians," he said. This statement, once translated, brought a chorus of disapproval from the assembly. Ritter also admitted for the first time that his weapons inspectors had been used to spy on Iraq. He told the Iraqi parliamentarians that they were justified in their concern about readmitting inspection teams because, in the past, the access granted by the Iraquis had been used to violate the UN mandate.

Ritter said that his former supervisor, Richard Butler, had ordered him to "provoke an incident with the Iraqis" in 1998. When Ritter refused, Butler had personally ordered the withdrawal of the inspection teams from Iraq. Subsequently, American and British forces launched air strikes against more than one hundred targets purported to be Iraqi weapon stores. According to Ritter, however, "the majority of the sites targeted had been, in fact, directed against the Iraqi leadership, not their weapons capability." Moreover, "acquiring those specific targets had been assisted by the inspection teams."

Although the United States had always maintained that Saddam had kicked the inspectors out of Iraq, the facts supported Ritter's version of events. In October 1998, the U.S. Congress passed the Iraqi Liberation Act (HR 4655), which was reluctantly signed by President Bill Clinton. The reason for his hesitation was that, while previously working in conjunction with Iraqi opposition groups, the CIA had suffered a number of embarrassing reversals in Iraq. The most notable occurred in 1996 when the CIA was heavily supporting Jalal Talabani's Patriotic Union of Kurdistan against rival warlord Massoud Barzani's Kurdistan Democratic Party. Not wanting to be pushed out, Barzani made a separate deal with Saddam Hussein. In a surprise strike north, Saddam's tanks assisted the Democratic Party's *peshmerga* fighters in pushing into Patriotic Union territory.

Unable to use air power in the no-fly zone to support one Kurdish faction against another, the U.S. could not intervene. As a result, Saddam's agents successfully dismantled the CIA's operation in northern Iraq. Without their own sources in place, the United States had put additional pressure on Ritter to use

251

his UN access to gather intelligence on the Iraqi president's whereabouts.

Despite this startling admission, Ritter believed that Iraq could trust a new set of inspectors. "The world knows about the abuse of access which occurred, and they would be carefully monitoring the situation," he said. "In this case they would not tolerate similar action."

DESPITE SADDAM HUSSEIN'S official calls to convert Iraqi cities into fortresses, no real defensive preparations seemed to have been made in Baghdad. The few measures underway were aimed more at boosting civilian morale than at providing any real military defence.

Dr. Hameed Saeed, director of the Baytol Hikma institute, was a prominent academic and a respected writer. Grey-haired, with a hefty paunch, the sixty-one-year-old had to spend three hours every morning doing military training, basic drills and rudimentary weapons practice. With the United States threatening war, Iraq had begun recalling its nearly three million reservists to active duty. The reservists in Saeed's unit were of all ages and included his son. "I'm a pacifist by nature, not a soldier," he explained. "If Iraq were declaring war on the United States, I would be the first one in the streets to hold a peace protest. But this is something different. If Iraq is attacked, then everyone must fight."

Iraqi border posts had been reinforced in response to increasing U.S. demands for a regime change, and manpower had been mobilized from the reserves. One call-up was Mohammed Noori, a forty-two-year-old father of four who had spent the previous twenty years working for the Iraqi Ministry of Information. The last time Noori had been recalled briefly to active duty was during the 1991 Gulf War in the air defence of Baghdad. Now, after having received his latest orders only a week earlier, Noori would spend the next two months bolstering border patrols along the Kurdish-controlled provinces of northern Iraq. In the event of war this was considered to be one of the most likely U.S. invasion routes.

"I have not been in uniform in twelve years," he said. "The Americans are professional soldiers, and they have the best equipment in the world." His voice trailed off before he nervously added, "Nevertheless, this is our country and we will fight them if necessary."

After years of embargo the Iraqi army was forced to cannibalize many of its tanks just to keep others serviceable. The shortage of replacement parts also prohibited them from conducting large-scale training exercises. While the best of Iraq's equipment was issued to the elite Republican Guard units, even they were hit hard by the shortages. With tightened security in effect throughout Baghdad, Republican Guard units, distinct in their desert camouflage, could often be seen patrolling the main streets in civilian pickup trucks mounted with light machine guns.

FOLLOWING THE CAMP David summit meeting on September 7, 2002, it was clear that British Prime Minister Tony Blair was fully aboard President George Bush's war wagon. For their part, Iraqi information officials were doing their best to undermine American efforts to drum up a coalition force. When Pentagon officials released a satellite photograph of a sixty-truck convoy purportedly leaving a chemical weapons plant, the Iraqi Ministry of Information moved quickly to squelch the allegation. Rounding up the tiny cadre of foreign journalists still in Baghdad on September 10, they drove us out to the site in question.

While the Iraqis openly admitted there had been a sixty-truck convoy at the site, we were able to report first-hand that the building was, in fact, a warehouse containing nothing more than tea,

253

sugar and flour. The vehicles in the satellite photograph had been delivering rations under the direction of the UN oil-for-food relief program. Given the time difference, the sluggish Iraqi bureaucracy and the increased security measures in effect in Baghdad, however, the news was forty-eight hours old by the time the Pentagon claim had been convincingly refuted. Needless to say, the correction made barely a ripple in the press.

In the interim, a second, more damaging satellite photograph had been released. This one, attributed to British intelligence, purported to show that Iraq was resurrecting its nuclear arms project. According to U.S. officials, Iraqis had rebuilt a research facility at the bombed-out Tammuz nuclear reactor site. It was here that the Israeli air force had struck in 1981, on the eve of the Iraqis making the reactor operational. The reactor was destroyed in that raid, but Iraq had contrived to continue developing nuclear technology.

When the Gulf War began in 1991, the Iraqis had a much smaller reactor, Tammuz II, in full operation. During the Operation Desert Storm air raids, this nuclear plant was targeted and destroyed. Recognizing that they could not let these new allegations stand unchallenged, the Iraqis again rounded up foreign journalists and arranged a visit to the site.

254   During our three-hour visit they opened all the buildings shown in the Pentagon's satellite photograph to media inspection. From the display of fertilizers and medicinal products, the facilities appeared to be used for agricultural and pharmaceutical research. The buildings contained none of the sophisticated hardware one would expect to find at a nuclear arms development site. In fact, the conditions were so primitive that we questioned whether the nuclear waste from the previously destroyed reactors was not creating an environmental hazard. In

the bathrooms, signs posted in English and Arabic explained how to flush the toilets—hardly the sort of direction one would expect top-level rocket scientists to require.

For the reporters who visited the Tammuz site, the openness of the Iraqi officials and the evidence provided brought the Pentagon's allegations into question. But then, as one of the British journalists quipped, "not being scientists, we wouldn't recognize anthrax from applesauce." We could report what we had witnessed, but contrary to the Iraqis' intent, we could not conclude that no nuclear research was being conducted at the site.

Many of the officials at the Ministry of Information were disappointed that our reports reflected this doubt. "What more can we do to prove this point to you?" asked an exasperated Uday al-Tai. In response, I said that, in my opinion, the only way to prevent a war at this eleventh hour was for Iraq to convince the world it had nothing to hide. Such reassurance, I said, could be provided only by qualified weapons inspectors, not a bumbling bunch of journalists.

ALTHOUGH PRESIDENT BUSH did not use the September 11 anniversary to launch a punitive attack against Iraq, a group of Commonwealth reporters staying in Baghdad decided to have a party that night—just in case. As a matter of courtesy, British, Australian and Canadian journalists invited their Turkish colleagues to attend.

255

Included in the Turkish delegation were Barcin Yinanc, whom I had met at the Hotel Moskva during the bombing in Belgrade, and Zeynep Tugrul, a reporter with the Turkish government newspaper *Sabah*. As a diplomatic correspondent in the Middle East, the fluent English-speaking Tugrul would prove to be a valuable contact.

We had presumed that since they were Muslims, the Turks would be teetotallers. To our surprise, they made a serious dent in our whisky stock beneath a dense pall of acrid blue cigarette smoke. Toby Dodge arrived late because he had been summoned to a meeting with Tariq Aziz. He excitedly told us about his ninety-minute tête-à-tête with the deputy prime minister. "They finally get it," he said. Over cigars and brandy, Aziz had confided to the British academic that Iraq was going to waive its demands and allow the weapons inspectors to return unconditionally.

On September 9, Aziz had returned from a meeting with UN Secretary-General Kofi Annan in Johannesburg, while Foreign Affairs Minister Naji Sabri had flown back from an Arab summit in Cairo. Both ministers had brought back some bitter truths for Saddam. Apparently, the British had met with French President Jacques Chirac and had convinced the French to support a framework agreement that would be in place by September 20. Under the terms of this proposal, Iraq would be given a three-week ultimatum to comply with weapons inspections.

This about-turn by the French shocked the Iraqis, particularly since it came on the heels of the Russian pullout. Over the previous few months, the Russians had signed nearly $40 billion worth of trade agreements with Iraq. The Iraqis had naively believed that this would buy them Russia's protection at the United Nations. Instead, the Russians had used the hefty price tag as a bargaining chip with the Americans, effectively putting a price tag on their Security Council veto.

Since it was generally agreed that the Chinese would never stand alone on the issue, the betting was that the Americans and the British would be cleared to obtain a UN resolution. Sabri had equally sobering news from the Arab council. While the council publicly denounced the American intervention, the consensus had been that Iraq must submit to new inspections. Dodge went on to explain that the only card the Iraqis could play would be relenting at the eleventh hour, thereby taking the wind out of Bush's sails. After months of international arm-twisting, Bush had finally sold the world on the need to resume weapons inspections.

The battle cry for weapons inspections quickly replaced the battle cry for regime change. With no concrete evidence of weapons of mass destruction to offer, America's strongest card became Saddam's refusal to accept inspections. If Saddam had nothing to hide, then why was he hiding it, spokesmen for the U.S. State Department asked at every opportunity. By agreeing to weapons inspections, Aziz and his colleagues knew that they would at least pull the rug out from under the American rhetoric.

The gamble worked—temporarily. When the UN inspection teams were readmitted, the impetus for further action against Iraq disappeared. Saddam had effectively stripped George Bush of allied support and all but guaranteed that the Americans would be denied a UN resolution against Iraq.

ONE MONTH LATER, in an attempt to show the world that he still had the faithful support of the Iraqi people, Saddam decided to hold a referendum on his leadership. Billed by Baghdad officials as a "demonstration of honest democracy," there could be no doubt that Saddam would be re-elected for another seven-year term in office: he was the only candidate on the ballot.

Nevertheless, Baath party officials staged large-scale political rallies across the country, and the main thoroughfares of Baghdad were adorned with gaudy, multicoloured election banners. Although portraits and statues of Saddam had always been prominently displayed in public areas, photographs of the president were now seen on every corner and storefront window. Large, hand-painted signs, many written in English, proclaimed "Yes, Yes to President Saddam Hussein" and "We Love the Leader," and

257

songs and poems paying tribute to the glory of Iraq and the vir-
tues of Saddam were played repeatedly over public loudspeakers.

To witness the presidential referendum, nearly one thousand
international observers and media had been invited to visit polling stations throughout the country. I had been surprised to
receive a personalized invitation from Vice-President Taha Yassin
Ramadan. Sami and his partner Mohammed greeted me when I
arrived at the airport. They apologized for General Hasan who,
they said, would be unable to meet with me during this visit
because, as head of Iraqi intelligence, he would be preoccupied
with monitoring the elections.

Although most of the invited foreign observers were from
neighbouring Arab countries, a large number of western journalists took advantage of the referendum to obtain an entry visa
into Iraq. Since the United States had stepped up its calls for a
regime change, security in the capital had been tightened and
the issuance of visas to media severely restricted. The sudden
influx of foreigners overtaxed Iraq's unwieldy bureaucracy. With
as many as four fully loaded, wide-bodied aircraft arriving daily
at Saddam International airport from Syria and Jordan, there
were interminable delays at customs and immigration checkpoints. The airport had been restored to only marginal capacity,
and the airport staff were accustomed to no more than a dozen
flights a week. As a result, some travellers had to spend up to four
hours just to have their documents processed.

In the days leading up to the referendum, Saddam Hussein
was committed to staging a demonstration aimed at convincing
the international community that he maintained a popular mandate, thereby undermining support for the U.S. campaign to oust
him. Many Middle East experts attending the referendum were
skeptical. Yoshiaki Sasaki, a senior research fellow with a Tokyo
foundation that specialized in Iraq studies, had been invited to

258

participate in the referendum as an official observer. We had first met on the flight from Amman, and due to the backlog at the airport in Baghdad, we were able to discuss the Iraqi situation at length. "The Iraqis claim that Saddam Hussein is not a dictator," said Sasaki. "Unfortunately, they don't understand the basic tenets upon which western democracies are based."

Under the terms of the referendum, Saddam's nomination was first put forward by the members of his Revolutionary Command Council, a group largely comprising Saddam's closest associates. It was, in fact, the cabinet that ruled Iraq. Following his nomination, the Iraqi National Assembly—all members of the ruling Baath party—approved Saddam's presidency in a unanimous vote. Under Iraq's constitution, the presidential candidacy had to be upheld by a public referendum within sixty days.

On the Royal Jordanian flight I had been fortunate enough to be seated next to a surprisingly outspoken resident of Baghdad. "I wish that he would step down from power immediately, but tomorrow I will cast a vote for Saddam Hussein," a former-pilot-turned-merchant told me. "This is not an exercise in democracy; it is simply a matter of Iraqis impressing the authorities. With the U.S. policy, the only way we can avoid complete destruction is if the current regime capitulates, but that will never happen. In the meantime we must somehow survive." Having worked for Iraqi Airways, he had been forced to seek an alternate career when the Americans imposed their post-1991 no-fly zones over Iraq. Despite the sanctions and without any Baath party loyalty to fall back on, he had managed to build a tannery business and a poultry farm. His English was excellent, and he invited me to visit his home anytime I was in Baghdad.

At a pre-referendum press conference, Mohammed Saeed al-Sahhaf, Iraq's minister of information, made the first of many classic denials to assembled western media. He categorically

259

denied that the leadership vote was being held to undermine President Bush's push for regime change. "We do not submit to outside pressures; that would be stupid," said al-Sahaf. "The people of Iraq will send their message of support for Saddam whether or not there is a threat of war. Whether this will be accepted in the West is irrelevant." However, when asked to explain why the majority of the election banners were in English and displayed in front of hotels housing foreigners, the minister refused to answer.

A large number of Turkish journalists were in attendance as well, and their questions were entirely concerned with the voting in Kirkuk. When I asked Zeynep Tugrul why they were so focused on this northern city, she replied, "Because that's were the Turkmen live." My next question was, "What's a Turkmen?" She patiently explained that there were approximately two million indigenous Turks in Iraq and that they could trace their roots in this region back approximately fifteen hundred years. I had always simply presumed that Turks came from Turkey, but in a quick *Reader's Digest* version of the region's history, Zeynep outlined how the Turkic tribes originated in Central Asia—present-day Turkmenistan. As a semi-nomadic people and a fierce warrior race, they had gradually migrated both east towards China and west to the current borders of Turkey. Those Turkmen living in northern Iraq were descendents of Turkic tribesmen who chose to settle and develop the land rather than seek further conquests. Although their population had been interspersed with both Arab and Kurdish residents, the Turkmen formed a narrow buffer zone between these two major ethnic groups.

Handouts provided by the Iraqi government officials showed 11,798,000 eligible voters, all residing in the fifteen southern provinces still under the central authority of Baghdad. Although technically part of sovereign Iraq, the three northern provinces—populated by an ethnic Kurdish majority and Turk-men minority—were under UN protection.

The nearly three million Kurds residing in the northern provinces had broken all ties with Baghdad in 1991. The two rival warlords—Massoud Barzani, leader of the Kurdistan Demo-cratic Party, and Jalal Talabani, leader of the Patriotic Union of Kurdistan—controlled this territory and aspired to establish an independent Kurdistan. When asked about the omission of these provinces from the voter list, al-Sahhaf replied: "The Kurdish voters who wish to support Saddam Hussein will be welcomed at polling stations across Iraq." As for the number of votes he expected to be cast, al-Sahhaf made a prophetic prediction: "There is no need for estimations. You will see the positive results."

THE CELEBRATIONS IN Baghdad continued into the next day. In anticipation of Saddam's win with a 100 per cent landslide majority, a state holiday had been declared so that all Iraqis could celebrate the "joyous triumph of honest democracy in Iraq." In floodlit stadiums in central Baghdad, thousands of rev-ellers were televised chanting praise to Saddam and dancing to the music of top-name Iraqi pop singers. In the rest of the coun-try, however, such festivities were uncommon. In the southern city of Basra, for example, there were no demonstrations at all of patriotic fervour.

Since arriving in Iraq, I had repeatedly asked Sami and Mohammed for authorization to visit Basra again, and they always assured me that this would not be a problem. I had visited this predominantly Shiite city on my first trip to Iraq in 2000, and given the Mukhābarāt agents' failure to raise any objections now, I booked myself on a ridiculously cheap (US$20) Iraqi Air-ways flight and headed off to the airport in the early morning hours. I knew that travelling without a handler—and without express permission to leave the capital—would be pushing the Mukhābarāt's patience, and I fully intended to beg forgiveness upon my return.

Although technically still flying within the U.S.-enforced southern no-fly zone, Iraqi Airways had started running daily flights to Basra about twelve months earlier. Twice a day, the U.S. Air Force and the Iraqi pilots played out the same ritual. "As soon as we cross into the no-fly zone, we are contacted by a U.S. AWACS radio operator," said Abid Ali Abud, a captain with Iraqi Airways. "They tell us that we are illegally entering U.S. airspace and should turn around immediately. We reply that this is sovereign Iraqi airspace, and continue to Basra." Although U.S. F-16 fighters stationed in Kuwait were frequently scrambled to escort passenger planes, to date no aggressive action had been taken. "The Americans will not dare shoot down a plane full of civilians," said Ali Abud. However, U.S. airplanes had already launched several major air strikes against the airport at Basra, completely destroying its radar system.

One of the first things I noticed on entering Basra was that there was little evidence of the pre-referendum banners and portraits of Saddam that had adorned Baghdad's main streets. The few posters that proclaimed "We love Saddam" were displayed only on federal buildings and only in Arabic. Knowing that none of the international delegates and journalists would be invited to Basra to monitor the referendum, Saddam's Baath party had targeted its campaign messages in the capital.

Although the previous day's official poll results had showed no dip in regional support for Saddam, many of the Iraqi officials I spoke to secretly admitted that there was little love for the Baghdad regime in Basra. As General Hasan had acknowledged during our earlier conversation, in the event of an invasion by the United States "the Iraqi army could not expect to hold the ground south of Baghdad itself, as local conscript soldiers are unlikely to put up much of a fight."

Many residents of Basra openly voiced these sentiments. Photojournalist Nabil al-Gorani told me, "The people of Basra are simply tired of war. It seems that we are always at the centre of these conflicts, and as a result, we suffer the most." Al-Gorani could barely recall a time in his life when his hometown had not been subject to regular air strikes. During the decade-long Iran-Iraq War of the 1980s, Basra was the most contested battleground. Strategically located on the Shatt al-Arab waterway, Basra was also the major logistic staging area for Saddam's ill-fated 1990 invasion of Kuwait. During the air strikes of Operation Desert Storm, allied bombers regularly pounded Basra. When the defeated Iraqi army fled north out of Kuwait, the coalition ground forces followed them to the outskirts of Basra, leaving behind a trail of death and destruction.

In response to the U.S. threat of regime change in Baghdad, Saddam Hussein inevitably issued brave statements about Iraqis resisting American aggression until "the last drop of blood," and many of the younger generation, those who had not experienced or were too young to remember the Gulf War, professed to embrace this defiance. For the residents of Basra, however, daily reminders of Iraq's human sacrifice in recent wars were a fact of life. Along the highway to Kuwait, thousands of destroyed armoured vehicles stood as grim testimony to the lethality of allied air power. Along the banks of the Shatt al-Arab lay rusting hulks of half-sunken tankers and warships, some from the Iran-Iraq War, a few actually dating back to the First World War.

Another reason for resentment towards Baghdad was the comparative poverty that southern Iraqis endured. The Shiite Muslim majority of this region had never been particularly loyal to

Saddam Hussein's primarily Sunni Muslim regime. At the end of the Gulf War, Iran-backed Shiite rebels had staged a bloody revolt in Basra. During the few days in which extremists held Basra, they exercised a terrible and violent vengeance on Saddam's captured Baath party officials. Many prisoners were reportedly tied between two cars and then ripped in half by the accelerating vehicles, to the cheers of fanatic onlookers.

After Baghdad re-established its authority in Basra, many residents felt they had been deliberately shortchanged in the national oil revenue distribution. "Admittedly, the twelve years of sanctions have severely hurt all of Iraq. However, we don't see the same number of palaces, public buildings or federal investment projects as in Baghdad," said al-Gorani. "The people here in Basra feel cut off completely from the televised images we see of Baghdad."

Things were even worse for the Marsh Arab tribes that had joined in the revolt. Following the return of Saddam's troops, Iraqi engineering efforts intensified to complete the drainage of the marshes—first begun by the British in the early 1950s—where the Euphrates and Tigris rivers meet at the Shatt al-Arab delta. This effectively took away much of the natural habitat that the Marsh Arabs needed to exist.

Although only 445 kilometres from the capital, Basra had remained relatively isolated from the control of central Baghdad. The national telephone system, largely destroyed during Operation Desert Storm, had not yet been repaired, and few lines were available between the two cities. Since my first trip to Basra, things had not improved: most senior Basra bureaucrats still had no way of calling Baghdad.

As a result, when I tried to visit the children's hospital, the director would not allow me to enter the facility without express

264

permission from his superiors. Unable to phone Baghdad, he explained he would have to draft a letter and wait for a reply. Although local government officials were still willing to rely on Saddam's regime for direction, I got the distinct impression that Baghdad's iron grip on the local population was starting to slip.

With U.S. ground forces already building up in Kuwait and President Bush armed with congressional approval for a military strike, most residents of Basra believed the next bloody round of fighting was only weeks away. Ali, a manager at the Sheraton Hotel in Basra, was nonplussed. "Everyone in Baghdad is yelling 'Nam, nam, Saddam' for the referendum," he said, "but they would be just as enthusiastically shouting 'Nam, nam, Tommy Franks' if the U.S. launched an attack."

Most Iraqis were well informed of America's proposal to establish a military command structure within an occupied Iraq. U.S. Middle East Commander Tommy Franks had been named as the most likely candidate for this post. With his hotel's occupancy down below 20 per cent, Ali said he would gladly open his doors to American soldiers. "Chanting slogans and professing a love for Saddam does not put food on my hungry family's table."

That evening, during my return flight to Baghdad, the tiny Iraqi Airways 727 encountered terrible turbulence and we landed at the airport in a full-blown desert storm. Throughout the night, gusting winds ripped at the shutters of my window while, in the streets below, merchants' kiosks were knocked flat. Swirling dust filled the air like a dense fog, giving the moonlit sky a strange orange glow.

When the winds abated in the morning, remnants of referendum banners and posters of Saddam were hanging in shredded tatters from branches and lampposts. For the superstitious doorman at the Sheraton, a desert storm blowing in to tear down

Saddam Hussein's proclamations of a continued presidency was a singularly bad omen. "This was Allah's will," whispered a bell-hop as he surveyed the garbage littering the streets. "Saddam has angered even God."

I didn't know it but I was about to face my own personal storm, one brought on by the Mukhābarāt. When I filed my story about the mood in Basra, I titled it "Iraqis Weary of War" and deliberately buried at the bottom the quote about Iraqis being just as willing to chant "*Nam, Nam,* General Tommy Franks" as they were to shout out support for Saddam. *Ottawa Citizen* editor Bruce Garvey, however, decided to play up that part of the article. The published headline read "No Love for Saddam in Basra: Unhappy Residents Debunk Claims of 100 per cent Voter Support." Upon reading the "offensive article," the Iraqi chargé d'affaires in Ottawa immediately faxed a copy of it to the Ministry of Information in Baghdad. Mohammed al-Sahhaf himself demanded an explanation from my handlers as to how I came to be in Basra without his department's knowing about it, let alone approving it.

Following al-Sahhaf's reprimand, Sami and Mohammed did not waste any time in tracking me down at the Sheraton. A prolonged shouting match that lasted several hours erupted in my room. The Mukhābarāt agents accused me of fabricating quotes, while in the same breath demanding that I provide them with my sources' identities. I reminded them that their own general had acknowledged that my assessment of Basra's questionable loyalty was correct.

In the mistaken belief that I was threatening to reveal publicly Hasan's private admission, Mohammed went berserk. We came close to exchanging blows, but in the end, calmer heads prevailed and we managed to come up with a face-saving solution.

To appease al-Sahhaf's anger, we agreed that they should expel me from Iraq immediately. Since I had already booked my return flight to Amman for the following morning, the expulsion was purely symbolic.

ON MARCH 17, 2003, George W. Bush announced that he was running out of patience and he gave Saddam Hussein the ultimatum to abdicate his presidency within the next forty-eight hours "or else." Saddam didn't budge, and on the evening of March 20, the United States and Britain launched a precision bombing attack on the outskirts of Baghdad. Although it was described by the coalition as a successful leadership strike, a visibly shaken but very much alive Saddam Hussein appeared the following morning on state television to denounce the attacks.

Within hours, coalition special forces and armoured columns began pouring into southern Iraq from jump-off positions in Kuwait. After the first few days of the campaign it was readily apparent that the Iraqi army had collapsed. Conscripts surrendered in the hundreds, and allied troops swept through vast tracts of empty desert.

The strongest opposition to the coalition's forces came in the form of the irregular volunteers who called themselves the Fedayeen Saddam. Fighting as guerrillas, the Fedayeen managed to win a few skirmishes against the advancing Americans. The most notable of these was the March 23 ambush of Private Jessica Lynch's 507th Maintenance Company near Nasiriya. Ten U.S. soldiers were killed in that battle, fifty were wounded, and a further twelve—including Private Lynch—were taken prisoner.

Despite the reversal, the U.S. vanguard had pushed close to the southern suburbs of Baghdad within seventy-two hours, and allied aircraft were pounding the Iraqi capital with impunity as part of its shock-and-awe bombing strategy. With reports that advance units of coalition commandos had been used to secure oil-producing and manufacturing infrastructures to prevent their sabotage, some reporters in Washington asked U.S. Secretary of Defence Donald Rumsfeld why the Americans had not used such tactics to secure the so-far-undiscovered Iraqi arsenal of weapons of mass destruction. In response, Rumsfeld testily retorted that those weapons would be found because "we know where they are."

As events unfolded dramatically in the south, the so-called northern front was strangely quiet. In the weeks before the war Saddam had ordered his army units out of their bases and into freshly dug trenches. When Anmar al-Saadi, my long-time driver and friend, and I had ventured north to Mosul in January, I was astonished to see that all of the defensive positions were manned but without any attempt at camouflage. When I had suggested to Anmar that U.S. and British air superiority would slaughter the soldiers stationed here, he quickly agreed. "But if they are in the trenches, then they have no choice but to fight," he explained. "If they were in the cities, they would simply take off their uniforms and escape to their homes. That would be more embarrassing for Saddam than to have them massacred in the front lines."

268   It quickly became evident that Saddam's intentions would not be realized. When they received word that U.S. troops had secured the Baghdad airport and made probing attacks into the capital, the Iraqi soldiers on the northern front began slipping away from their bunkers. On April 6, when U.S. special forces allied with Patriotic Union of Kurdistan *peshmerga* and began to attack south from the Kurdish autonomous region of Iraq towards Kirkuk, they met very little resistance from Saddam's forces. Inability to find Iraqi armoured units puzzled U.S. special forces Sergeant Fred Walker, whose unit operated with a

peshmerga detachment. "Our guys knocked out twelve Iraqi tanks with hand-held missiles, but we sure as hell didn't kill them all," Sergeant Walker told me. "Hell, there was supposed to be an entire armoured division here—its just up and gone. It sure is one hell of a mystery."

The Kurdish *peshmerga* advanced quickly and without a fight took control of the village of Chemchemal on the outskirts of Kirkuk. The Iraqi army had already withdrawn from the area. At this point in the war, the Turkish government again warned that Kirkuk was not to fall into the hands of the Kurdish warlords, for if they controlled the oil riches of northern Iraq, the Turks feared this would provide them with the economic engine to facilitate the declaration of an independent state. If that were to occur, then there was a strong possibility it would reignite the separatist Kurdish movement in eastern Turkey. After enduring a decade of bloody inter-ethnic violence spearheaded by the Kurdish Workers Party, the Turks were anxious to ensure that the lid remained in place on this simmering conflict.

Just forty-eight hours later, Saddam's regime collapsed in Baghdad. As if on cue, all organized resistance simply ceased, and only handfuls of Fedayeen Saddam paramilitary fighters fought on. The Iraqi president himself had allegedly fled towards Tikrit, his hometown stronghold. The U.S. media had already declared Saddam toppled—just like his statue in Firdos Square, which was pulled down live on CNN the next day. The Iraqi army in Kirkuk also had disappeared by the night of April 8, and Kurdish *peshmerga* moved forward past their abandoned trenches.

THE TOPPLING OF Saddam's statue on April 9, 2003, created a false sense of achievement and caused the U.S. media to issue premature declarations of total victory in Iraq. Fedayeen fighters and even some units of the Republican Guard continued to

269

fight rearguard actions as they retreated towards Tikrit to make their last stand. Saddam's hometown was not declared secure by coalition troops until April 28. Only seventy-two hours later, President Bush gave his "mission accomplished" speech aboard the aircraft carrier uss *Abraham Lincoln.*

Although the American commander-in-chief declared an end to combat operations in Iraq, the Iraqi resistance did not abide by his assertion. With the collapse of Saddam's Baathist regime and its security forces, the citizens of Iraq went on a massive looting spree. Since Secretary of Defence Rumsfeld had overruled the advice of his top generals and conducted the Iraq campaign with just 120,000 troops—not the recommended 275,000—the coalition forces were much too thin on the ground. The technological superiority of the American military made the destruction of Saddam's ill-equipped army very easy, but to replace the disbanded Iraqi police and military in the streets required far more personnel and would expose U.S. soldiers to far greater risks.

As a result, Rumsfeld did nothing to inhibit the looting, and quipped to reporters that the Iraqi thieves were simply "enjoying their freedom." With all government functions suspended and the occupation troops unable to intervene, Iraqi utilities shut down and Iraq descended into a state of anarchy.

270 In some places, like Fallujah, Iraqi resistance fighters collected abandoned military hardware and attacked American patrols. For the most part, however, in the first weeks after Saddam's regime had collapsed, the fighting was largely conducted between roving bands of *schroogs* (thieves) and civilians trying to protect their property.

As violence continued to spread through Iraq, it became increasingly difficult for the Bush administration to justify its intervention to the world. Its claim that the mission had been accomplished was contradicted by the facts that no weapons of mass destruction had been located and the Iraqi dictator still eluded capture.

Almost immediately, the White House and the Pentagon began to change their spin on the reasons the war had been waged. The focus shifted from Iraq's possession of weapons of mass destruction to the discovery of mass graves by U.S. troops. Given the media hype on this new twist, one could be forgiven for beginning to believe that George Bush had gone to war to prevent Saddam from committing genocide against his own people.

The first revelation of an alleged slaughter came during the initial week of fighting. In a warehouse outside of Basra, American troops found four hundred corpses, and the discovery of the decomposed bodies was filmed by embedded journalists. Brigadier General Vince Brooks, the U.S. military spokesman in Qatar, briefed the international press corps on the discovery. During his dramatic presentation Brooks made a point of telling reporters that "many of the dead had been . . . executed" and that the site had since been sealed as it was a "possible war crime."

What Brooks neglected to clarify was *which* war. The U.S. authorities already knew that these were the corpses of Iraqi soldiers that had been killed during the Iran-Iraq conflict nearly twenty years earlier. The bodies had been stored in the Basra warehouse—tagged and identified by the International Committee of the Red Cross—as part of ongoing efforts to repatriate Iraqi war dead. Similarly, many of the other mass graves discovered by the U.S. military and reported to the media were those of Shia, Kurdish and Turkmen rebels killed during the 1991 post–Gulf War uprising.

There was no denying that Saddam's security forces had exacted a brutal revenge on those involved in the revolution, but

271

at the time of the killings some 500,000 U.S. coalition troops had been still based in the Persian Gulf and allied aircraft were routinely flying overhead on patrol. When an international intervention could have easily been mounted against Saddam to save the lives of the rebels, America had turned its back on them.

Without facing probing questions from the media, the U.S. State Department was now using these deaths as justification for its invasion of Iraq. To perpetuate this myth, senior spokespersons reiterated the genocide spin as often as possible. Before he was replaced as interim governor in May 2003—after acting for just five months as the U.S. civil administrator in charge of reconstruction and humanitarian aid in post-war Iraq—Jay Garner told the media that "up to one million bodies" would be found buried in Saddam's mass graves. Vice-President Dick Cheney added to the chorus by proclaiming that regardless of whether or not weapons of mass destruction were ever found, had the U.S. not intervened when it did, "the torture chambers would still be operating" and Saddam would be on target to kill his annual "ten thousand innocent civilians."

Of course, it was difficult to explain why occupation troops were being attacked if Bush's coalition of the willing had indeed just saved the Iraqi people from a genocidal maniac. To further convince the American public that some Iraqis were greeting U.S. troops as liberators, interim governor Jay Garner went so far as to stage a victory parade through the streets of Sulaimaniyah. Still eager to curry U.S. favour, Jalal Talabani and his Patriotic Union of Kurdistan supporters willingly complied with the governor's request. Thousands of Kurds lined the streets to wave flags and throw flowers at Garner as he walked along, shaking hands and smiling to the crowds. It was a wonderful photo op, and not a single U.S. reporter noted that the flags being waved were not Iraqi

but had the distinctive sunburst pattern of the Kurdish nationalist party. Nor was it mentioned that Sulaimaniyah had not been
under Saddam's control since 1991 when the region had been
"liberated" by Kurdish *peshmergas*—not by U.S. troops in 2003. As
the three northern provinces remained under tight Kurdish control, the U.S. occupational force considered them to be stable,
and therefore they required only minimal military presence.

Despite the apparent calm in the region, below the surface
interfactional rivalry had started to simmer. Thousands of Kurds
clogged the roads as they headed south into Mosul and Kirkuk.
The Americans simply saw this as a reversal of Saddam's thirty-
year Arabification policy. The Iraqi dictator had made a concerted
effort to transplant impoverished Shiite Arabs from the south
into the northern cities. The U.S. troops thought that these people were heading home to reclaim their lost property. In some
cases this was true. But with the great effort taken by the *peshmerga* to eradicate all registration and land deeds, a much more
sinister program of ethnic cleansing was underway.

"If they can flood the area with enough Kurdish settlers prior
to a census, then they will be able to substantiate their claims
that Kirkuk is a Kurdish city," said Mustafa Kemal, the director
of the Iraqi Turkmen Front office. "At the same time, because the
Kurds control the borders, they are preventing Turkmen exiles
from returning home."

During my first post-war trip back into Iraq, I had witnessed
this first-hand. However, travelling back through the same border region in southern Turkey a little more than a month later,
in May 2003, was almost a surreal experience. A land that had
previously been bustling with wartime activity had returned just
as quickly to being a sleepy little corner of the world. All of the
American transport aircraft and freight containers I had seen on

my last trip—which were never officially authorized to be there in the first place—had since left the Diyarbakir airport. Although the U.S. troops had gone, Turkey's 7th Armoured Corps remained biv-ouacked in the area, but its state of alert had been greatly reduced. These soldiers now lounged in the sun or played soccer, while most of the armoured vehicles were covered by tarps. Before the war this border crossing had been a virtual rolling pipeline as tank-ers delivered oil exports out of Iraq. Now, thousands of oil trucks sat idle in parked columns stretching back some thirty kilometres because the crossing point was still officially closed.

It was still difficult to enter Iraq at that time, and Zeynep Tugrul had again directed me to the Iraqi Turkmen Front in Ankara for its help in arranging a special clearance for me. It took several days to process, but in the end the Turkish general staff allowed me to accompany a few returning expatriate Iraqi Turkmen as a "tourist." On the Turkish side of the border I met with Muaffaq Hacioglu, the representative of the Iraqi Turkmen Front responsible for all transit arrangements. Tall, thin and sporting an oversized Ottoman-style moustache, Muaffaq spoke little English but was genuinely friendly. As a resident of Zakho, just inside the Iraqi boundary, Muaffaq had earned himself well-deserved popularity as a goalie on the local football team. About a dozen of us were making the crossing that day, and our group formed a small convoy of vehicles. Muaffaq had arranged our exit visas and cleared us through Turkish MIT (intelligence).

Once we had crossed the border and were on the Kurdish side I was surprised to see that there was no U.S. military presence, only *peshmerga* belonging to Massoud Barzani's Kurdistan Democratic Party (KDP). Given the animosity between the two ethnic groups, I found it odd that a Turkmen Front representative like Muaffaq could have facilitated our passage. I quickly realized that passage

274

through this border crossing presented a perfect opportunity for Barzani's ruling faction—and a very lucrative one at that.

While the KDP's Asaish secret service recorded and searched everyone entering "Iraqi Kurdistan," Barzani's "customs officials" were free to levy their own entry taxes. For an individual visa the cost was US$50, which amounts to a princely sum in a country where policemen often made only US$10 a month. However, the real money-maker for the KDP was the amount of "duty" assigned to imported goods, which seemed to be predicated on one's ability to pay. "Welcome to the new liberated Iraq," said an Iraqi Turkmen who worked as one of Muaffaq's drivers. "We are now free to charge and be charged for just about anything."

One of my travel companions was Zygon Chechen. A Turkmen resident of Kirkuk, Chechen had fled to Toronto after the collapse of the 1991 uprising. When he had left Iraq, he had been robbed at gunpoint by Kurdish *peshmerga*; this time, it was at the hands of Barzani's customs officers. Chechen had purchased a used Opel station wagon in Germany for US$3,000. He and his nephew had then driven the vehicle to the Iraqi border, intending to visit relatives in Kirkuk and Erbil. After hours of negotiations the Kurds levied a US$1,600 tariff on his vehicle and possessions. After Chechen paid the fine, he was left with exactly US$22 in his pocket. As he had no means of getting funds to replace the money or even the ability to use credit cards while in Iraq, that money would have to last him for the duration of his two-week visit. "Not exactly a grateful welcome home for an old soldier, is it?" asked Chechen.

I got to know that old soldier quite well over the next five hours. Since the rest of the Turkmen delegation had already departed, Chechen's vehicle was my last hope for a ride to Kirkuk. I agreed to pay him US$20 for gas and buy him and his

275

nephew lunch in exchange for a lift. The only problem was fitting me in the car, because the Opel had been overloaded to the point where you could not see out of the rear window. For an ex-soldier, Chechen was of considerable girth, possibly tipping the scales around three hundred pounds, while his nephew had a slender build. Although tall and lean, I could not manage to squeeze in between the car's small bucket seats. In the end, we placed a small cooler between the two seats; by straddling it and lifting my head and shoulders out through the sunroof of the car, I was able to cram myself between the two men. In the 40°C heat, however, this was decidedly uncomfortable, not to mention very dangerous. "No police, no problem!" shouted the robust Chechen. Speed, however, was also a problem as it became difficult to breathe when we went faster than sixty kilometres an hour. But we had struck a deal: Chechen needed the money and I needed the ride. So we plodded onwards to Kirkuk.

Because we could not travel at top speed and had been delayed at the border, we did not arrive until well after dark. With the electricity not yet restored, Kirkuk was pitch black on this hot summer night. We could barely make out the outlines of shadowy figures as they moved along narrow alleyways, and we could hear the rattling of occasional gunfire. The worst part was that, within minutes of entering the city, Chechen was hopelessly lost. He had not been here since leaving twelve years earlier and quickly became disoriented in the darkness. At one intersection a number of armed men demanded that we stop. One of them started to approach our car with his Kalashnikov pointed at the windshield. Chechen's alarm quickly turned to glee. "Ahmet! Ahmet! You are a fucker of goats!" he yelled in Turkish. Translating his greeting, Chechen happily explained to me that Ahmet was his cousin. After years of exile, Zygon Chechen was finally home—and among friends.

When I learned that this armed detachment was a security force from the Iraqi Turkmen Front, I realized that I had successfully reached my destination. I was informed that Mustafa Kemal and Dr. Mustafa Ziya were expecting me and that I should meet with them in the morning. I was then taken to a nearby hotel. The place was filthy; there were stains on the rugs and fleas in the bed, and I found a four-inch cockroach in the shower stall. On the plus side, it had a generator, but the air conditioner was broken. Nearby, on the darkened city streets, the shouts of looters were occasionally punctuated by bursts of gunfire. For US$6 a night—including breakfast—I figured I couldn't complain.

The next morning I ate an early breakfast of boiled eggs, flatbread and tea al fresco. From my table I saw a long queue of angry drivers waiting at a gas station. A small unit of American troops was present, but the female military police officer in charge had difficulty coping with the waiting motorists' rising tempers. And without a translator, the soldiers could not communicate with them. Shortly after the pumps opened at 7:00 AM, a fistfight broke out between the gas station attendant and an angry customer. Shouts and punches flew. The angry mob of fed-up drivers physically manhandled the abusive man to the roadside. Almost hysterical at being expelled from the queue, he pleaded his case to the American soldiers. "I have been waiting in line for four days, and now they say they won't serve me because I'm a Kurdish *schroog* (thief)," he said. "Please do something to help me."

The young military policewoman whom he had asked to intervene on his behalf appeared both exasperated and a little frightened at the events unfolding around her. "We can't help you. This is an internal problem," she told him. "We are here only to provide security, and we don't have enough people to help you." The Kurdish driver was led away from the pumps without any gasoline. A Turkmen waiter at the hotel then approached my

277

table. "Do not feel any pity for that man," he said. "He is a *schroog*. We know who is from Kirkuk, and which of these Kurds came after the war to steal from us. Unfortunately, to the Americans all Iraqis look the same."

The shortage of gasoline across the country was a new phenomenon for Iraqis, and while some post-war confusion was to be expected, the failure of the U.S. authorities to ensure adequate distribution had caused tensions to mount. After my breakfast I walked to the gas station and discovered that the lineup stretched back nearly six kilometres. Because I looked like an American, I was heckled in Arabic, Kurdish and Turkish by many of the frustrated drivers.

Near the end of the line, things became much more tense when a giant of a man blocked my passage. In fluent English he demanded, "Where the fuck is our gas? What have you Americans done with all of Iraq's oil?" Before I could respond, other drivers began to gather round and started yelling at me in a variety of languages. Before the situation could turn violent, a passing U.S. special forces patrol braked to a halt to investigate the commotion. The .50-calibre machine gun mounted on top of the vehicle proved enough of a threat to disperse the mob.

Staff Sergeant Al Tifton offered me a lift and asked me what had caused all the fuss. When I explained the situation, Tifton laughed and said, "We've got plenty of gas up at our air base. Hell, we'll probably have to start drinking the stuff now that we've run out of places to put it."

278

THE INTER-ETHNIC VIOLENCE of the Kurds and the Turkmen continued. The Coalition Provisional Authority brought in a number of Kurdish policemen from Erbil and Sulaimaniyah to patrol the streets and monitor traffic, but any action against insurgents was to be undertaken only by the U.S. 173rd Airborne Brigade.

While both of these forces maintained their own separate check-points and patrols, the third level of authority established in Kirkuk was that of Jalal Talabani's Patriotic Union of Kurdistan (PUK) *peshmerga*. Independent of the Central Provisional Author-ity and of any U.S. command, the armed Kurdish militiamen had virtual control over Kirkuk because they were free to stop and search civilian cars.

In September 2003, I returned to Kirkuk in the company of Laci Zoldi, a Hungarian colleague and friend, and we discovered for ourselves the level of control that the PUK exercised in this northern Iraqi city. Laci and I had originally gone to the large, heavily guarded PUK headquarters in Kirkuk to ask about the possibility of interviewing Jalal Talabani in his office in Sulai-maniyah. Since the telephone systems were unreliable, we had hoped to have a definite appointment before undertaking the two-hour drive. We presumed that the local commander would at least be able to put us in touch with Talabani's aides. There appeared to be some confusion about our request, however, and we were told to come back the following morning for a personal audience with Jalal Jawhar Aziz, the governor of Kirkuk.

Our curiosity somewhat piqued, we returned the next day at the arranged time and were ushered into a large waiting room, where a number of Kurdish civilians were already seated. Ser-vants brought us each some tea. All those assembled seemed apprehensive about their imminent audience with Aziz. Eventu-ally the elegant, grey-haired, self-appointed governor of Kirkuk entered from a side room and took up his position behind a desk as though he were a judge presiding over a courtroom. As we watched the first few Kurdish presentations, it became clear that Aziz and the PUK were as powerful in this region as any feudal lord. A cousin to Jalal Talabani and a former *peshmerga* colonel, the governor resolved issues as trivial as business disputes and marriage arrangements. After hearing brief submissions, he would pass judgement with a wave of his hand and a few words to his clerk, who dutifully recorded the proceedings. Without a word of rebuttal or challenge, plaintiffs and defendants alike were then escorted from the room by *peshmerga* guards.

After the crowd had thinned, Aziz looked up and noticed Laci and me. He issued a flurry of questions, and an officer who also acted as a translator approached us. "Are you the journalists who were requesting a highway pass to Sulaimaniyah?" he asked. While we noted that Aziz was also in the business of selling passage on what were ostensibly free roads, we hurriedly clarified our request. Again, the translation left much to be desired, because Aziz now believed that we wanted to interview him. Obviously flattered that foreign media would seek him out for comment, he clapped his hands to adjourn the proceedings and invited us into his private chambers.

Throughout our interview Aziz maintained the PUK party line that the Kurds wished only to operate within a central Iraqi federation. When I asked him why the flag of Kurdistan flew over the building, he became visibly nervous. "That will be replaced tomorrow," he assured us.

Earlier that month, the U.S. ambassador and administrator of the Coalition Provisional Authority, Paul Bremer, had instructed the removal of all partisan flags from public buildings in northern Iraq. When the demand had not been met, an American patrol had attempted to forcibly carry out the order in the city of Sulaimaniyah. In response, a mob of Kurds had attacked the U.S. soldiers, rolled their Humvees over and set them ablaze. The soldiers wisely beat a hasty retreat. This incident had gone largely unreported in the media, but it had badly shaken Bremer's relationship with the PUK, and obviously Governor Aziz did not want to reignite the issue in Kirkuk.

ALTHOUGH THE AMERICANS may have been temporarily placated, other local factions were not fooled by the gesture. On November 21, 2003, shortly after ten o'clock in the morning, a tremendous blast detonated outside the PUK headquarters in Kirkuk. Estimated to contain no less that one ton of nitroglycerine, a car bomb shattered the eight-foot-long garden wall and destroyed Aziz's office suite—the same rooms where Laci Zoldi and I had chatted with him in September. Chunks of twisted granite and burnt furniture now littered the street. Three *peshmerga* guards who had been patrolling the garden were killed instantly in the blast. Aziz, who was not in his office at the time of the attack, believed he was the intended target.

When I arrived on the scene the following day, I was greeted cordially by the officer who had acted as translator during my interview with Aziz. He smiled often enough, but his eyes held a steely gaze that could be quite unnerving. On this day, however, he wore sunglasses and appeared to be visibly shaken by the bombing. As he showed us the extent of the devastation, he stated that his agents were examining the remains of the car. All the evidence and clues that were found had been collected and piled in the garden next to the PUK offices. Workmen were already rebuilding the protective outer wall, while scores of armed *peshmerga* provided security from the rooftop and adjacent bunkers. The officer spent a few minutes combing through the collected auto parts before he discovered what he had been looking for. The grisly objects he held up were a couple of vertebrae held together by some burnt skin and muscle. A small patch of cloth embedded in the skin appeared to be that of a red and white headscarf.

"They want us to believe that this was the work of a suicide bomber, and that is why they put an Arab's body in the car," he said. "However, the remains of the remotely controlled detonator would suggest that this man didn't know the purpose of the mission." When asked who he thought had tried to assassinate Governor Aziz, he did not hesitate to reply, "Turkish intelligence."

Although he could offer no direct proof to support his allegations, he said that his agents would continue to investigate the car bombing based on this assumption. "The Americans announced that this was the work of al Qaeda Islamic fundamentalists, but they did not even approach the bomb site," he said. "In fact, they still believe that the U.S. headquarters [just five hundred metres away] was the intended target and that the bomb detonated prematurely."

The Americans in Kirkuk had good reason to feel threatened. Although the stiffening resistance was gaining momentum in the central Sunni triangle of Iraq, it had yet to spread north. But anti-occupation violence was on the increase. A major incident had been the September 10, 2003, bombing of a U.S. safe house in the city of Erbil. It was estimated that nearly eight tons of explosives packed into a truck had caused the devastating blast. While several CIA and Mossad intelligence agents inside the house at the time of the explosion were killed, the destruction had not been limited to the target. When the dust settled and the bodies were counted, it was believed that three Iraqi civilians, including a two-year-old boy, were dead and another fifty-five were wounded. The combined U.S.-Israeli intelligence casualties were never revealed, but they were estimated to number more than two dozen. It had been a well-planned and carefully executed strike.

Attacks against American soldiers in northern Iraq were now becoming commonplace. Earlier in November, resistance fighters had riddled an SUV driven by two U.S. special forces soldiers. After bringing the vehicle to a halt, the Iraqi fighters pulled the wounded soldiers from the vehicle and slit their throats. Crowds of onlookers cheered and danced at the spectacle.

"We are certainly not being greeted as liberators," my old

282

friend Eddie Calis told me when I met up with him in Kirkuk on November 22. A Palestinian-American and a mutual friend of Ben Works, Calis had been deployed to Iraq as a civilian security adviser at the Kirkuk airfield. When U.S. forces began launching major counteroffensives against the resistance fighters in hotbeds such as Fallujah, many of the guerrillas headed north to find softer targets. The Kirkuk airfield was soon coming under almost nightly mortar attacks.

"As a demonstration of U.S. determination we have begun firing our own mortars in return," said Calis. When I asked him just what it was they fired at, he smiled and said, "Would you believe, an empty field? . . . We want to be certain that we don't create any more collateral damage among the Kirkuk citizens. Our blasting away is to bolster the morale of the local population [to get them] into thinking that it's a two-way fight. The truth is, we don't have a clue where the terrorists are."

AS U.S. TROOPS in the north came under increased attacks, the various Iraqi factions stepped up their own turf wars. On February 1, 2004, Barzani's KDP and Talabani's PUK were simultaneously attacked. At two separate events in Erbil, suicide bombers gained entry to the crowded garden where a reception was taking place. Since security at both functions was tight, it was believed that the assailants had entered with the compliance of treacherous *peshmerga* guards. The results were terrifying and brutal. Perhaps sixty-five Kurds were killed and another two hundred were wounded in the two blasts, making the combined attack the bloodiest in post-war Iraq to that date. Many of the casualties were senior members in the parties.

Driving through Erbil the next night, I learned first-hand just how edgy and vengeful the *peshmerga* had become in the wake of the bombings. After our car was halted at a KDP checkpoint,

283

about a half-dozen armed Kurdish fighters emerged from the gloom to surround us. With a Kalashnikov pointed at the driver's head, the *peshmerga* demanded to know if there were any Arabs in the car. One of my travelling companions joked, "What about a Canadian?" In response we heard the distinctive metallic click as the assault rifle was cocked. The Kurds were obviously in no mood to joke. Once our identification had been examined, they waved us through the checkpoint.

As we were pulling away, we realized that the car in front of us had not been so lucky. Two male occupants were dragged from the vehicle and thrown to the ground. Several *peshmerga* started viciously kicking them. In the back seat a young woman wept as she tried to comfort two infants. Just past the KDP checkpoint sat an Iraqi police vehicle, but the Kurdish policemen inside it made no effort to intervene.

ACCORDING TO OFFICIALS, the February 1 bombing of the KDP and PUK gatherings had been the handiwork of the Ansar al-Islam, a Kurdish Islamic extremist group with links to al Qaeda. However, from the rounding up and beating of Arab suspects, I had to conclude that the Kurds had a different idea about who the actual culprits were. "They know the truth, but they also know that right now there is so much anger that the people cannot be told," said Mahmud, a thirty-five-year-old Kurdish expatriate who lived in Sweden. "Otherwise the streets of Erbil will run red with the blood of Arabs."

I had met Mahmud at the Turkish border crossing, and we agreed to share a taxi to Kirkuk. He had been en route to a family reunion when he had learned that his brother was one of those killed in the bombing. "My brother was a senior official in the KDP, and I assure you his death will be avenged," declared Mahmud. "I will carry on his work to ensure that his sacrifice is ultimately rewarded with the creation of an independent Kurdistan."

This trip into Iraq, in June 2004, was to be the final research-gathering venture that would enable me to write about the forgotten Turkmen. At an Iraqi Turkmen Front (ITF) meeting in Kirkuk I expressed a desire to visit the entirely Turkmen city of Tal Afar. My request was referred to the organization's executive, and after several minutes of discussion they asked me where I would stay. As I had never before been to Tal Afar, I naively said, "Oh, I'll just take a hotel room. Please don't worry about that." The translator looked at me curiously and said, "There are no hotels in Tal Afar." Somewhat taken aback, I replied, "You mean to tell me that in a city of 400,000 inhabitants there is not a single hotel?" "No," he said, "and there never has been." Doctor Yashar Talafarli, the head of the ITF in Tal Afar, cordially invited me to stay at his home. "You will be safe there," he said.

Before arriving in Tal Afar, I had not really had any concerns for my safety. I knew that all of central Iraq was incredibly volatile and that since the U.S. had ignited the Shiite followers of Muqtada al-Sadr in April 2004, most of the heretofore dormant south had also become very dangerous for a foreign journalist. However, of all the cities in Iraq I had never heard of any violent attacks occurring in Tal Afar. "That is only because the Americans don't report their losses from here, and not a single journalist has bothered to come here," Doctor Talafarli explained as we toured the central core of the ancient city.

Pointing to the shattered remains of a large walled compound, he said, "That used to be the American headquarters until it was hit [in July 2003] by a suicide car bomb. Dozens were killed and perhaps fifty wounded. The helicopters were evacuating casualties for hours. But there was never any media report about it."

285

Following this attack and others, the U.S. authorities had eventually abandoned all of their facilities in the city and withdrawn their military to the airfield.

The former Iraqi air force base was situated approximately five kilometres from the town limits and completely isolated from the town itself. "Saddam's helicopter gunships could safely operate from there to keep us in line," said Doctor Talafarli. "And now the Americans are using the base for the same purpose."

Since July 2003 the resistance in Tal Afar had increased steadily. "When the U.S. troops first came to Tal Afar, the Turkmen citizens were very happy to see them because it meant that the terror of Saddam had ended," said Talafarli. "But as U.S. vehicles crushed civilian cars, soldiers shot civilians by mistake and houses were searched at random, we began to resent their presence."

When I visited the Turkmen enclave in June 2004, relations between the people of Tal Afar and the U.S. military had been severed almost completely. To allow me to walk the streets safely, Talafarli had two of his ITF subordinates accompany me at all times. The crowds stared at me with open hostility, and on several occasions my guides had to hurriedly explain that I was a guest of Doctor Talafarli, to avoid violence. "I'm sorry, but they think you are an American and right away they want to kill you," explained Omar, one of my beleaguered escorts.

When I requested that a taxi take me out to the U.S. airfield, it caused considerable concern among my ITF handlers. Several cabs were hailed to discuss a fare, but all refused. "No local drivers will take you to the American camp, because they don't want to die," explained Doctor Talafarli. "There are an average of two U.S. soldiers killed in Tal Afar every week in ambushes, and the Americans are eager for revenge. But more dangerous than that is the fact that the resistance fighters watch the airbase twenty-four hours a day. Any Turkmen seen visiting the gate will be presumed to be traitors and will be killed upon their return home."

That evening the Talafarli family prepared a veritable feast. As is the Turkmen custom, the women cooked the meal and laid out the dining room table for the men to eat first. As we ate, the children brought their friends into the doorway to catch a glimpse of me. Whenever I glanced at them, they would giggle and scatter back to the safety of the kitchen. I realized that in my western-style suit I must have looked like something from Mars to them. It was a game that continued well into the night. Once we had finished our meal, the men retired to the garden while the women and children ate. As we sat under the stars, many of Tal Afar's community leaders and intelligentsia came to visit Talafarli—and to practise their English on me. The power shortages in Tal Afar were far more acute than in Baghdad, and in this impoverished city only the wealthiest residents could afford generators. It was a clear night, but without streetlights it was eerily dark.

The Turkmen apologized that they could not offer me a shower after my travel on such a very hot day—Tal Afar had an acute water shortage. As the population grew over the centuries and Tal Afar was transformed from a village into a city, the wells and spring-fed streams were unable to meet the increased demand. Plans had been drawn to build a pipeline from the Tigris River. Saddam's engineers had actually started construction of the twenty-two-kilometre-long conduit, and sections of pipe had been dropped off all along the Mosul–Kirkuk highway. That, however, was just before the 1991 Gulf War and subsequent uprisings.

With sanctions in place, Saddam had neither the material available nor the desire to waste precious resources on the welfare of a potentially disloyal faction, and the project was abandoned. As such, the pipe still sat along the highway and water continued

287

to be rationed in Tal Afar. "It would have taken very little money for the U.S. to have revived the pipeline project, and we would have eagerly supplied the workforce," Talafarli said. "But we soon learned that the American military was first and foremost concerned with the safety and welfare of its own soldiers, not of the Iraqi people."

All of the police and armed security personnel in Tal Afar were at this point Turkmen, recruited locally following Saddam's ouster. However, when Iraqi troops had discarded their uniforms and fled the Tal Afar airbase in April 2003, the Turkmen had no organized force to replace them. Seeing a power vacuum open up, Kurdish *peshmerga* from Barzani's KDP pushed into the territory and met no opposition. "They came to loot the Baath regime offices and to steal all the former government's vehicles and supplies," said Doctor Talafarli. "There were a few small skirmishes when they tried to rob private Turkmen homes, and they soon knew better than to try and remain inside our city. The Kurds took what they could and left."

Having visited Iraq's only purely Turkmen city, I felt that I had enough material for my book. I spent the next two months hammering out *Among the Others: Encounters with the Forgotten Turkmen of Iraq*. My one brief travel break was to visit Slobodan Milosevic in The Hague. I did not know it at the time, but I was destined to return to Tal Afar and break my promise to him to stay safe.

288

I was in Kosovo with the Serbian forces when NATO ground troops first entered the embattled province in 1999. Emboldened by the presence of allied troops, the Albanian Kosovars embarked on a wave of revenge against ethnic Serbs. Here a former Serbian military headquarters burns in downtown Pristina.

NATO's seventy-seven days of continual air bombardment of Serbia in 1999 effectively disabled the country's transportation and utility infrastructure. Here commuters cram aboard an overcrowded ferry to cross the Danube in the city of Novi Sad. Visible in the background are the remains of one of the three bridges destroyed by NATO planes.

In Baghdad in May 2003, anarchy and violence erupted in the wake of the U.S. invasion. Without any police on the streets and with all utilities shut down, looting and arson went unchecked.

A U.S. M1 Abrams tank roars down the Kirkuk–Baghdad highway in June 2003. Even at this early stage of the occupation of Iraq, snapping such photographs was a risky business because jumpy American troops had very aggressive rules of engagement. A soldier who felt threatened could resort to the use of lethal force.

In March 2004, Albanian Kosovars launched a pogrom against the Serbian enclaves remaining in Kosovo. Despite the presence of NATO troops, hundreds of Serbian homes and a number of ancient religious sites—such as the Prizren monastery shown here—were vandalized and set ablaze.

By April 2004, the Iraqi insurgency had coalesced into a deadly foe for the American and coalition occupation forces. Outside the protected green zones, Iraq's roadways became the new battlefield. Here the remains of a CIA SUV litter the airport road in Baghdad.

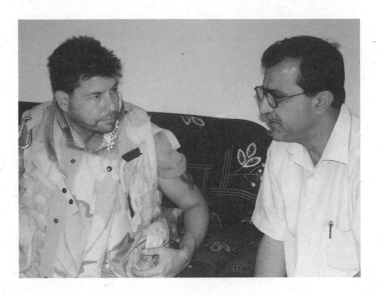

In September 2004, it had been my intention to meet with Dr. Yashar Talafarli in Tal Afar, Iraq. Instead, I was captured by Ansar al-Islam and held
hostage for five terrifying days. My eventual meeting with Dr. Talafarli was
facilitated by the U.S. 3rd Armoured Cavalry in July 2005, when his first
words to me were "You're late."

In January 2007, I trav-
elled outside the wire in
Kandahar with the Senlis
Council and was able to
speak with many Afghan
villagers who had been
displaced by the recent
fighting. Most of them
were almost entirely igno-
rant of the reasons for the
ongoing insurgency.

Most of the media coverage from Afghanistan comes from journalists embedded with the Canadian battle group, but I have tried to obtain a more varied perspective. In May 2007, I interviewed Taliban cleric Abdul Salam Zaeef in his Kabul compound. PHOTO: SASHA UZUNOV

As commander-in-chief of the Canadian Forces, Governor General Michaëlle Jean agreed to give *Esprit de Corps* a special Christmas interview in December 2007. As the magazine's publisher, I had the honour of interviewing her. PHOTO: DARCY KNOLL

The front-line hardships of war reporting are balanced by the less-trying social obligations of being an Ottawa-based publisher and author. Here my wife, Katherine, and I attend a military black-tie fundraiser in 2007.

Of all the senior officers I have encountered over the years, none has made such an impression as General Rick "The Big Cod" Hillier. His was a very difficult interview: his charm and charisma allowed him to seize complete control of the conversation. PHOTO: DARCY KNOLL

In 2008, I continued to visit Afghanistan as an unembedded reporter, having developed an extensive network of contacts there. In June, I was the guest of General Abdul Rashid Dostum, one of the most controversial warlords in the country, at his private compound in Kabul. PHOTO: SASHA UZUNOV

In January 2007, I met with a Kandahar warlord known as Commander Blue. Considering him a loyal ally, the U.S. appointed "Blue" as police chief in the town of Arghandab. The locals thought otherwise, and Blue was assassinated later the following year.

9

AMONG THE MUJAHEDEEN

Sleep now, and I will check your
story. If you are telling the truth, we
will release you. If not, you die.

TURKMEN INSURGENT LEADER

ON JUNE 16, 2005, I received a telephone call from Zeynep Tugrul
asking me to have a look at the photograph on the front page of
the *International Herald Tribune.* In the photograph, four Iraqi men,
identified as insurgent suspects captured in the city of Tal Afar,
were huddled together in the back of an American vehicle. The
individual on the left of the photograph—even with B-5 scrawled
on his forehead in grease pencil—was instantly recognizable as
one of the mujahedeen who had beaten me during my captivity
the previous September.

289

On the morning of June 18, I was still trying to figure out
whom to provide with this information when I received a phone
call from Major Gary Dangerfield of the U.S. 3rd Armored Cavalry
Regiment in Tal Afar, inviting me to make an "all-expenses-paid
visit" back to Iraq. As a result of the regiment's commanding
officer having read my book *Among the Others: Encounters with the*

Forgotten Turkmen of Iraq, I was being asked to come and provide a briefing to the 3rd Armored Cavalry. After accepting the proposal and being assured that I would have "more fucking protection than the president," I pointed out to Dangerfield that his regiment had arrested one of my tormentors. Although he was aware of my having been taken hostage, Dangerfield was not aware that prisoner B-5 had been involved. As a result, B-5 was relocated and isolated from the other prisoners until I could arrive to give a 100 per cent identification and statement.

True to their word, the Americans sent a Black Hawk helicopter and an Apache gunship to pick us up at the Iraq-Turkey border. Sasha Uzunov had agreed to accompany me on this trip, and Stefan Nitoslawski was filming the entire venture for a CBC documentary entitled *Targets: Reporters in Iraq*. I had already signed a contract and begun participating in *Targets* before receiving the call from Dangerfield. The producers had wanted me to venture to Iraq on my own for the movie, but after two sleepless nights of anxiety at the prospect I told them I could not do it. I was prepared to travel right up to the border but not beyond it. The offer of flying in by helicopter changed all that.

Almost immediately after the chopper had delivered us to Forward Operations Base Sykes, we were issued with protective gear and sent out on a patrol into the centre of Tal Afar. The gunner in the rear hatch suddenly ducked down inside the armoured fighting vehicle and hand-signalled me to do the same. When our column of five Bradley personnel carriers had rumbled along this narrow street just thirty minutes earlier, a large number of Iraqi civilians had been clustered in doorways. Dozens of young children had waved enthusiastically at the U.S. soldiers, running beside the vehicles in hopes of having candy or toys tossed in their direction.

By the time we returned along this same route, all evidence of the local citizenry had disappeared behind closed doors and shuttered windows. Sensing that Iraqi insurgents in the vicinity had prompted the exodus, the patrol commander ordered all the troops to duck down as we sped through the now ominously quiet streets. Thankfully, our patrol returned to the U.S. base without receiving any hostile fire. The troops of the 3rd Armored Cavalry explained that spending a day in Tal Afar without being attacked was a rarity.

The purpose of our trip into this volatile northern Iraqi city was to retrace the route taken by my captors when I had been abducted and held hostage the previous September. Although I could make general presumptions about locations based on my memory and satellite imagery, once I returned to the site, a lot of landmarks came rushing back to mind. Many changes had occurred in the past eleven months because of the continual fighting and the shifting political fortunes, and the police checkpoint where Zeynep and I were first taken had long since been dismantled. Nevertheless, after viewing the same approach road we had taken from Mosul, I remembered the large Hitachi neon sign that stood in the centre of the checkpoint. Once this vital starting point could be confirmed, it was amazing how the detailed memories came flooding back.

Our armoured patrol followed the main boulevard that the terrorists had used, and I could recall where they had crossed the median and then driven uphill into a tightly packed suburb on the outskirts of town. At that point, our patrol veered back onto the main route. Before our departure I had been told that there were still two large areas in Tal Afar that the U.S. military would enter only with a full combat mission, including tanks and helicopter gunships. To know that after eleven months of often heavy

291

fighting the area in which I had been held hostage remained a heavily contested zone brought home the magnitude of the good fortune that I had been released alive.

That evening I met my host, Colonel H.R. McMaster, the commander of the 3rd Armored Cavalry Regiment, who explained that I would be making a special presentation to at least three hundred members of his regiment on the following day. After McMaster excused himself from the table, his executive officer, Lieutenant Colonel Joe Armstrong, said he wanted a private discussion with me in his office. Once the door had been closed, Armstrong got straight to the point. "The boys here love Colonel McMaster, and I want you to assure me that he didn't make a mistake in bringing you here," he said. "I've read your stuff—all of your stuff, including the Al Jazeera features—and I know you're not a believer in this intervention."

I was surprised at how much research Armstrong had conducted, and was shocked to learn just how far McMaster had stuck his neck out to arrange this trip.

"The Pentagon would never have approved this, so the Old Man [McMaster] did this on his own hook," Armstrong said.

That certainly explained the confusion at the Iraq-Turkey border when we had shown up at the American military office and said we were expecting a helicopter pickup. The U.S. soldiers had been amused and had explained that American helicopters were not authorized to operate in this airspace. Their smugness had turned to awe when an Apache suddenly swept in over the border checkpoint, and a Black Hawk landed at a nearby soccer field. There were plenty of curious stares from the Kurdish and Turkish border guards as Sasha, Stefan and I strutted out to the Black Hawk, carrying a briefcase and camera bags.

I assured Armstrong that I respected McMaster's initiative in bringing me to Tal Afar, and I promised him I would not use the opportunity to do anything but tell the story of what had happened to Zeynep and me the previous year.

IT WAS JUST after lunch, and the mess hall had been converted into a mini-auditorium. At least three hundred U.S. soldiers filed in to take their seats. When Colonel McMaster strode into the room, the entire assembly stood to attention. In introducing me, the colonel praised my courage for returning to Iraq and instructed his officers to pay close attention to my tale.

Stefan Nitoslawski was filming the whole thing, and I'm sure that most of these soldiers were wondering, *Just who the hell is this Canadian civvy who brings his own cameraman to tape his performance?* Always a nervous public speaker, I mumbled my way through an opening joke—I likened my thanking them for being there to the way the padre always thanked us for attending the church parades that we had no option but to attend. Once I started telling the story, though, I had their undivided attention.

I started by telling them a little bit about my previous involvement with the Turkmen of Iraq and how in September 2004 I had found myself in Ankara to discuss the details of publishing and shipping my recently completed book *Among the Others*. While conducting business in Turkey, I heard a couple of sketchy news reports about a violent flare-up in Tal Afar between insurgents and U.S. troops. The reports from Baghdad claimed that foreign fighters were responsible for the violence—and most media outlets had no idea where Tal Afar was.

I had a five-day window in my schedule, and through the Iraqi Turkmen Front I arranged yet another trip into Iraq. As a matter of mutual convenience, Zeynep Tugrul joined me on this fact-finding mission into Tal Afar. The Turkish media were certainly keen to learn more about the possible suffering of the Turkmen, and there was absolutely no reliable news coming out of that

293

region. From their sources, the Iraqi Turkmen Front knew that things were very dangerous, and promises were made to provide us with an armed escort. Zeynep and I made an uneventful border crossing and arrived in Mosul at around noon on September 7. Our driver dropped us off at the U.S.-controlled green zone at the airport, where I had made prior arrangements to meet with Phil Atkinson for lunch.

Phil was a retired Canadian soldier and a subscriber to *Esprit de Corps.* He had taken a job working with General Dynamics Land Systems in London, Ontario, where the Stryker light armoured vehicles are manufactured. The twenty-two-ton wheeled personnel carriers were the controversial new addition to the U.S. Army inventory, and this was the first time the newly formed Stryker Brigade had deployed to Iraq. Atkinson's job wasn't just to repair any battle damage suffered by the vehicles; he was also required to recommend possible improvements to the armour protection.

On my previous visits, Phil's workshops in Mosul had been beehives of activity, but on this day when Zeynep and I visited, the place was like a ghost town. I asked him if there was a special holiday, and Phil dropped his voice to a conspiratorial whisper. "Can you guys keep a secret?" Assuring him that that's what journalists do best, he proceeded to tell us that everything had been moved forward to Tal Afar. "We're gonna mount a major offensive up there in the next twenty-four to forty-eight hours, and you guys won't want to be anywhere near that place when that happens."

Of course, that's exactly where we headed as soon as we left the Mosul airport's front gate.

As I explained this part of the story, I saw an American captain's hand shoot up in the front row. Although it had been explained beforehand that I would field questions at the end of my talk, I could see this guy's query wasn't going to wait that long. As I acknowledged him, the captain asked, "Why the hell would you do that? Why wouldn't you listen to his advice?"

I explained that as a Turk and as a Canadian, Zeynep and I were unembedded and that both our countries were neutral in the conflict. Our plan had been to push down the highway as far as we could. If the Americans were about to attack, we thought they would have the city cordoned off and would deny us entry into Tal Afar. If that was the case, we planned to wait behind the U.S. troops and follow their attack from behind. If we actually got inside the city, we were going to look up Doctor Yashar Talafarli and hole up at the hospital throughout the American attacks.

In the past, I had found the hospitals to be about the safest places to gain up-to-date and accurate assessments of the fighting. In April 2004, when the United States announced its intention to arrest Shiite cleric Muqtada al-Sadr, spontaneous violent attacks against American troops erupted in Baghdad and Najaf. My driver had called his Shiite contacts to ensure us safe passage, and he drove us to the hospitals in both locations. When the United States launched counter-strikes against the Shiite militia, we had seen the dead and wounded civilians and insurgents being rushed in for treatment.

I explained to the audience that this really wasn't as danger-ous as it sounded and that the toughest challenge we faced as unembedded journalists was the fact that the U.S. military did not like to admit its own setbacks. Bristling at this suggestion, the captain asked me to give an example. I told him of an occasion in November 2003 when Sacha Trudeau and I had teamed up again in Baghdad. Trudeau had been anxious to get embedded with the U.S. 82nd Airborne division that was reportedly having a hairy time securing the city of Fallujah. He was becoming frustrated as the Americans kept putting off his request. I convinced Anmar and Sacha that we should just drive out to this hotbed of insurgency and visit the 82nd Airborne on our own initiative.

We spent a considerable amount of time driving around the streets of Fallujah, observed by increasingly hostile crowds of locals, but saw no sign of any U.S. presence. In fact, all we found was a padlocked compound where the paratroopers used to reside. The American army in Baghdad was telling journalists that they were on a waiting list to be embedded in Fallujah, instead of admitting that its troops had already abandoned the city. Only weeks later, when the Americans tried to re-enter Fallujah, did it become apparent how lucky we had been to get in and out alive.

I explained that it had been a similar situation in Tal Afar for Zeynep and me on September 7, 2004.

It was nearly dusk when we arrived at the outskirts of Tal Afar. On the highway to Mosul, a checkpoint had been set up, and about a dozen Iraqi policemen were supervising a frightened exodus of civilian refugees. Over the past week there had been local reports of escalating violence between resistance fighters and U.S. troops in Tal Afar, and many of the residents were fleeing the embattled city.

It had not been easy to find a taxi driver willing to take us to Tal Afar. All the drivers in Mosul had been warned that the mujahedeen were in control of the city and that it was too dangerous. One Kurdish fellow disagreed with his colleagues and said that their fears were unfounded. With daylight fading, we quickly made a bargain on the fare and set off.

The sight of U.S.-paid Iraqi police forces monitoring traffic had seemed like a good sign that things were still under control, despite the recent fighting. Since I did not have an exact address for my contact, I approached a police checkpoint to ask for assistance. When I asked the policemen about contacting Doctor Talafarli, they recognized his name as that of a prominent local Turkmen official. A senior police officer was summoned, and he instructed Zeynep and me to climb into a nearby car containing four armed and masked men. As we clambered into the back seat, one of the gunmen said in excellent English, "We will take you to Doctor Talafarli. Please do not be afraid."

I had presumed these men were part of some sort of special police force—our own Canadian Joint Task Force 2 counterterrorist teams often wear ski masks—so I had no immediate cause for concern. As soon as we entered the city, however, I saw that the streets were full of similarly masked resistance fighters armed with Kalashnikov rifles and rocket-propelled grenades. I suddenly realized that we were in the hands of the resistance. Still believing that they were taking us to Doctor Talafarli's house, we were instead ushered into a small courtyard outside a walled two-storey building. There were about a half-dozen armed men inside. None of them was smiling.

As soon as the metal door had clanged shut behind us, the English-speaking leader said, "You are spies . . . and now you are prisoners." All of our cameras, other equipment and identification were taken from us, and we were told to sit on a mat with our backs to the wall. "The Americans will attack soon, and I have to see to my men," said our captor. "I will deal with you when I return."

Shortly after nightfall they brought a platter of food into the compound and, in what would soon become a routine pattern, served us first before eating dinner themselves. I did not have much of an appetite.

The plates had just been cleared away when another car pulled up outside and four more gunmen came quickly through

297

the door. Before I could react, I was pulled to my feet and pressed with my face against the wall and my hands on top of my head. Almost immediately I heard the distinct sound of a Kalashnikov being cocked about a metre behind me. Realizing that they were about to execute me, Zeynep screamed in Turkish, "Don't shoot him . . . He has a son!" The outburst was enough to distract them, and they began to explain to her the necessity of killing a "Jewish spy."

Thankfully, I had no idea what was being said. The brief discussion was still taking place when our original captor returned. Harsh words were exchanged between the two groups of gunmen, and it seemed as though my fate was in the hands of those who had made the capture. The would-be executioners left.

Now Zeynep was blindfolded and taken away for questioning. The remaining guards—their ages ranging from fifteen to fifty—took turns watching me and crouching behind the second-floor parapet, looking at the sky for signs of a U.S. attack.

About two hours later it was my turn to be blindfolded and roughly manhandled into what felt like an SUV or a Land Rover. At the second house I was rushed through several doorways and up several stairs. With my hands tied behind my back and unable to see, I stumbled and fell several times, only to be pulled forcibly back to my feet and once again shoved forward. "Hurry, hurry, you bastard Jew," one of my guards whispered as he slammed my head into a door frame.

I was forced to lie face down on a mat, and two men carefully searched through my pockets. Finding my money inside my sock (about US$700), they laughed and said, "Your money is our money. You won't need cash in heaven."

It was difficult to gauge how long I lay there in the dark, but my shoulders were aching when my hands were finally untied and I was brought to another room for interrogation. They removed my blindfold and shone a bright flashlight directly into my eyes. Two men were questioning me: "Which intelligence agency are you working for?"

For about an hour I did my best to answer all their allegations and explain to them that my intention in going to Tal Afar was as a journalist. In what seemed like a bad Hollywood comedy, when someone started a generator outside, the lights came on immediately and the two interrogators clumsily tried to pull their ski masks back on before I could see their faces.

The one who identified himself as the emir actually started to laugh and, with the tension broken, left his mask off. This man had been among the group who took us at the police checkpoint. "Sleep now, and I will check your story," he said. "If you are telling the truth, we will release you. If not, you die."

AT ABOUT SIX o'clock the following morning I was kicked awake, rolled onto my stomach, blindfolded and bound. This time Zeynep and I were transported together. Although the vehicle roared through the streets at top speed, I could hear the engines of U.S. unmanned aerial vehicles flying overhead as they watched every move made by the resistance. Knowing that these Predator vehicles have the capability to not only transmit video images but also launch guided missiles, I felt extremely vulnerable during that short drive. At the third house our blindfolds were removed, and we were fed a generous breakfast of fried eggs and flatbread.

After drinking a cup of tea, I was escorted into a small room with barred windows. There were three guards at this facility, which appeared to be a small house or workshop. Two of them were middle-aged men, while the other was just a fifteen-year-old

299

boy. They were obviously not front-line mujahedeen but support-
ive of the resistance.

In the first hours they were very strict in enforcing the rules.
I was to sit on a broken chair in the middle of my cell. However,
as the temperature rose to about 45°C and my sun-baked room
became an oven, they compassionately allowed me to venture
outside. By nightfall everyone was so relaxed that Zeynep and I
ate dinner and talked to our guards. The young boy stated that
his only ambition in life was to "die a martyr." Soon after dark
the emir returned and informed us that he had confirmed that
we were not spies. He gave a "Muslim promise" to set us free in
the morning; on this night, though, Zeynep and I would remain
his "guests."

JUST PAST MIDNIGHT, American Apache helicopters attacked.
Their arrival over Tal Afar was greeted by a heavy barrage of
rocket-propelled grenades and cannon fire. We could hear the
distinctive *crack, whump* sounds of the Iraqi grenades being
launched, and then deafening bursts of fire from the Apaches.

We could not see the battle's progress from inside the workshop's open courtyard, but from the sounds of the gunfire we
could plot its course. On several occasions the mujahedeen fighters all across the city screamed, *"Allah akbar! Allah akbar!"* (God
is great!). I had first thought that these cries were in response
to their downing a helicopter, but our young guard explained
that they were cheering the deaths of their own, newly created
martyrs.

At about three o'clock in the morning we heard a loud banging on the courtyard gate. Our guards let a mujahedeen fighter
inside, and he spoke quickly with them in Turkish. Hurriedly a
storeroom was opened and the fighter helped himself to three

rocket-propelled grenades, which he tucked inside his belt. I was able to see inside the small room, which was packed with munitions, and I realized that we were being held captive in one of the resistance's ammunition depots. The fighter took a bowl of water, drank thirstily and rushed back out to the darkened streets. Minutes later, he was on a rooftop about fifty metres away. He managed to launch only two of his rockets before disappearing in a burst of 25-mm cannon fire from an Apache helicopter that blew him to pieces. Following a brief silence came a chorus of "*Allah akbar!*"

IN THE MORNING Tal Afar was strangely quiet except for the continuous buzzing of unmanned Predators overhead. The Apaches had gone, and the resistance was licking its wounds. It was reported that 50 mujahedeen had been killed and another 120 wounded. The worst news was that the emir had been killed—found by a Predator missile that had successfully destroyed his Land Rover. Although his followers celebrated his martyrdom, his death left a power vacuum among the mujahedeen.

Around midmorning a group of gunmen arrived at the workshop to take us away. Zeynep pleaded with them in Turkish, saying that we were to go free—but to no avail. "We received no such instruction," said the man who now appeared to be in charge. "You are spies."

This time they were extremely rough in applying my blindfold. It was tied so tightly that I could sense I was losing blood circulation in my brain. Our captors pushed and prodded me blindly towards a car and then deliberately bashed my head against the door frame. "Jewish pig!" spat one of the guards.

At the fourth house, which smelled like some sort of farm complex, I was once again rushed through doorways and then down

301

into the cellar. In addition to making me wear the blindfold, they placed a hood over my head. I felt I was suffocating in the heat and dust. I could feel the fear well up inside me as one of the gunmen forced me onto a mat and placed the barrel of a Kalashnikov against my neck. "Don't speak," he said. "Don't move."

Another group of men entered the cellar and began questioning Zeynep about our identity. She told them of the emir's promise and advised them that our papers, identification cards and passports were all at the first house. Finally, she and I were allowed to remove our hoods and blindfolds while the mujahedeen left to check our story. I saw that there was another prisoner in the room with us. He was an Iraqi from Mosul who was also accused of spying. He had not been allowed to remove his hood.

Throughout the rest of the morning there was plenty of activity in the resistance bunker. About thirty fighters were busy transferring stockpiles of rocket-propelled grenades and explosives. In addition to hearing the gruff male voices, we could hear an elderly woman shouting encouragement to the men. "They call her *mother*," Zeynep whispered. "She is encouraging her 'sons' to go out and become martyrs and die in battle. Can you believe it?"

Our previous interrogator returned to our makeshift cell to advise us that all the belongings we had been forced to leave behind—our bags, cameras, and identity papers—were now buried in a heap of rubble because a precision-guided bomb had destroyed the first house. With no proof of our nationality or profession, a heated debate erupted among the fighters outside in the corridor.

Overhearing their conversation, Zeynep suddenly gasped, "Oh, my God, they're going to shoot us!" I fought to suppress the panic I felt. It was then that the other prisoner spoke for the first time. In good English he said, "Are you sure?"

The door burst open and several men stepped inside. "Stand up," one of them said to me. "You are the first to die, American pig." My hands were still tied, and I felt helpless as one of them approached me with a blindfold. I told them I did not want a blindfold—not out of any bravado but because I found that my sense of fear was magnified by the inability to see. I received a punch to the head for my protest, and a blindfold was pulled snugly into place. This time they added a gag and a black hood.

Once again, I could feel the claustrophobia and the fear building to panic, and I struggled to maintain some composure. Zeynep's cries of fear and alarm caught the attention of the elderly woman, who apparently had not realized that the men were detaining a female. She entered our cell, and a heated discussion took place between her and the fighters. I was struck several times during this conversation, and I still believed I was about to die. Finally one of the mujahedeen came close to me and whispered, "I have a brother in Canada . . . I have just saved you, my friend—at least for now."

Instead of shooting us, they decided to take us with them. They had learned that the Americans were about to bomb their complex, so they were going to leave Tal Afar until the air strikes were over. The hood and mask remained in place, and the man who said he'd saved me warned me not to make any noise. "If my people hear someone speak English, they will beat you to death before I can stop them. Now move!"

Once again I was manhandled through the passageways and pushed into the back seat of a car. I was shaking uncontrollably as I realized that I was not going to die—at least not at that moment.

ALTHOUGH THE AMERICANS claimed that they had sealed off Tal Afar before launching their offensive, it was nothing more than

303

wishful thinking. In the car it took some time before the mujahedeen relented and allowed Zeynep and me to remove our
hoods and blindfolds. The other hostage had been put in another
vehicle. Our hands were still tied, but I had sweated so much in
the 45°c heat that the moisture had loosened the straps binding my hands. I was able to free them easily and, in an effort to
gain my captors' trust, showed them that my bonds needed to be
retied. The man next to me simply laughed and instructed them
to forget about it. After all, where can you go in the desert?

In a six-car convoy we had left the bunker and were making
our way northward into the open desert. With short grey hair
and a close-cropped beard, the man sitting next to me informed
us that the emir had been his brother. "I'm sorry about his death,"
I said, to which he replied, "Why be sorry? We celebrate his entry
into heaven."

What was reassuring to me was that, as the brother of the
former leader, this man appeared to have filled the immediate
leadership void in the group. I was especially relieved to learn
that his brother had told him of the decision to set us free. He also
said that once our identities were confirmed—via a Google search
on the Internet—he would keep the promise of the martyred emir.
In the meantime, we would remain with the mujahedeen.

AT AROUND TWO o'clock in the afternoon the convoy stopped
near a remote desert house. Nearly thirty fighters had assembled around our car, and they began to conduct a mass prayer.
Zeynep and I were instructed to remain in the car. It was while
they were engrossed in their prayer that I spotted two American
helicopters coming out of the south—low and fast and headed
straight towards our parked convoy. I cried out in alarm. At
first the mujahedeen were angry at the interruption, until they

spotted the approaching threat. Caught out in the open, we were sitting ducks. Nobody could move; we simply watched the helicopters steadily bearing down on us.

At about eight hundred metres' distance the gunships inexplicably banked away to the east without so much as a reconnaissance overpass of our mysterious group of vehicles in the middle of the desert. We had to have been in plain view, but the Americans had turned away. "They always fly the same patrol routes," explained one of the fighters. "They see nothing."

Shortly after the helicopters had veered off, two cars joined us, and the mujahedeen hastily began transferring huge stockpiles of explosives and rockets into them. "We are making them into suicide bombs," said Mubashir, the emir's brother, of the cars being loaded and wired. "These men will head back into Tal Afar and use the vehicles to destroy American armoured vehicles." Four mujahedeen climbed into the suicide cars. As they drove back into the battle, their comrades shouted a final encouragement.

We proceeded on through the desert towards the northern outskirts of Mosul. Along the way we stopped at several farmhouses, where the residents eagerly offered food and water to the fighters. When we passed a Mosul checkpoint, the Iraqi police appeared to take no notice of the dusty column of cars that were packed with bearded men armed with Kalashnikovs and rocket-propelled grenades. A gauntlet of young boys lined the route to cheer our convoy and offer water and cigarettes. Instead of entering the city, however, we headed farther north, to a deserted house that was still under construction. We were ordered inside the building. I now realized that the other hostage, a driver for UNICEF, had spent the entire three-hour desert transit in the trunk of one of the cars. He emerged from the vehicle still blindfolded, covered in dust and sweat and without his shoes. He was in terrible condition but made no complaint as they hurried us into the empty house.

There was some confusion among the fighters because they were eager to return to Tal Afar, not to sit out the battle in a safe house. Soon, all but one of the cars had left. Now only two armed guards remained with us, and the possibility of escape certainly crossed my mind. It was the hottest part of the day, and the sentries were exhausted. The Mosul highway was clearly visible about two kilometres away. With all the passing traffic it would be possible to flag down a ride—if I could only survive the run across the open ground.

Before I could give much thought to such a plan, another car had pulled up at our hideout. Four new mujahedeen strode into the building and immediately began berating the two guards for being lenient with us. The leader of this group was a short, stocky man who strutted about with his ski mask on. He wasted no time in making his thoughts known. "The Turkish girl will live . . . you two will die," he said, pointing at me and the UNICEF driver. "I will cut off your heads at dusk, and you will be buried there." He pointed to a freshly dug grave-sized ditch at about twenty metres from the house.

Zeynep was moved to another room, and we were told to prepare ourselves to die. Although we were forbidden to talk, whenever the guard was distracted the driver and I tried to encourage each other. "At least we will not die alone," the driver said.

As dusk approached we were offered a final meal of flatbread, roast chicken and tomatoes. The maniacal little leader came to watch us eat, all the while aiming his gun at us. "Eat, eat . . . Why do you have no appetite? Are you afraid, American pig?" He laughed at his own joke.

Although I was certainly not hungry, I did my best to choke down a few difficult mouthfuls. Inside, I had to stifle a trembling fear. My fellow prisoner began to sob, and I reached over to take his hand.

"How long do you think the pain will last?" he asked. It was something I had also been carefully considering, and I replied, "About three seconds." The sun was starting to set on the horizon when Mubashir returned. He entered into a heated argument with the leader of the new group. Reassured by the sound of his voice, I risked a glance out of the window—just in time to see the ceremonial dagger being returned to the trunk of the car. We had been spared once again.

IT PROVED IMPOSSIBLE to enter Mosul safely, so we circled back into the desert and spent the night at another farmhouse. The scorching heat of the day had been replaced by a cool breeze, and after a meal of lamb and rice we spent a relatively relaxing eve-ning under the stars. It was the first good sleep I'd had in days, and I began to believe that with Mubashir here to protect us, we might survive this ordeal.

It was during some candid conversations at this farm that I finally learned the identity of my captors. As we talked about the various ethnic factions and politics at play in northern Iraq, I mentioned the group Ansar al-Islam. Mubashir looked surprised at my comment and said, "Don't you know? We are Ansar al-Islam." My heart sank when I heard this because I knew that this group of fundamentalist extremists had links to al Qaeda. "Yes," confided Mubashir. "Osama is our brother in Afghanistan, and al-Zarqawi is our brother in Jordan."

This group had never before released a foreigner, a fact that explained why they had never mentioned ransoming us off as

307

hostages. The Ansar al-Islam fought for their religious beliefs, not money. Although I expressed my fears to Mubashir, he once again stressed that his brother's wish would be granted—provided we were telling the truth.

The farmhouse itself was a simple mud-brick structure with two small rooms. A plastic tarp provided the roof. The house had no actual windows or doors, just openings in the walls. There were only two metal cots, without mattresses, and the mujahedeen brought these outside for Zeynep and me to sleep on. They also provided us with a couple of filthy blankets. The UNICEF driver was kept inside the hut. The enormity of their generosity became apparent when the Ansar al-Islam fighters began preparing their own bedding. They had straw mats, under whose edges they carefully placed small rocks so that the edges were raised off the ground. It was explained that this was a precaution against scorpions and camel spiders. These dangerous creepy-crawlies obviously elicited more fear in the mujahedeen than American attack gunships did.

In the middle of the night I awoke, chilled by the night breeze. I rolled onto my other side, thereby putting the wind against my back, and clutched my blanket tightly around my shoulders. As I did that, I noticed my ski-masked antagonist standing guard at the roadside about twenty metres away. Sensing my movement, he got up from his seat and moved towards me. I feigned sleep as he stood directly over me, watching me on the cot. After what seemed like a long time, he disappeared into the farmhouse. I heard his returning footsteps and realized that he was now standing behind me. I felt a slight movement and then realized he was gently placing another blanket over me. His task complete, he strutted back to his roadside post.

We spent Friday morning at the farm awaiting word that we could enter Mosul and be granted an audience with the new emir. Again, everything seemed to be relaxed, and although the notion of having someone pronounce a live-or-die sentence upon me was still very frightening, Mubashir assured us that his brother's promise would be kept. Unfortunately for us, Mubashir had become quite ill and was complaining of stomach pains. He was sleeping fitfully in the room where Zeynep and I were being kept, and through an opening we could see the other prisoner in the adjacent room. We had been told repeatedly not to communicate with him, but when the guards' backs were turned and Mubashir was definitely asleep, Zeynep would exchange mime gestures with him.

Zeynep had learned that the reason the mujahedeen believed that the UNICEF driver was Jewish was because of his long sideburns, which they thought resembled Orthodox Jewish ringlets. By making a chopping gesture with her hands, Zeynep thought she could warn him of the danger and perhaps entice him to shave them off. It was obvious that he did not understand what she implied, because he soon became visibly panicked. The more she tried to illustrate the shaving of sideburns, the more frightened he became. Finally, with the guards out of earshot, he asked, "Why are they going to cut off my ears?"

Once this misconception had been hurriedly cleared up, the UNICEF driver took the next opportunity to shave his sideburns off completely, by using the communal razor at the wash station—a water pump with a basin and a small mirror. In fact, he shaved them a full inch above his ears.

Throughout this period of forced inactivity, Zeynep and I began watching a large black ant in its effort to drag the carcass of a dead cockroach up the wall of our room. Amazingly, the ant succeeded time after time in getting its heavy load to the top of the wall, but it would fail to find a passage under the tightly drawn plastic tarp roof. Eventually, the dead cockroach would slip the ant's grasp and plummet back to the dirt floor. The industrious ant would climb back down, locate the body and start all over again. "That ant is like us," said Zeynep. "Every time we get close to being released, the whole process starts all over again."

We vowed to take our inspiration from that ant, and as corny as it seemed, we believed it was a sign not to lose hope.

We got the word at around two o'clock that the emir would see us. We climbed into one car—the UNICEF driver in the trunk, Zeynep and I along with Mubashir in the back seat and two guards in the front. Our hands were not tied, and we wore no blindfolds; everything seemed to be going well. However, once we were inside Mosul, it became apparent that something had gone wrong with the plan.

We stopped at several homes and picked up different guides at various locations. Eventually we were taken to a large house in a northern suburb. The UNICEF driver was released from the trunk and taken into a small anteroom beneath the staircase while Zeynep and I were made to sit on the floor of an empty room. There were about a dozen young men inside this house, and they were extremely hostile towards us. Blankets were placed across all the windows despite the soaring temperature. Zeynep whispered that these men were not Turkmen but Arabs and that she no longer understood their conversation. Complaining of being ill, Mubashir now seemed uninterested in our fate. He made some sort of statement to the Arabs on our behalf and then bade us farewell. He and his men were heading back into Tal Afar to join the fight.

Within minutes of his departure the Arabs burst into the room and roughly blindfolded me. When I tried to protest, I was kicked in the ribs, the wind knocked out of me. "Shut up, American spy!" my assailant shouted.

For the next hour I was interrogated. Again my captors began with the presumption that I was either a CIA or a Mossad spy. I gave them all the details of my identity and, when asked how I could confirm these "lies," told them to research my writings on the Internet. In particular, they could not believe that I had written features for Al Jazeera's Web site. Although it was intense, the questioning ended without any physical force being used. I was greatly relieved but I soon realized that my relief was premature.

IN THE MESS hall the American soldiers listened intently, and as I detailed the torture I had endured, they were transfixed and often gave involuntary shudders in empathy. I told them of the men in masks, the ropes, the clubs beating my feet, the reeds whipping my feet, and I admitted my belief that I was going to be killed.

I also acknowledged that I had lost all track of time. I could have been tortured for five minutes or twenty-five; I had no real conception of the actual duration of the beatings. I did remember that despite the excruciating pain in my legs, I always feared that the next blow would be to my genitals. Upended and with my legs splayed apart, I felt extremely vulnerable. When the beating finally stopped, I felt a tremendous sense of relief that they had not used the batons on my crotch.

After my feet were cut loose I was roughly pulled upright, and the interrogator handed me a pen and paper. "You will write down all the Web sites you think might help to confirm that you are in fact a Canadian journalist," he said. I made some remark that I would have gladly done so without the beating, but my attempt at black humour was ignored.

I had been badly beaten, and as I walked out of the anteroom back into the main parlour, most of the Arab guards gathered to

311

see my reaction. I tried my best not to let them see any weakness, by pressing the pen hard against the paper so that they could not see my hands shaking. Taking the list of Web sites from me, the interrogator said, "If this checks out, you'll live . . . If you lied— you die." Although this threat was becoming a familiar one, it was no less convincing for that.

A few minutes later I was ushered into an adjacent room and told to lie face down on the floor. A gun barrel was placed against the back of my neck. It was Zeynep's turn to be beaten, and as she cried out in pain, the guard behind me kept repeating, "You can spare her the pain. Simply confess that you are a spy." I con- tinued to utter denials, so he spat on my head and said, "Only a dog would let a woman suffer like that!" I thought to myself, And what kind of animal would torture a woman?

For several hours after the beating I was kept alone in that room. My legs were aching and would occasionally seize up on me. I tried to stand, but the guards insisted that I remain seated on a mat. When the interrogator finally re-entered my holding cell, he said, "You failed the test on the Internet. Prepare yourself to die—tonight." As the door banged shut behind him, I again had an all-consuming sense of dread. The next time the door opened, it was an armed guard and one of the Students of Islam carrying a platter of food. Once again I was being encouraged to eat my final meal.

Although I did not know it at the time, Zeynep and the UNI- CEF driver had been set free, and both of them were told that I had been beheaded. Zeynep had seen my shoes, sportcoat and bloodstains on the floor, and she was convinced I had been killed.

AFTER I HAD picked away at my food, the dishes were cleared away and a heavy-set young Arab entered the room. He was grinning from ear to ear, and I recognized him as one of my torturers. "I am the lucky one who has been chosen to kill you, American dog," he said.

It was at this time that I decided to play my final card. Zeynep had always told me that I should tell our captors that I wished to convert to Islam. Even if I wasn't sincere, she thought it might buy me time, if not freedom. I said, "I want you to teach me an Islamic prayer before you kill me. A man about to die should have a God to pray to, shouldn't he?" Other guards and students overheard this, and they seemed excited at the prospect of converting a *kafir* (infidel) and then executing him.

As they started to explain the conversion process and necessary prayers, the leader of the group returned. He put an end to the commotion by informing me that my religious conversion was no longer necessary as I was "free to go." Thinking this might be yet another test of my resolve to convert, I explained that in that case it was even more important "because a man needs a God to thank for sparing him his life."

I was advised that the procedure would have to be performed at a later date because a car was waiting to take me to a safe house in preparation for my release. Once again, I dared to start believing that I might survive this ordeal.

MY EYES WERE taped shut with electrical tape, and sunglasses were placed overtop the tape. I was then led gently outside to a car. The night air felt cool and refreshing, and I tried to keep my euphoria in check, reminding myself that it was not over yet.

However, by the time we had driven several kilometres and my escorts had led me inside a new house, I felt certain that I had been saved. The glasses were taken off and the tape removed. I found myself in a clean home, sitting on a bed, looking at three smiling Arabs. My guards from the other house were in the doorway, and one of them waved his hand in a fluttering motion, smiled and said, "Free . . . Bye-bye." The door shut behind them, and all of a sudden the three Arabs stopped smiling. The big man standing in the centre of the room pulled a pair of handcuffs from behind his back and strode towards me. The nightmare started all over again.

THEY CUFFED MY hands behind my back and instructed me to sleep. Two of them—armed with pistols—slept in the same room with me, and the homeowner took the precaution of padlocking us in. It proved impossible to sleep with my arms pinned back like that, and after two hours I felt a stabbing pain in my shoulders. In an attempt to alleviate the pressure, I tried to sit up on the edge of the bed. Startled by my movement, one of the Arabs put his pistol to my forehead and motioned for me to lie back down. For the next six hours I could only try to block out the pain.

The following morning it became clear that instead of being taken to a safe house en route to freedom, I had been transferred to yet another fundamentalist faction. At about ten o'clock I was "prepped" for my new interrogation by having my feet and hands chained to the bed and my eyes once again taped firmly shut. At least three additional terrorists had entered the room and begun talking with my guards. Anticipating yet another beating, I fought to control my fear. One man simply stated in excellent English, "We know that you are a Mossad spy." As I started to protest, he interrupted me: "Don't waste your breath. You have twenty-four hours to decide whether to tell the truth and die with a clear conscience . . . or go to your death as a liar. That is your choice. Think it over." With that said, the newcomers promptly left the house.

I spent that entire day chained to the bed and, for the most part, blindfolded. As a gesture of compassion my captors occasionally freed my eyes so that I could watch the television. All the programming was focused on the anniversary of the World Trade Center attacks. It was September 11, and I was tied to a bed in an al Qaeda cell house in Iraq. I felt my fate was truly sealed.

With so many hours to once again contemplate my imminent demise, I began to think of all the practical aspects that would be attendant upon my death. Zeynep would inform my family of my capture and death—if she had been released, as my guards had told me—so my thoughts drifted to things such as, How would they repatriate my body? Was there a process for moving corpses out of Iraq? Who would take care of the funeral arrangements? And so on.

That evening I was asked once again what I would prefer as my final meal. After arguing, again, that my appetite wasn't exactly stimulated by the prospect of death, I asked for roast chicken. When the food arrived, my captors kept one of my hands tied to the bed and a pistol aimed at the back of my head. It seemed that they were taking no chances of letting me escape execution.

It was only 9:00 PM—just eleven hours after they had first come, not the promised twenty-four—when the three terrorists returned. I did not feel cheated out of the time as I was dreading the thought of another night of agony in the handcuffs. I had made my peace with God and, if necessary, I was prepared to die. Another thirteen hours of mental anguish were not necessary.

As soon as everyone had settled around my bed, the interrogator said that I did not have to fear any torture, because this round of questioning would be far more straightforward. "It is either life or knife, with each answer that you give us," he said, "so please relax." For more than an hour I carefully answered all their questions, being careful to avoid the obvious traps. For instance, when asked, "Have you ever visited the State of Israel?" I answered, "No, I have never been to the occupied State of Palestine."

I had no idea whether or not my answers were convincing—in fact, I suspect that the decision to release me had already been made at some higher level—but during what would be the last of my lengthy replies the interrogator suddenly said, "Stop. Get your things. You will live. You are free."

Once the handcuffs had been removed, I was handed my shoes and jacket, and it now seemed as though my captors were the ones anxious to be rid of me. With my eyes again taped shut, I was driven to a main road where one of the guards flagged down a passing taxi. Another man ripped the tape off my eyes, pushed 10,000 dinars (US$6) into my shirt pocket and pushed me head first into the back of the cab.

I was free.

ALTHOUGH MY PHYSICAL presence in front of them should have removed some of the drama as to how my story concluded, the American soldiers were quick to start asking me a barrage of questions. The most obvious, of course, was, How had my release been secured? I explained that, unbeknownst to me at the time, the Turkish government was not only aware that Zeynep and I were being held hostage, but actively negotiating for our release. Zeynep's employers had noticed her failure to report from Tal Afar, and our prolonged absence had prompted her government to mobilize its intelligence resources in northern Iraq.

Other American soldiers wanted to know if the experience had "fucked me up mentally." I confessed that in those first few days following my release I had difficulty accepting the reality that I had survived, and each time I awoke I had to suppress the panic evoked by the belief that my transit to safety had been just a dream. This panic disappeared the minute I returned home, to familiar surroundings and a place of security.

When my story had broken in the international media, one of the most persistent questions was, "Would you ever go back?" At that time my categorical response was, "No—absolutely not." The hostage taking had occurred on my twentieth trip into Iraq. Since August 2000, I had reported on the situation before, during and after the U.S.-led intervention, and I realized that each visit was becoming more dangerous than the previous one.

Despite my multitude of contacts and my knowledge of the various factions, particularly in northern Iraq, I had not been able to prevent my own capture. The fact that it had been the U.S.-organized Iraqi police that had handed Zeynep Tugrul and me over to the Ansar al-Islam mujahedeen illustrated the rapidly blurring lines. During our captivity we were privy to a rare inside perspective on the collaboration that existed between police and insurgents and on how surprisingly widespread and multilayered these links were. When you realize you can no longer identify the players, it is time to get off the field.

This response naturally led one lieutenant to ask what had changed my mind and brought me back to Tal Afar. Without hesitation I replied that journalists can achieve no greater success than to have their work make a difference. By reading my material and flying me in to brief his troops, not only had Colonel H.R. McMaster only complimented my work but he had validated the pain and suffering that I had endured to obtain such a rare insight.

AFGHANISTAN FOLLOWING THE U.S. INTERVENTION, 2001

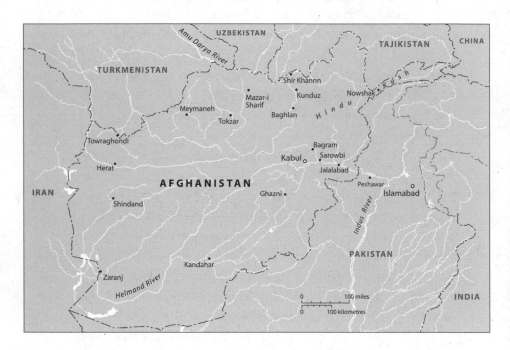

10

BACK ON THE HORSE

The Taliban is number one. That's
why they are always kicking our ass.

RAMIN, AFGHAN NATIONAL ARMY SOLDIER

THE HOSTAGE ORDEAL CERTAINLY SHOOK my sense of invincibility, and on my return to Canada it was a tremendous challenge for me to compartmentalize my field experiences. It was also a tremendous emotional shock to my family, friends and staff members.

When the *Ottawa Citizen* published a full front-page photograph of me with the headline "Tortured and Beaten," Katherine was deluged with calls of concern and e-mails of support. Although he was just ten years old at the time, Kirk took things in stride. That day at school his principal, teachers and a counsellor brought him in for a private interview. They asked him if he understood what had happened to his father, and Kirk replied in the affirmative. When asked how that affected him, Kirk shrugged dismissively and said, "That's what my dad does. He's a war correspondent." My mother was far less understanding, and although I was forty-three years old, I had to endure a full-scale maternal guilt assault for putting my family through such a terrible ordeal.

For her part, Katherine had been worried sick, but her confirmed knowledge that I was being held hostage had only lasted a few hours. When Zeynep was released from captivity, she had been taken to a halfway house—presumably for insurgent sympathizers—to await being picked up by Turkish intelligence. She managed to gain access to a computer and sent a short e-mail to the *Esprit de Corps* office. Zeynep believed I was dead then, but she felt the authorities might work harder to secure the release of my body if they thought I were still alive. Owing to the time zone difference, her e-mail arrived just after the staff had left work on a Friday afternoon. Although everyone was a little uneasy that I had missed the deadline for my weekly column and had not been in contact with the office for four days, they assured Katherine that everything would be okay.

It was not until mid-morning of the following day that Kath and Kirk opened the office in the hope of receiving word from me. Instead, they found Zeynep's e-mail, which contained a clever reference to Kirk's birthday and convinced Katherine that it was not a hoax. Katherine informed the Canadian Department of Foreign Affairs of my circumstances and brought them up to speed on the crisis.

Phil Atkinson in Mosul—the last person known to have seen us alive—was e-mailed, and the U.S. authorities in Iraq were alerted to our abduction. Katherine was also able to contact someone who confirmed that the Iraqi Turkmen Front in Ankara was aware of the terrible fighting in Tal Afar and of the fact that Zeynep and I had disappeared. It was news to them that, according to Zeynep, I was being held in Mosul. By the end of the day a Canadian Foreign Affairs representative had called Katherine to say that there was still no news. As the staff and neighbours began organizing a round-the-clock watch on the phones and computers, Katherine received a call from Aydemir Erman, Turkey's ambassador to Canada. "Our intelligence agency has secured your husband's release. He is safe," was the most welcome news he could have told her.

I still had no access to a telephone then, but I had been taken to the Iraqi Turkmen Front office in Mosul. A handful of security guards provided me with a hot shower and a fresh shirt. Through a few words of English and sign language, they told me that a Turkish intelligence operative would pick me up the following morning. When the agent arrived, I had to be assisted to his car because my legs were seizing up from the beating.

It was not until we had driven to Erbil and I was reunited with Zeynep that I finally had access to a telephone. It was around two in the morning when I called Katherine in Ottawa to reassure her that I was indeed alive and free. Our conversation was very brief, but that connection to a different world allowed me to relax a little. As soon as I hung up the phone, my legs simply collapsed and I realized that my mind had been overriding my pain threshold to keep me moving until I felt safe. Hearing Katherine's voice flicked that switch, and the floodgates of pain were flung wide open. Still to come were hours of clandestine road travel through northern Iraq, a border to cross without identification, a lengthy debriefing session with Turkish intelligence—complete with a review of mug shots of suspected al Qaeda members—acquiring a temporary passport and rebooking a homeward flight, but that single phone call home was the moment that I really began to believe I would survive to tell the tale.

Since I had not been able to file any stories from Iraq and we were still on a shoestring budget, I had to write my account of the ordeal as soon as I returned to Ankara. Despite my injuries and mental exhaustion, I did not have the luxury of delaying this task. *Esprit de Corps* needed my five-thousand-word report to offset the travel expenses, so I had no option but to start writing. In the midst of all the writing I was deluged with media requests from around the world. Often interviewers asked if I would continue in my profession, and I once again announced that I was giving up war reporting for good. I was sincere in that sentiment.

In my first few months back in Ottawa I concentrated on revitalizing *Esprit de Corps* magazine. We had broken off the crusade against corruption in Department of National Defence Headquarters in 1998. After the extensive recommendations of the Somalia Inquiry and the resulting reforms, other oversight agencies such as the Canadian Forces ombudsman were now in place.

That we had stopped fighting did not mean that the brass suddenly supported our publication wholeheartedly. So we decided to rebrand, and although we had never ceased publication, we relaunched *Esprit de Corps* in April 2005. We changed the logo, revamped the format, added to our page count and hosted a large, formal reception—complete with a pin-up calendar for the troops and with Miss Universe Canada in attendance as a hostess. Thankfully, the defence industry responded to this make-over in a positive fashion, and our advertising roster began to grow. With the hatchet publicly buried, it was once again safe to be seen supporting *Esprit de Corps*. For the first time in a decade the magazine became self-sustaining.

One of the key guests of honour at our relaunch party was Turkish Ambassador Aydemir Erman. Since the hostage ordeal Erman had become a personal friend, and the embassy had helped to promote the book *Among the Others* across Canada. While I wasn't heading back into Iraq, I didn't consider Turkey

322

off limits, and I often travelled back to Ankara and even visited the border area. Through Ambassador Erman I made the acquaintance of the Azerbaijani ambassador and his counsellor, who had a keen interest in my writings about the Turkmen of Iraq—the Azeris of Azerbaijan, also a Turkic people, feel they are part of a common brotherhood. Their small embassy in Ottawa was aggressively trying to promote wider Canadian interest in Azerbaijan and hoped to make our business leaders aware of the opportunities in their country.

I was invited to participate in a small press tour of Azerbaijan in the summer of 2006. At first I intended to decline because my reporting so far had focused primarily on conflict, not on the development of trade and diplomatic relations. However, the counsellor explained that this angle could also be pursued because Azerbaijan and Armenia were still engaged in what could be described as a frozen conflict. Not knowing the background of this 1992–94 war—I had never heard of it—I was intrigued. Plus the fact that Baku sounded like an extremely exotic port of call. I agreed to tag along.

The Azerbaijan trip proved to be a plunge into the deep end of a complex economic and strategic situation. Awash in oil revenues from newly discovered offshore deposits in the Caspian Sea, the former Soviet republic was rife with corruption and political intrigue.

The war with Armenia had been a disastrous defeat, resulting in the occupation of 20 per cent of Azerbaijan's sovereign territory and the displacement of more than 800,000 civilians. Azerbaijan's secular Muslim regime was proclaiming a commitment to Western democratic reform, and as a result neighbouring Russian and Iranian intelligence services were certainly complicit in monitoring and manipulating the underlying instability.

For me, it was a steep and challenging learning curve. Although I was granted rare access to the Azeri front lines which surrounded the disputed Armenian-occupied territory of Nagorno-Karabakh, media features on this frozen conflict proved a difficult sell in Canada—particularly when Canadian troops were being increasingly drawn into a very hot combat zone in southern Afghanistan.

While at Baku International Airport I noticed that Azerbaijan Airlines offered direct flights to Kabul, Afghanistan. By the summer of 2006, a Canadian battle group had completed its move south from the capital to Kandahar, and the casualty count had begun to escalate. The newly elected Conservative government in Canada had not called into question its Liberal predecessor's decision to take on a combat role. Instead, Prime Minister Stephen Harper embraced the new mission by flying to Kandahar Airfield, where he declared that Canada would not "cut and run" from the dangerous mission. This declaration was followed by members of Parliament from all political parties taking turns praising Canada's troops and pledging to support them.

The entire Afghan mission was dumbed down to a simple equation wherein the Taliban was bad—and therefore fighting was good. Fearmongers in the pro-war camp raised the spectre of Canadian women being forced to wear burkas if we didn't stop the Taliban in their own backyard. It was a ridiculous notion, but as I voiced that opinion through my commentaries in the media, my arguments were undermined by the fact that my experience had been in other conflict zones and not Afghanistan. Believing that our soldiers were going to be sacrificed in a far-off land without Canadians understanding the bigger picture, I decided in the Baku airport that I would once again head back into a hot war zone.

REMAINING FASCINATED WITH the cultural and political intrigue of Azerbaijan, I continued to use Baku as the staging area for my trips into Afghanistan. I also relied upon my Turkish and Turkmen connections to mitigate some of the risk of travelling on my own. Ambassador Aydemir Erman had been Turkey's representative to Afghanistan during the Taliban regime. In the course of those six years spent on the ground, Erman had made a tremendous network of connections among the northern Afghan leadership, who had subsequently replaced the deposed Taliban. He provided me not only with letters of introduction to key officials but also with gifts to bear on his behalf to his old friends. The Turkish foreign ministry maintained an embassy in Kabul and a consulate in Mazar-i-Sharif. They were given advance notice of my impending visits and offered full co-operation in return.

In addition, I was assisted by Thomas Hutson, a diplomat who had resigned from the U.S. State Department in 1999 to protest the decision to bomb Yugoslavia. As a result of my Balkan reports, I had met Hutson at a black-tie dinner in Chicago in 2001 where we were both honoured by the Serbian-American community. At that time Hutson had spoken of his experiences in Afghanistan and, in particular, his close friend General Abdul Rashid Dostum.

Dostum was a renowned warlord and a friend of Aydemir Erman. It was my plan to interview Dostum and write a detailed profile of one of the most notorious characters in the past three decades of Afghan history. A biography of Dostum would be a useful vehicle to illustrate to Canadians the nature of the Afghan warlords and the complexity of the ethnic and tribal divisions in Afghanistan. I had pitched this story to a number of editors, and with assurances from Dostum's handlers that he would meet with me, I felt I had a solid base to launch a trip into Kabul. As with any well-prepared plan involving Afghanistan, everything went wrong before it even got underway.

I scheduled my flight from Baku to Kabul to round out a full Middle East tour in January 2007. After a trip to the Iraq-Turkey border, I met with Azeri officials in Baku and was allowed to visit the demarcation lines at Nagorno-Karabakh. The last leg of the tour was the jaunt to Kabul, which was scheduled to last only five days. Unfortunately, the first three of those days were spent in Baku, waiting for the crews in Kabul to clear a massive snowfall from the runways. This setback ended up proving incredibly fortuitous in the end because the cast of characters on that delayed flight was a unique assortment of trades and nationalities. The initial atmosphere of suspicion and mistrust was soon broken down by our shared circumstances and duty-free booze.

By the time we were finally cleared for takeoff, I felt far more confident about my travels and I had made some fantastic new friends. Among them were a former Russian helicopter pilot who had flown combat missions in Afghanistan and who was now a marketing representative for a mobile phone company, and an American Vietnam veteran who now worked as a contractor in northern Afghanistan. The veteran had also had plenty of dealings with Dostum and a had tremendous network of former special-forces types and contractors in Kabul. I soon learned that everyone in the international community looked out for each other's security because it was in their collective best interests.

This became evident from the moment we landed in Kabul. As this primitive airport operated only daylight flights and in clear weather, every incoming aircraft arrived daily at virtually the same time. Of course, this created a massive influx of people at once that completely overwhelmed the customs and immigration kiosks. Every policeman and official worked the crowd,

326

demanding baksheesh to move people to the front of the queue. Since our little group refused to pay any money, we were among the very last people to be processed.

Once through the checkpoint, we proceeded into an unlit hall where the handlers had simply dumped all the baggage. Again, people with flashlights sought baksheesh to help travellers find their own suitcases. It was a complete madhouse, and one of my companions pointed out that after six years of U.S. occupation, if the Afghans had wanted to light the baggage carousels, the carousels would have been lit. Instead, the darkness and confusion made it a pickpocket's dream come true.

I was supposed to have someone waiting to pick me up, but as the last of the travellers departed and the parking lot emptied, with no sign of my driver, my new friends insisted that I travel with them to the four-star Serena Hotel. As darkness closed in on the Afghan capital, a lone foreigner stranded at the airport would have been a sitting duck, so I readily agreed. The Serena was an absolutely stunning hotel for any location, but set against the backdrop of war-ravaged, poverty-stricken Kabul, it was like a mirage. During our prolonged stay in Baku we had not had access to our luggage, so I took this opportunity to shower for the first time in four days and change into some fresh clothes. My temporary host, who had been one of the men I had spent the past few days with in the Baku airport, was a secretive New York lawyer who kept telling me not to get too comfortable. When I finally emerged from the refreshing shower, he was beaming. "Your missing contacts just called. They're coming to pick you up."

My new digs were at a small guest house run by ACTED, a French non-governmental organization. The main building was a former mansion, but my quarters were to be the old gardener's shack across the walled courtyard. The price was right—about us$25 a night—but I quickly discovered that my hut had only a wood stove for heat. That first night the temperature plunged to −27°C, and the last of my logs had burned out by three in the morning. With absolutely no insulation and with doors that did not even come fully to the floor, this shack brought back memories of my freezing tent experiences in Shilo, Manitoba. As I warmed up in the main house the next morning, I learned that I had even worse news to deal with. An aide calmly told me that General Dostum had waited for me, but after two days he had flown to Uzbekistan and was no longer in the country.

The only other story I had pitched before leaving Canada was that of an outside-the-wire, unembedded trip down south into the volatile Kandahar region. It was dangerous, and I still had reservations about making this trip as a result of my Iraq experience, but I needed to make it economically viable.

So on January 22 I found myself on a UN-operated Dash 8 flight from Kabul to Kandahar. Seated next to me was Emil, an Afghan from Jalalabad. I had arranged to travel with the Senlis Council, one of the few civilian agencies operating in the Kandahar region. Emil was a member of the Senlis team, and one of his responsibilities was to provide security for his co-workers when they ventured out of their compound to ply their trade.

328   Our discussion centred on the violent instability and growing insurgency in Kandahar. "You are lucky, sir, because you are a foreigner," Emil said. "If the Taliban captures us, they will either kill you right away or hold you for ransom. For Afghans caught working for the infidels, it will mean torture before they finally kill us." He was lost in thought for a moment and then he looked at me solemnly and said, "Promise me that if we are taken, you will kill me before they torture me."

I mumbled an affirmative, but this morbid exchange left me further unnerved. The inherent danger of venturing into the heartland of the Taliban was illustrated by Kandahar's tiny civilian air terminal. There were only a handful of westerners in the group waiting for their luggage, and even they had transformed themselves with headscarves, turbans and, in the case of two women, burkas in order to blend in with the locals.

The drivers and contacts waiting to meet the arriving passengers were all armed, even though they were civilians. The Senlis delegation was no exception. Jorrit Kamminga came forward to greet us, wearing a Muslim cap, baggy pants and the flowing shirt-dress that is the standard Pashtun attire. Despite his clothing, the thirty-year-old native of the Netherlands could not disguise his blond hair and pale complexion. "They call me the Tal-albino," he said, laughing.

Emil and I piled our gear in the back and clambered aboard the Land Cruiser. In addition to carrying Kamminga and the driver, the vehicle contained one other passenger. Wynand Lamprech, known as Vinno, was a former South African army officer turned security consultant and was employed by Senlis to organize its protection force. Vinno was armed with a Kalashnikov and a side arm, but our real security materialized once we had crossed the airport's boundary. He uttered a few commands via walkie-talkie, and two additional Land Cruisers manoeuvred onto the Kandahar highway—one in front, one behind and both crammed with Afghan gunmen. As I had not yet acquired local clothing or headgear, Kamminga advised me to wrap a blanket around the back of my head and to keep low in the seat. "We cannot be invisible, but we don't want to broadcast the fact that we are foreigners," he said.

The traffic was light as we entered the city. The few police checkpoints that we passed were manned by indifferent Afghans who simply waved everyone through. Only once did I see a small coalition force manning a hillock, well back from the highway.

Otherwise, there was absolutely no international presence visible on the streets of Kandahar. Unlike Kabul, where you constantly saw foreign military and civilian vehicles, here only the local cars, bicycles and tuk-tuks clogged the narrow streets around the central market.

Upon arriving at the unmarked Senlis compound, the three vehicles in our small convoy took up positions to block the road and then backed in through the gateway in rapid succession. As we dismounted, Vinno gathered his guards to debrief them on the patrol, and I was ushered inside the building by Kamminga to meet the other Senlis team members.

The introductions were brief as word had been passed that the entire crew would be heading out again in less than an hour. In that time, I would have to be transformed into a passable Pashtun. More importantly, lunch was to be served before our departure. Everyone on the team, from Afghan guards to European researchers, ate together. "This is essentially an Afghan house—we respect the Afghan customs and eat Afghan food," said Norine MacDonald, the Senlis Council's president and founder, as I took my place on the cushions. After the dishes were taken away and the traditional green tea had been served, Vinno got to his feet and announced that the convoy briefing would be in twenty minutes. Another flurry of activity was set in motion by this directive; guards checked their weapons, researchers packed their video equipment, and foreigners were turbaned-up by Afghan compatriots. The convoy would include seven vehicles and seventeen armed Afghan gunmen. In addition to this escort, each western Senlis member carried a weapon for self-defence.

Norine MacDonald was the only woman in the group, but she dressed as an Afghan boy and carried her own Kalashnikov. It is not the custom for non-governmental organizations conducting aid work to carry such an arsenal, but the security situation in southern Afghanistan made it necessary. "If the Taliban really want to take us, they will succeed," said Vinno. "The weapons provide a deterrent, in that an attack on us will cost them their lives as well."

This mission was to be mounted in the volatile Panjwaii district, which in previous months had been devastated by fighting between coalition forces and Taliban supporters. The Senlis team was bringing a truckload of food to a camp of displaced Afghans who had been forced to flee their homes. In addition to delivering food, Senlis would establish a small temporary medical clinic at the site to give some primary treatment and dispense some medicine.

However, the true purpose of the Senlis team's foray into Panjwaii was to collect information from the locals in order to assess the extent of the overall crisis. The survey conducted by the team would examine the effectiveness of both the insurgency and the coalition forces' counterinsurgency efforts. In 2006, the Senlis Council had tabled an extensive report showing that the Afghan government's policy of poppy crop eradication only exacerbated the economic hardship of an already impoverished nation, because there had been no compensation for the farmers whose crops had been destroyed. Although it was difficult to acquire a wide range of input due to the security constraints, the Senlis team would try to talk to as many people as possible at the camp.

When we arrived at the cluster of mud huts and tents, Vinno established a central vehicle park and then sent his gunmen to establish a loose perimeter. Although there was no advance notice, word spread quickly and a crowd soon formed. As well as watching for any signs of Taliban activity, some of the guards needed to remain close to the distribution point in case things became unruly. It seemed that everyone knew the drill, as Afghan men quietly assembled in two long seated rows to await their food bundles. A large group of women and children formed in separate rows.

The medical clinic was up and running in a matter of minutes. Senlis used an Afghan doctor, who was assisted by Ed McCormick, an advanced-care paramedic from Vancouver. Given the volume of patients and the short time available, the examinations were cursory and the prescribed treatments rudimentary, but because these people had no other access to medical care, the Senlis care was well received.

Behind a small hut just out of sight of the food line, Kamminga had established an area where a Senlis video cameraman recorded interviews with the Afghans to substantiate their reports. Out along the lengthening queue Norine MacDonald and her translator conducted their own questionnaire. One of the gimmicks MacDonald used to endear herself to her interview subjects was to snap Polaroid photographs of them. Invariably, the recipients stared intently as their own images appeared, and then they continued to hold their photographs by the corners, fascinated. Distracted in this manner, the Afghans freely gave answers.

332 There was no sign of either the Taliban or the coalition forces. Several young Afghan men ominously observed the proceedings from a safe distance before riding off on their motor scooters. Regardless of how safe and secure things may have seemed, Vinno set a maximum of two hours on site. "Any more than that and you're just giving them [the Taliban] time to get themselves sorted out," he said. When the time was up, the food bags in the truck had nearly gone. Since the queue remained as large as ever, he ordered the Senlis team to pack up. As the last of the food was

emptied from the truck, people who had waited in vain predict-
ably began to vent their anger and frustration.

Once we were back at the Senlis compound, the process of col-
lating the data and photographs began immediately. A lot was
learned this day—particularly just how little the locals understood the nature of the fighting that had uprooted their lives.
Kamminga observed, "For the most part, they don't know who
is doing the bombing—either the Taliban or the Afghan government troops. They don't even comprehend the role of the
coalition forces for the simple reason that they never see them."

The data collected over the previous few months would be
analyzed and tabled in conjunction with the 2007 International
Institute for Strategic Studies in London. Owing to such tight
timetables, eighteen-hour days were the norm for the Senlis
team, and there was no such thing as a day off. "It really isn't
that difficult for us," said Kamminga. "It's not like we can just
head downtown and hang out at the local bar."

Security remained tight around the compound at night, with
twenty-four guards posted around the perimeter and observation
posts. On average, Senlis Council members spent one month in
Kandahar before returning to the head office in Paris.

Norine MacDonald's first trip into Afghanistan had taken
place in January 2005, but by 2007 she lived in Kabul almost
full time. A very youthful fifty, MacDonald kept fit with a row-
ing machine in her personal quarters. Despite the overt sexism in
the Afghan culture, she was easily able to exert her authority over
her locally hired employees. "They accept me as the boss because
they understand that I'm committed to the people of Afghanistan," she said. "They're also very protective of me as a woman."

Since almost all international non-government organizations
have withdrawn from southern Afghanistan or are employing

only a caretaker staff of locals, one would think that the information being collected by Senlis would be a vital resource for the coalition forces. However, getting its message through to the local military commanders proved to be one of the council's biggest obstacles. In the past, whenever Senlis released a report, NATO spokesmen were quick to attack the source.

"One Canadian officer went on television suggesting that we were fabricating our data from air-conditioned offices," said Kamminga. "He suggested that we should see things first-hand on the ground—and yet that is exactly what we do."

I WOULD DISCOVER just how wide the divide was between the military forces and the civilians who operated in the Kandahar region on my second morning. As we were looking to touch base with some nearby Canadian troops, Norine arranged for us to travel to Fort Wilson, a forward operating base in the Panjwaii district.

We arrived in time to witness a touching scene, the likes of which public relations teams only dream: two Canadian army medics were attending to an injured Afghan child as his father thanked them profusely. The previous evening, the young boy had scalded his feet when he upset a pot of boiling water. With no access to medical attention, the father had put his son in a wheelbarrow and brought him to the one place he knew he could get help: the Canadian outpost on the edge of the Panjwaii district.

The medics cleaned the boy's burns and applied antibiotic ointments while the father nodded his head, muttering, *"Teshekura"* (thank you) over and over again. Once the treatment was complete, the beaming Afghan man happily wheeled his son back to their village. Unfortunately for a Canadian military hard-pressed to win a hearts-and-minds campaign both in Kandahar

334

and at home in Canada, this success story was not captured on film. Not because no one got the story out (I did), but because the military brass ordered me not to film the event. I was told not to film Canadian soldiers administering first aid to an Afghan child.

The saga had started at about ten o'clock that morning when we had pulled up in front of the base and dismounted from our vehicles. Leaving our Afghan security detachment and our personal weapons behind, five of us advanced on foot to the front gate. As we approached, two young soldiers and a warrant officer greeted us cordially. Despite the fact that our arrival was unannounced and that we were dressed as local Afghans (complete with Pashtun-style beards), the senior non-commissioned officer recognized me. "Hey, I just finished reading your [Halifax Chronicle-Herald] column on-line," he said. The warrant officer also recognized my companions from their previous visits to Fort Wilson. Our group consisted of Norine, a paramedic and two South African security consultants. Our intention had been to visit the Canadian camp and chat with the soldiers, but when we saw the first-aid scene being played out right in front of us, we asked for permission to film.

"I'll check with the base," said the warrant officer, disappearing behind the barricades. When he reappeared a few minutes later, he was shaking his head. "Sorry folks, it's a no go. We checked with the public affairs office at [Kandahar airfield] and they said that since you're not embedded, you get no access." When I explained that the public affairs officers not only knew I was in Kandahar but were going to embed me that evening, it didn't change a thing. "Get yourself embedded, get them to organize a military convoy, come on back out here and I'll be happy to let you film," he said. "But right now, I have to ask you to leave the premises."

In December 2006, I had advised Canadian army commander Lieutenant General Andrew Leslie of my intention to make an unembedded visit to Kandahar to assess the situation from the Afghan perspective. He had suggested that, if possible, I should get onto the Kandahar base to record the accomplishments of our troops. In Kabul I had interviewed Canadian personnel, and upon arriving in Kandahar I had been in phone contact with public affairs officers at the airfield. They were aware that I was outside the wire and fully intended to sign my embed agreement later that night.

The dangers of travelling on roads in the Kandahar district have been amply illustrated by the level of casualties sustained by our troops. That being said, an inconspicuous civilian motor-cade (such as ours) would attract far less attention than would a military convoy. In this case, the thought of travelling to the Kandahar airfield, processing the embedding paperwork and organizing a patrol back to Fort Wilson to record an incident that had already concluded was absurd. Besides, Senlis already had a full schedule lined up for me: our next stop was to be Arghandab.

A VISIT TO police chief Abdul Hakim Jan's compound had been prearranged, and a security vehicle full of gunmen met our small convoy at the outskirts of his village. Following the Afghan police's 4 × 4s, our four Land Cruisers—also crammed with armed escorts—bumped slowly along a deeply rutted dirt road. When we reached a large villa and parked in the dust-filled compound, the metal gates to the main house opened to reveal an extensive garden.

Surrounded by a group of Afghan fighters, a middle-aged man in a flowing blue robe and matching turban came forward to greet us. Not very tall and somewhat rotund, "Commander Blue" (as he was better known) nevertheless presented an imposing image. His Kalashnikov assault rifle had a gold-plated forestock (to match his front teeth) and the shoes beneath his baggy blue trousers were silver, with their fronts curled up like a genie's slippers.

As the purpose of this visit to Arghandab had ostensibly been to provide a medical clinic for Commander Blue's fighters, an Afghan doctor and the Canadian paramedic Ed McCormick had come to assess the men. Although the Senlis Council hired local Afghan guards and South African security consultants, it would not last a minute in its unmarked Kandahar city compound if the group did not curry personal favour with the local leaders.

Recently appointed police chief for the Kandahar district by Afghan President Hamid Karzai, Commander Blue was a particularly key player in this equation. In the early 1990s, Blue had been a prominent warlord in the region. After helping force the Soviets out of Afghanistan in 1989 and topple President Mohammad Najibullah's communist government in 1992, Blue and his militia became part of what became known as the mujahedeen regime. By 1996, the brutality and ruthlessness of this fractious collection of warlords had led to the emergence of the Taliban movement. As these religious extremists—led by Mullah Mohammed Omar—resisted the warlords, volunteers flocked to the ranks of the Taliban.

Although Commander Blue was revered by his young fighters as an anti-Taliban warrior, his militia was destroyed by Mullah Omar's forces. As the Taliban secured Kandahar and marched north to Kabul, Blue fled the region with a handful of followers. Before the U.S. intervention in 2001, Blue and his small entourage were members of the Northern Alliance—virtual exiles in northeastern Afghanistan. After the collapse of the Taliban he returned to his home village and steadily reasserted his influence in the Kandahar region. His militiamen were now "policemen," and his vehicles were provided by the Kabul administration. Nevertheless, his followers made their loyalty known by taping portrait photographs of Commander Blue in the front and back windshields of their Russian-built 4 × 4s.

In a country where 72 per cent of the population is illiterate, the word *police* in both English and Pashtu script meant less than the picture of Commander Blue with his gold-accented Kalashnikov. While the NATO officers at the Kandahar airfield knew him as the new police chief with a strong anti-Taliban background, the residents of Kandahar still remembered him as a ruthless warlord.

As the Senlis Council's doctors set up their clinic, about sixty Afghan fighters milled about the inner compound waiting for their cursory checkup. Many of the young Afghan men had decorated the ends of their Kalashnikovs with colourful ribbons, emulating their leader's flamboyant style but without the expensive gold plating. On the grounds of the expansive garden could be seen Commander Blue's collection of massive fighting dogs, exotic animals and cages full of fighting birds (a popular sport in rural Afghanistan). The sprawling estate also held a small lake and a massive well. "He's sitting on top of all the water in this area," explained Vinno. "After five years of drought, water is a vital commodity in Kandahar."

By controlling the police force and the water supply, Commander Blue had firmly re-established his authority over the locals—regardless of the presence of NATO soldiers. I realized that if the followers of Blue abused those powers as they had in the past, it would only exacerbate the current security situation. Violated villagers would again turn to the Taliban to protect

338

them from a brutal warlord, and NATO would then support Commander Blue as a vital anti-Taliban ally.

As the Senlis Council's clinic wrapped up, the doctors provided a general assessment of the Afghan fighters' health. Although no chronic illnesses were reported, those with high blood pressure had their arms marked to indicate that they should be on a no-salt diet. The rest were advised to cut out cigarettes. The doctor's advice was translated into Pashtu, and the sea of gap-toothed smiles indicated that the well-intentioned advice would be promptly ignored.

We posed for some photographs with Commander Blue, remounted our vehicle and left his villa with an escort of police vehicles—all adorned with photographs of the "former" warlord.

MY FIRST VISIT to Afghanistan gave me some tremendous insight, but more importantly, it allowed me to lay down some substantial groundwork for my subsequent visit. In May 2007, I headed back to Kabul, again via Baku but this time accompanied by seasoned war correspondent David Pugliese and my old friend Sasha Uzunov. Vince Scopa, the Vietnam veteran I had met on my first visit, had arranged a meeting with Wardak Rachat, a young Afghan journalist and Kabul native. Wardak agreed to work as our driver, translator and all-around adviser. As soon as we arrived we changed into the local garb, which complemented the long hair and beards we had grown before the trip, and we managed to look like average Afghans—at least from a distance.

I planned to follow through on my interview with General Abdul Rashid Dostum during this trip. With Dostum tucked away in his northern stronghold of Sheberghan, we decided that this would be our first stop on our road trip. Although the Taliban insurgency was not much of a factor in the northern provinces,

339

banditry and kidnappings were still commonplace along the main highway. Wardak was armed, and Vince arranged to furnish us with a Kalashnikov assault rifle and a pistol, along with the necessary permits.

"No one travels in Afghanistan without weapons," explained an Australian contractor who had spent the past three years living and working in Kabul. "If thieves try to block the road, don't stop. Drive right over them." One of our concerns about carrying weapons with us was what might happen if we were stopped by Afghan police. As it turned out, although we did encounter numerous police checkpoints along the route, usually the policemen were too preoccupied with openly demanding and receiving cash bribes from truck drivers to bother searching our vehicle.

Encountering NATO troops was another worry that proved to be baseless. During our return trip, which required approximately eighteen hours of driving along Afghanistan's primary highway, we only encountered one small convoy of Norwegian troops. After they noticed us photographing them, the lead vehicle, full of Norwegian special forces, blocked the road and halted our vehicle at gunpoint. Part of a provincial reconstruction team based in Mazar-i-Sharif, the Norwegians were not patrolling the road; they were simply driving to Kabul as part of their scheduled rotation. While our clothing certainly would not fool the locals for long, the Norwegians thought they were being filmed by a carload of Afghans and were naturally inquisitive to find out the reason.

Unlike similar experiences I had had with U.S. troops while reporting from Iraq, the Norwegians were extremely courteous, and the drama evaporated as soon as they saw our press passes. Once our identity had been established, even the special forces troops had no objection to being photographed—another major departure from the no-media policy of similar U.S. and Canadian commando units.

We spent a night at the Turkish consulate in Mazar-i-Sharif, just seventy kilometres from Dostum's hometown. The Turkish diplomats provided us with a fantastic meal, and tucked away inside their protected perimeter, we were relaxed enough to indulge in some of their excellent wine and raki. The following morning we ate breakfast in Aydın Acıkel's private apartment, but despite the hospitality he offered, the consul general had bad news for us. He told us that the interview with Dostum had been cancelled because the warlord was not feeling well. We asked Acikel to do what he could to pressure Dostum's people. We had driven seven hundred kilometres of dangerous highway to meet him, and this was my second such venture.

While waiting for Dostum's final response, Acikel arranged for a driver to take us to the Qala-i-Jhangi just a few kilometres northwest of Mazar-i-Sharif. It was here, in 2001, that Dostum's forces had gathered up a large number of Taliban prisoners whom the CIA had been interrogating. When the Taliban fight ers realized that, after being questioned, most of their comrades had been executed, they staged an impromptu uprising. Over-powering Dostum's troops, they seized their weapons, killed a CIA agent and briefly took control of the fort. However, since they were completely outnumbered, it was only a matter of time before the Taliban were overwhelmed. We visited the site of their final stand, a small underground bunker that Dostum had ordered to be flooded. An estimated three hundred trapped Tali-ban drowned in the concrete stronghold, which still bore traces of the corpses.

Among Afghanistan's warlords, Dostum was believed to be one of the most ruthless in dealing with his captured enemies. I

341

spoke to Thomas Hutson about the incident at the Qali-i-Jhangi fort, and he confirmed that it was also a sore point for the United States because American special forces had been present when the atrocities were committed against the Taliban prisoners. To keep things quiet, Hutson had offered Dostum a retirement package to the Caribbean island of Grenada. In addition to the promise of a beach house and a healthy pension, the U.S. training hospital would have ensured that he got full medical treatment into his old age. I asked Hutson what Dostum's answer had been, and he said that Dostum turned down the offer flat. "He has always been a warlord, and he will die a warlord," said Hutson.

As we were preparing to leave Qala-i-Jhangi, our driver received a phone call from Aydin Acikel. "Dostum will host you at his guest house in Sheberghan at 1400 hours today," he said.

We were about to meet a legend.

THE GATES OF the compound were hurriedly pulled aside, and three black armoured Lexus 4 × 4s raced into the courtyard. Braking hastily, the vehicles disgorged a dozen heavily armed guards who immediately established a protective cordon. With the dust still settling, a giant of a man in a flowing green-striped robe strode through the parked convoy. General Abdul Rashid Dostum had arrived for an interview. After a brief introduction Dostum made it clear that his consent to this meeting was only out of his respect for Aydemir Erman. I told him that I brought greetings from our mutual Turkish friend, and we walked through Dostum's garden to a table prepared with green tea and ice water.

As the primary commander of the Northern Alliance, Dostum explained how his troops had been instrumental in helping the United States bring about the collapse of the Taliban in

2001. However, in the post-war cycle of violence, instability and insurgency the general had played only a marginal role. Despite winning a million votes in the 2004 election process, Dostum was excluded from President Hamid Karzai's cabinet. Appointed to the symbolic post of army chief of staff, Dostum said that he felt the time was right for him to once again enter the fray. "I'll collect ten thousand fighters and you give us ten thousand fighters, from the international community... and then you'll see what will happen in just six months," said Dostum. "I would use five thousand fighters as a reserve and five thousand as an offensive force to push the Taliban. I am sure we would push the Taliban even out of Waziristan [region of northwestern Pakistan], not just Afghanistan."

The creation of a force of veteran Afghan fighters would buy time for the fledgling Afghan National Army (ANA), allowing them to better prepare for combat with the Taliban, he said. "Every day, the ANA is engaged in the fighting—but just ten Taliban can disrupt an entire battalion of troops. What will happen if you stage a wrestling match between a twelve-year-old and a six-month-old infant? Obviously the ANA cannot match the experience of those soldiers who have fought before." He added that the tactics employed by the Taliban against the ANA and the coalition forces were the same ones that Afghan fighters had used to oust the Soviets. "In these days, one hundred Taliban fighters attack a district and destroy everything, kill the police chief, kill the governor and then simply vanish. Then the army comes," explained Dostum. "The Taliban withdraw, and the only people left to die are the civilians."

Dostum's criticism of the ANA's inability and unwillingness to enter into combat also extended to the foreign coalition forces, which he said had a mixed record of battlefield efficiency. "I have

343

friends who have given me intelligence that the people from the international community who are really fighting the Taliban are the United States soldiers and the Canadian soldiers. Other nationals are not fighting. They are just in defensive positions." (Dostum held meetings with a number of foreign ambassadors and military commanders from the international community.) "If President Karzai gives me the power, I can guarantee him, and assure the international community and the people of Afghanistan, that we can play a significant role in defeating and breaking the back of the Taliban," he said.

Another concern for the Afghan administration about providing Dostum with a ten-thousand-strong army is the potential for him to stage a coup. In the past thirty years of fighting in Afghanistan, Dostum had often changed sides and violated agreements with previous regimes. When I asked him about such a scenario, he reassured me, "President Karzai has the support of the international community, and there are thousands of International Security Assistance forces here. How is it possible that someone can perform a coup against such a government? I'm not crazy enough to do that." He threw back his head and laughed heartily at his own joke. After two full hours of confiding in us, he politely excused himself and we headed back to the Turkish consulate in Mazar-i-Sharif.

344

After the extreme rush of having achieved our objective to meet and speak with an elusive warlord, the road trip north was almost anticlimactic and thankfully devoid of any major incidents, outside of a flat tire and a faulty radiator. On our way back to Kabul, we stopped to let our engine cool down before passing through the famous Salang Tunnel, high in the Hindu Kush mountains. Here, we decided to test our weapons and fired a few rounds at an old, destroyed Soviet tank. Only then did we discover that our driver's pistol had a faulty firing pin and was useless.

BACK IN KABUL our next mission was to get the perspective of the Taliban. Wardak had informed us that he could bring us to one of their religious leaders who resided in the Afghan capital. However, we were not allowed to bring weapons with us, and our team was more than a little apprehensive about taking that risk. In the end, we had to put our faith in Wardak.

Although there were armed Afghans inside the courtyard, I think what put us most at ease was the tacky plastic flower arrangement inside the main parlour and the non-threatening appearance of our Taliban host. Agreeing to speak on the record, and in fluent English, Mullah Abdul Salam Zaeef launched straight into his spiel: "The people in Kandahar are thinking that the Canadians, the British and the Americans are all enemies since they are killing us, they are destroying our villages. They are capturing us and they are abusing us."

In his large private mansion in the western suburbs of Kabul, Zaeef resided under virtual house arrest. Before September 11, 2001, he had been a senior official in the Taliban regime. As ambassador to Pakistan when the United States launched its military intervention into Afghanistan in 2001, Zaeef had been the last public spokesman for the rapidly collapsing Taliban. Arrested by Pakistani intelligence in January 2002, he was subsequently handed over to the Americans and interned at Guantánamo Bay detention centre for three years and ten months. Although he was eventually cleared of terrorism charges and returned to Afghanistan, Zaeef was forbidden to return to his home in the volatile Panjwaii district. Monitored in his movements by the Afghan authorities, he nevertheless received regular visitors from the Kandahar region.

"The problem increases day by day, and the distance between the government and the people has become worse," he explained. "I think the foreigners, especially the Americans, had the

345

opportunity to do something in Afghanistan last year and in 2002, 2003 and 2004. I think they have no opportunity now. They killed a lot of people, and still the struggle is continuing."

Throughout the interview Zaeef repeatedly made the point that he no longer spoke on behalf of the Taliban and that since his incarceration in Guantánamo Bay he had not had contact with his former colleagues. In a meeting with Hamid Karzai, Zaeef had implored him to open a dialogue with the insurgents and had not ruled out playing a role in those peace talks. "Negotiation and dialogue is the solution," he said. "The solution is not with the foreigners. The foreigners had six years, but they didn't bring security, they didn't bring stability and they didn't satisfy the people."

One of the obstacles to a negotiated settlement between the Taliban and the Karzai government was the fragility of the current Afghan administration. "The government has no control; they have no power," said Zaeef. "They have no independence to negotiate. They want to talk to the Taliban; they want a solution. He [Karzai] is not able. He is crying in front of the media. He is powerless."

If the U.S. military were to withdraw, the Karzai government would not last a week, Zaeef said. The Americans had repeatedly stated they would not negotiate with terrorists, and in Afghanistan that meant the Taliban and al Qaeda. "Terrorism, in this case, is an American definition," said Zaeef. "Now in Pakistan, in Arab countries, in Iran, people are thinking this is not fighting against terrorists; this is fighting against Islam."

Although Zaeef urged a negotiated settlement, he warned that the window for such a possibility was not open ended. "After two years, then there will be no more opportunities," he said. "If the country is being bombed, if someone is being killed, if a village is destroyed, if the situation becomes worse, it is Afghans

346

who suffer. Canadian soldiers are killed here, but our casualties are more." Zaeef estimated that since the American intervention in 2001 more than fifty thousand Afghans had died in the fighting. As the killing continued, those Afghans joining the insurgency were increasingly doing so for reasons of personal revenge. "Americans are enemies, Canadians are enemies," said Zaeef. "They are supporting each other. There is no difference."

We asked him what he thought about General Dostum's plan to march south with NATO air support. The cleric's eyes widened. "He is a big killer," said Zaeef. "But if he comes south, all of Pashtunistan will resist him; he would drive millions of volunteers into the ranks of the Taliban."

THE THIRD PERSON on my wish list in Kabul was another one of Aydemir Erman's contacts. On my previous visit I had only managed to deliver the introductory letter and a small gift from the Turkish ambassador. As the security surrounding this individual was so extensive, Dave Pugliese and Sasha Uzunov were told they could not attend the meeting.

When I arrived at the office of this senior Afghan government official to conduct an interview, I was thoroughly searched, had my camera and recorder taken away, and was ushered into a large meeting room. Following a considerable wait Amrullah Saleh purposefully strode into the room and introduced himself as the head of the Afghan National Directorate of Security—essentially, the Afghan secret service. Saleh spent several minutes asking about my background and quizzing me on my knowledge of Afghanistan. Following this brief question-and-answer session I was told that there would be no formal interview but I should return in four days so that he and I could "go for a walk up the mountain."

347

Dutifully, I returned at the appointed time and found my contact and his entourage ready to depart. For security reasons the vehicles were full of heavily armed bodyguards. In the company of such a senior individual, navigating the clogged afternoon Kabul streets proved less difficult than usual. Whenever traffic stalled, two guards would dismount and race to the source of the congestion. With the help of traffic police our little convoy would then speed through the intersection.

Our destination was the base of Radar Hill, one of the tallest summits among the mountains that ring the Kabul basin. Leaving the vehicles guarded by the drivers, Saleh and I proceeded on foot with a half-dozen bodyguards spread out in a rough circle around us. The slope was gentle at first, but as we approached the top, the climb required us to use our arms and legs to pull ourselves up certain sections of the rock face. Of the entire group I was the only one wearing traditional Afghan clothing—baggy pants and robe. Saleh wore a crisp white shirt, western-style suit pants and expensive leather shoes. Thankfully, I had changed into sneakers from my sandals before the start of our walk.

The wind picked up, creating a massive dust storm across the cityscape below us, and storm clouds hovered ominously above the peak of the mountain. Even as the rain started and the lightning flashed dangerously close to us, none of the Afghans gave any notice of alarm or concern. Taking my cue from them, I acted as if this were an everyday occurrence for me as well.

As we closed on the summit, another half-dozen individuals appeared from a different path, hauling kettles of hot tea, cold pop and cakes. Overlooking the entire city, we sat on rocks in the rain, eating snacks. Finally, Saleh told me what he felt about the situation in Afghanistan. He explained that one of the major obstacles preventing a successful solution to the current crisis was the American insistence that everything be viewed as either black or white. "Afghanistan is a very complex mosaic," he explained. "If we are going to succeed, we need to recognize the grey areas and be flexible enough to deal with them."

The Taliban crossing into Afghanistan had long been noted as a major problem in combating the insurgency. Sealing the border was possible, but the United States was rejecting a proposed solution, he said. "When the Soviets tried to seal the border, they offered huge bribes to the tribal leaders in the region. However, those tribes refused the money and the border stayed open. Now we have these same tribes offering their services to President Hamid Karzai, and the Americans will not let us accept their participation."

The Americans were reluctant to empower tribal militias and insisted that all security operations be conducted by either the U.S.-trained Afghan National Army (ANA) or the Afghan National Police (ANP), Saleh noted. "The same thing happened in Helmand Province, where the recent crisis became much bigger than was necessary," he explained. "The local warlord offered to eradicate the Taliban with his own soldiers, but the U.S. insisted on deploying the ANA and the ANP. Feeling snubbed and ostracized, the warlord was now hostile to the international forces." Recognizing that the Afghan security forces were still dependent on NATO troops, Saleh predicted it would be at least another two years before self-sufficiency could be attained. "At that point [in spring 2009] the international troops must leave, and Afghanistan will have to decide on an Afghan solution."

Before heading back down the mountain I raised a sensitive issue with Saleh. Over the previous weeks the Canadian media had portrayed the Afghan National Directorate of Security as "evil torturers" and their detainee prison as a "living hell." Anxious to set the record straight and to improve its tarnished image, Saleh quickly agreed to provide my colleagues and me with three hours of unrestricted access to the infamous detention centre in Kandahar. All we had to do was get ourselves safely to the most dangerous place in this wartorn country.

Wardak was able to find us a flight from Kabul to Kandahar on Ariana Afghan Airlines. The price was right, at about US$50, but the agent claimed that we could only purchase a one-way ticket in Kabul and that the return portion had to be purchased in Kandahar. However, upon arriving in Kandahar, we learned that this was not possible immediately because there would not be another flight to Kabul for at least seven days. Despite this initial setback, the trip south would prove fruitful right from the very beginning.

WHEN WE FIRST met them at the Kabul airport check-in line, the three young Afghan men were wearing traditional civilian clothes—white robes and baggy pants. What set them apart from the rest of the crowd waiting to board a Kandahar-bound flight was that they were speaking English among themselves. When I inquired about their identity, Ramin—at twenty-two, the oldest of the group—explained that they were ANA soldiers returning to duty after taking leave in Kabul. Their unit was based in Tarin Kot, in support of the Australians, and after flying to Kandahar on our Ariana flight they would travel in a convoy to their forward operating base.

Informing them that I was a former Canadian soldier, I tried to spark their martial pride by asking them to compare the ANA to other armies with which they had worked. All three of them looked at me in disbelief before Ramin replied, "The Taliban is number one. That's why they are always kicking our ass."

With three years of combat experience, Ramin had just re-enlisted for a second tour. He was a first sergeant and the most senior ranked among the trio, yet Ramin explained that he had been given this authority as soon as he had volunteered for the army: "Because I was one of the few recruits with secondary education, I was made first sergeant for my company." Simply for being literate, Ramin had been promoted upon enlistment to a position of authority that would require at least ten years of experience to attain in any Western army. Only recently has the ANA altered its policy of training and fielding completely inexperienced *kandaks* (battalions).

In the past, the NATO-supervised Kabul Military Training Centre (KMTC) had pushed out complete *kandaks* of six hundred men after a seventeen-week training course. Any soldier who showed initiative during training—or who, like Ramin, was literate upon enlistment—would automatically be given a senior rank. In an attempt to resolve the shortage of experienced soldiers, the KMTC was trying to send its graduates to already formed veteran *kandaks*. The problem with this was that only a relatively few ANA soldiers re-enlisted for a second tour of duty. Ramin explained that his circumstances were slightly different from those of his colleagues. "My father was a warlord, and I'm carrying on a family tradition with my military service," he said. "I intend to become an officer and make this my career." While commenting on the performance of his ANA unit, Ramin made a final statement: "We run away from the Taliban because we want to live. What's hard to understand about that?"

Another obstacle to attracting new recruits to veteran units was that the ANA was expanding so quickly that there simply were not enough units in existence to make this possible. At that point, it was estimated there were 35,000 trained members of

351

the ANA. The goal was to boost that number to a target of 70,000 as quickly as possible. To achieve this objective, U.S. President George W. Bush increased funding to the KMTC. Since January 2007, the KMTC had graduated two complete *kandaks* (1,200 troops in total) every four weeks.

The pay for ANA recruits was US$115 a month, so in a country where 40 per cent of adult males were unemployed and US$300 per capita was the average annual income, there was no shortage of enlistees. However, with the pressure to produce such a vast number of troops in such a short time frame, the KMTC had a no-fail policy.

The drawback to this everyone-graduates policy was evident when we encountered an ANA guard at the Qala-i-Jhangi fort in Mazar-i-Sharif. Walking in circles, shaking his fists and talking to himself in angry tones, it was apparent that this soldier was completely witless. Yet, armed and in uniform, he remained a statistical contribution to the magic number of 70,000 ANA soldiers that the Pentagon believed would result in the self-sufficiency of the Afghan security forces.

WE BADE FAREWELL to the Afghan National Army soldiers at the Kandahar terminal and met up with Tamer, a Turkish national and another one of Vince Scopa's contractor contacts. We had met Tamer in Kabul, and he had agreed to assist us in getting into downtown Kandahar. Since no specific location had been given for the National Directorate of Security (NDS) detention centre, we first met with several Afghan secret servicemen at the governor's guest house, a well-known landmark. From there, the NDS agents drove us to the prison compound. After pleasantries had been exchanged and we had been offered bowls of sheep livers in gravy, the deputy director voiced his opinion.

"Many of the stories broadcast in Canada are lies or fabrications," said Colonel Noor Mohammed Balak Karzai, deputy director of the NDS in Kandahar. "When I saw these reports I was very angry, and it made the people of Kandahar very angry as well." One reason the directorate was taking such unprecedented measures to open the facilities to us was a desire to maintain good relations with the Canadian battle group in Kandahar. "The Canadian [soldiers] have a better attitude than some other NATO troops have, including the Americans, and people will pass along advance warnings to the NDS if they suspect Canadians are being targeted," said Colonel Karzai. "That is why we are angry that the Canadian media did not observe the reality before publishing their negative stories."

Although a series of road barricades had to be negotiated before the main vehicle gate, the detention centre was surprisingly free of heavy security. There were no guard towers or bunkers—just a walled compound topped with razor wire, not unlike any other government building in Afghanistan. While discreet in appearance, the detention centre's location was certainly not secret. The families of suspected Taliban detainees were allowed to visit prisoners and bring them food once a week; a number of these visitors were at the compound when we arrived.

Centre officials said they could hold suspects for seventy-two hours. If they believed a case warranted further investigation, the suspect could remain at the facility for fifteen days. Any incarceration beyond that point required a court-ordered extension. "If we [the directorate] have made the arrest, the processing procedure is usually quite quick as we make sure we have sufficient evidence prior to apprehending them," said Karzai. "The delays occur when we receive prisoners from other agencies, such as

NATO troops, and we have to begin an investigation with very little information."

The tour began in the basement cells where eight shackled men sat or reclined on their dirty bedding. This was the general population area, and while it was evident that the facility had been recently cleaned, there was no lingering odour of human excrement or filth, which would have been difficult to mask for the benefit of our tour. Some prisoners seemed amused at the intrusion, while others stared blankly at us as we filmed and photographed them.

On the other side of the basement were the solitary cells. Narrow enough for each occupant to barely lie down on his grubby mat, all inmates in this section had shackled feet and were kept behind locked doors. The doors were opened for us to inspect the conditions in the cells and examine the state of the prisoners. In each cell the prisoner had reading material—usually a copy of the Koran—water bottles and a few personal items. Although some of the solitary cells were kept darkened, we were allowed to light these in order to view and photograph them. Nowhere in the entire complex was there any sign of the cages in which detainees were allegedly confined.

Following the prisoner inspection we were shown the guards' quarters on the second floor, where the security force lived eight to a room, sleeping in bunks lined with bedding just as filthy as that of the prisoners. The interrogation room was a spartan office with a couple of desks, like any police station interview room, only with more battered furniture. While the security directorate denied that they beat or tortured suspects to extract confessions and intelligence, they did not divulge what they did to coerce prisoners.

The prisoner in the interrogation room during our visit was a suspect in a kidnapping. As the night watchman at the school where the kidnap victim had been held, the prisoner was believed to be implicated in the crime. Through an interpreter he told us that his family was aware of his situation and had visited him in the prison. Not evident were any of the alleged ceiling chains from which prisoners claimed to have been suspended during interrogations. In fact, the cracked plaster ceiling looked barely capable of supporting the weight of the flimsy light fixture, never mind the weight of a man.

Every office, cupboard and toilet facility was opened for our inspection, which included a visit to the roof and the dining facility. Huge chunks of a freshly slaughtered sheep were being boiled in an immense cauldron over an open fire. "The prisoners receive the same food as the guards and prison staff," said Colonel Karzai. "They receive bread and tea for breakfast, and meat and rice for lunch and dinner." The yogurt that the prisoners would be consuming was heavily watered down in a large pot. Admittedly, the food appeared to be unappetizingly thin fare, but the prisoners' families and friends often supplemented the daily ration.

At the conclusion of the tour Colonel Karzai again pointed out the importance of maintaining good relations with Canadians. He said he would also be willing to negotiate a new arrangement whereby the Canadian military could routinely access the facility to monitor the prisoners whom they had handed over.

"The detention centre is not a nice place to be," said one senior security directorate official. "It's not supposed to be. But we do not do those things which the [Canadian] media have accused us of having done."

NOW THAT WE knew there was no return flight for several days, we had a serious problem. Without much time in our schedule, because we all had connecting flights to catch out of Kabul, it seemed as though we would have no choice but to hire a driver to get back to the Afghan capital.

Following our tour of the National Directorate of Security's detainee prison we asked Colonel Abdul Razzaq, the intelligence officer responsible for security in the entire Kandahar province, what safety precautions we should take to minimize the danger to ourselves while driving to Kabul. Pondering our question for a moment, Colonel Razzaq responded with a single word: "Fly."

This was the same person who only minutes earlier had proclaimed his province to be safe and secure. This was the reality of Afghanistan: they told you what they believed you wanted to hear, until they realized that you actually believed what they had told you.

Fortunately, the stars aligned in our favour and we were able to heed his advice. We found three last-minute seats on a British air force plane out of Kandahar airfield.

11

TAKING STOCK

The only locals who were organized and
funded to run a campaign in post-war Kosovo
were the warlords, thugs and drug dealers.
As a result, Kosovo went from a state full of
criminals to a legitimate criminal state.

AN AMERICAN UN POLICEMAN

WHEN THE SUGGESTION WAS FIRST made that I should write a
memoir, my initial reaction was that at the age of forty-six I was
far too young to start looking back. I felt I still had a lot of learning and exploration to do before I started trying to make sense
of it all. That belief was shaken at 6:10 AM on October 20, 2006,
when a pickup truck made a left turn through an intersection
and accelerated straight into me. I was thrown about twenty
feet—still astride my bicycle—and my world became a blur of
headlights, twisted metal and the screeching of brakes. The
truck ended up on top of my buckled front tire, and somehow
the chain sprocket rolled up the front of my shin, leaving a gap-
ing, bloody gash. My hands and arms were scraped as well, but
through the blood pounding in my ears I could hear the pickup

truck driver shouting something about calling 9-1-1 and a pass-
erby screaming, "He's been killed!"—I realized I was still alive.

Waiting to get stitched up at the hospital emergency ward, I
decided that perhaps it was never too soon to start writing up my
experiences. I called Scott McIntyre at Douglas & McIntyre that
afternoon and told him I was on board for the project. The only
proviso I requested was that the last three words would be *to be
continued*. Once the writing and research had begun, however, I
realized just how many chapters of my life had already come to a
natural conclusion and how, as the old adage goes, the mistakes
of the past that we refuse to recognize become the genesis of the
mistakes that we are destined to repeat in the immediate future.

On March 11, 2006, before I could testify at The Hague's International Criminal Tribunal, Slobodan Milosevic died in his jail
cell of an apparent heart attack. Although the international community had already passed judgement on his guilt prior to the
trial, Milosevic's death was a blessing for the prosecutors. Only
months later the tribunal ruled that there was not enough evidence to prove that Serbia bore state responsibility for genocide
during the Bosnian war from 1992 to 1995. The Kosovo parliament had already ruled that with a total death count of 2,700
people during the conflict in 1998 and the NATO intervention in
1999—including some 900 Serbs and non-Albanians—the term
genocide did not apply to the crisis. As the president of the Republic of Yugoslavia, Milosevic could not have been convicted of
the crime of genocide, a crime for which his state was absolved.
Neither could he have been punished for urging a genocidal campaign in Kosovo, which the Albanian officials acknowledge did
not occur on a scale to warrant that moniker.

His death before his defence could be concluded also meant
that The Hague's International Criminal Tribunal was spared

the embarrassment of having to explain why certain individuals were being protected from justice. I never did get the opportunity to remind the judge about the atrocities that Agim Ceku had committed in the Medak Pocket, and his deliberate shelling of innocent Serbian civilians who were fleeing the Krajina in 1995. In fact, around the time I was to testify in the spring of 2006, Ceku was serving as the prime minister of Kosovo and meeting with international heads of state.

The U.S. State Department may have deliberately overlooked Agim Ceku's crimes, but they will never be forgotten by those Canadian peacekeepers who were forced to sit idly by and bear witness to the carnage. Canada did recognize the heroism of our soldiers at the Medak Pocket with a Governor General's unit citation that was presented to the 2nd Battalion, Princess Patricia's Canadian Light Infantry, on December 1, 2002. However, as a nation we have failed to follow up on that proud service by demanding that the perpetrators be brought to justice. In fact, Canada should have made the handing over of Agim Ceku to face a trial for war crimes a prerequisite to the recognition of Kosovo's independence in February 2008. That it meekly acquiesced to the U.S. demand to recognize Kosovo without reminding people of the criminal activity of the Albanian leadership was a disservice to all involved.

Another missed opportunity came as a result of the U.S. State Department believing its own propaganda about the success achieved in Kosovo, while it was planning to wage a war in Iraq. Although the media prematurely declared victory in Kosovo in 1999 and headed home, the international observers who remained behind to police the resultant anarchy had a completely different viewpoint. I remember interviewing an American UN policeman in Pristina in the summer of 2003. The

U.S. forces had just toppled Saddam Hussein, and the insurgency had yet to begin in Iraq. The American was blunt in his assessment of the situation, and he recommended that his leaders not make the same mistake as they had in Kosovo, by rushing to hold an election. "The only locals who were organized and funded to run a campaign in post-war Kosovo were the warlords, thugs and drug dealers," he said. "As a result, Kosovo went from a state full of criminals to a legitimate criminal state."

Since the Albanian leaders were holding public office and making the laws, the hands of the UN police had been tied. As no one openly admitted this massive failure of forethought, the Americans in Iraq repeated the mistake. The average Iraqis, being completely unfamiliar with the basic tenets of democracy, rallied around their tribal and religious leaders. The result was a deepening of the divisions within Iraq's societal mosaic, rather than a unifying exercise in creating responsible government. As history would record, the opening of those old wounds resulted in the eruption of a bloodbath.

Although American planners claimed that they would be welcomed as liberators in Iraq, my discussions with Iraqis prior to the invasion showed that they thought otherwise. Everyone knew that if the iron fist of Saddam were removed, it would have to be replaced by an equally firm grip or civil war would be the result. My Mukhābarāt agents prophesied in the spring of 2003 that there would be a battle in the south between secular and fundamentalist Shiite factions for the control of Basra's oil wealth, while in the north Sunni Arabs, Turkmen and Kurds would fight each other over the oil fields of Kirkuk. It was also widely understood that the American troops could enter Iraq but that if they decided to remain as occupiers, they would pay a hefty price.

In March 2008, on the fifth anniversary of the U.S. invasion of Iraq, the death toll of American service personnel stood at 4,000, with an additional 30,000 wounded. Those who tracked such things were forecasting that the ultimate financial cost of the war would be as high as US$3 trillion.

Nobody in the Pentagon was cautioning Americans about such a potential quagmire back in 2003. In an effort to drum up support for the war, George Bush's advisers warned about the threat of weapons of mass destruction, and Deputy Secretary of Defence Paul Wolfowitz claimed that the intervention would not last more than six months. Of course, no weapons of mass destruction were ever found, and once the American troops were on the ground, they could not be safely withdrawn; they continued to be unable to create a stable environment in Iraq.

It would be smug of us as Canadians, however, to point to the American fiasco in Iraq and pride ourselves on the fact that we turned down George Bush's offer to join in the fun. We have become embroiled in our own Afghanistan quagmire, which, given our relatively small military resources, is a blunder of equal proportions. In the immediate wake of September 11, 2001, the U.S. launched Operation Enduring Freedom, which succeeded in toppling the Taliban regime in Afghanistan in a matter of months. Canada did not participate in that initial offensive, but it did contribute a seven-hundred-strong light infantry battle group in 2002 to help mop up Taliban holdouts around Kandahar. These troops encountered little resistance and spent most of their time chasing shadows on long-range patrols.

The following year, Canada was asked to contribute a sizable contingent to the International Security Assistance Force. This mission was to take place under NATO command and was primarily concerned with securing the Afghan capital so that the fledgling government could get itself established and an Afghan security force could be trained and equipped. The Liberal finance minister, John Manley, set aside an initial budget of $270 million, and Canada agreed to a two-year troop commitment to the rebuilding of Afghanistan. At that point Canada had suffered four soldiers killed by U.S. friendly fire and two others killed by a mine strike on their Iltis vehicle. None of its casualties had been the result of being targeted by hostile Afghans; they were mishaps in a dangerous environment.

During the summer of 2003, critics warned that Canada's death toll "may climb as high as ten killed" if it kept troops on the ground through 2005. Manley's first year budget of $270 million for the mission had doubled before the first soldier had boarded an Afghanistan-bound aircraft. Military analysts suggested that due to our having to rent strategic airlift from the Russians, the total cost might reach the staggering sum of $1 billion.

Fast-forward to the spring of 2008, when Parliament agreed to extend Canada's commitment to Afghanistan until December 2011. In 2006, the Canadian contingent moved south from Kabul to Kandahar, and the casualties have climbed to over 80 killed and more than 650 wounded. Manley's projected $200 million had become an actual expense of $7.5 billion for the military mission—nine times the amount spent on civilian aid to Afghanistan. The situation on the ground was less stable than it had been in 2007, and it was far less stable than when Afghans still had post-Taliban hopes for a better future in 2002.

Like the response of the Americans in Iraq, one of the primary rationales our parliamentarians used for extending the mission was that it was easier to do this than to admit we had failed to achieve our stated goal of assisting Afghans to provide their own secure environment. One of the classic quips uttered by Prime Minister Stephen Harper to help sell the war was "Canada doesn't cut and run." While the media allowed this to go unchallenged and the retired colonels took it up as a battle cry, the fact is that Canada has cut and run from every overseas deployment it has undertaken since the Korean War. There are still UN peacekeepers in Cyprus, and NATO security forces in Bosnia and Kosovo—even though the Canadians have packed up their tents. Aussie soldiers are still deployed in East Timor, and Norwegians are patrolling Haiti—yet Canadians have long since walked away from those hot spots. In 1993 in Somalia, the U.S.-led coalition suffered some serious casualties at the hands of the warlords, and the entire allied force cut and ran—including Canada.

The fact that we have been in Afghanistan now for seven years does not mean that our military fully understands either the conflict in which we are engaged or the people whom we are attempting to assist. One clear example of this is the suicide bombing that killed Commander Blue and one hundred of his followers on February 17, 2008. Neither the Taliban nor any of its followers laid claim to this incident. The attack was mounted by an Afghan who remembered the brutality inflicted by Blue's men on the local population before the Taliban took control. A person whom NATO had found to be a convenient ally, Commander Blue, had turned out to be a liability to the allied forces. By arming and equipping this old thug to fight the Taliban, NATO was seen to be embracing a ruthless killer. That is not exactly a sound recipe for winning over hearts and minds.

By and large, Canadians recognize the wilful blindness of their American neighbours who proclaim their militaristic nationalism to be a proud patriotism and who describe their aggressive foreign policies as cautious self-defence measures. What we see in them we do not wish to see in ourselves; yet the Canadian government continues to largely follow in lockstep with the U.S. State Department's direction.

Our military is also in the middle of a massive transformation that will turn our armed forces into a much more American-style organization—moving away from the more traditional British composition and philosophy. Without being able to rely on an independent intelligence-gathering service such as the CIA or MI6, Canada's deployment of expeditionary forces into counter-insurgencies such as those in Afghanistan amounts to little more than the provision of highly trained and well-equipped mercenaries to serve the political interest of our allies.

In my short lifetime I have seen a lot of this planet, from a variety of perspectives. As an artist, soldier and war correspondent I have observed the extreme ends of the human spectrum. I can attest that life-and-death conflict certainly brings out both the best and the worst traits in people. That being the case, the single lesson my father taught me when I was a toddler was that courage is the one virtue without which all others are worthless.

Knowing the truth is not enough; we must have the conviction to act upon it.

AFTERWORD

IN THE FALL OF 2004, shortly after my hostage incident, a Serbian film producer approached me with a proposal to make a film about my life. In sharing the news about this project with friends and family, I soon realized that while flattering in concept, the reality of this film was something of a poison pill. Following a brief congratulations, the immediate question they usually asked was, Which actors were going to play them in the movie? I realized that condensing 47 years of living into a 47-minute documentary could not be done without some serious editing and omissions.

Although this written memoir, *Unembedded*, provides me with a much more in-depth manner in which to recount some of my trials and tribulations, it still required a number of rather painful edits. No passage was more difficult to omit than the account of my son's difficult birth, his congenital anomaly and the subsequent surgeries to save his life. That Kirk's birth defect may have resulted from my 1991 exposure to depleted uranium on the Kuwaiti "Highway of Death" left me feeling guilt ridden, and my inability to assist him in the healing process left me feeling completely incapable. Those months of impotent worry over my son's fate far outweighed the intense strain of anticipating my own execution ten years later in Iraq. Nevertheless, editor John Eerkes-Medrano convinced me that such personal revelations were exceeded by the import of recording for a larger audience the more newsworthy events that I had witnessed. Given the vast number of conflicts I have covered over the years, even these campaign stories have had to be prioritized.

As such, I have reduced my six trips into Cambodia to a couple of sentences, and three visits to Azerbaijan to three paragraphs. My front-line experiences in Macedonia in 2001—the genesis for my book *Diary of an Uncivil War*—have been cut in their entirety. Numerous other adventures—from suffering the freezing climes of the high Arctic to surviving a near disaster aboard a Canadian submarine—also have to be saved for the sequel.

In my many travels I have been fortunate to meet a large number of individuals, ranging from the influential to the infamous. There was no way that every one of them could be included without reducing the book to a catalogue of dropped names. Such tales as my participating in a sanction-busting flight to Iraq in November 2000 with the former first lady of Greece, Margarita Papandreou; a clandestine meeting with the notorious Sierra Leone war criminal Sam Bockarie in a Baghdad hotel room and my travels through wartorn Kosovo with Serbian Crown Princess Linda Karadjordjevic do not appear here, for the simple reason that not enough space is available to give them a proper telling.

Since delivering the manuscript for this book, I have made subsequent trips into the Balkans, another unembedded foray into Afghanistan and an extensive fact-finding tour of the wartorn Caucasus region. It remains my intention to make the proviso mentioned in the previous chapter a prophetic reality:

To be continued.

ACKNOWLEDGEMENTS

FULL CREDIT HAS TO BE given to Scott McIntyre for conceiving the notion of my writing a mid-life memoir. It had been my intention to write a detailed account of my five-day hostage ordeal, but after an extended lunch at an Ottawa pub Scott convinced me to widen the scope to include my numerous other adventures and mishaps. Julie Simoneau and Darcy Knoll assisted with the initial research and editing to ensure that the first draft was in manageable and legible form. Editor John Eerkes-Medrano had the unenviable task of chopping down the manuscript to its present form, and I applaud his splendid efforts.

Without *Esprit de Corps* none of this story would have been possible. Far more than just a magazine, *Esprit de Corps* is truly a spirit for those who have contributed to its survival and success. This extended family of supporters and contributors over the past twenty years has enabled me to bear witness to a world at war.

Also worthy of recognition is the courage and sacrifice made by my wife, Katherine, and my son, Kirk, who understand and accept the necessary risks I must take in order to ply my trade.

367

INDEX